Leadership
on the Line

Leadership on the Line

Staying Alive through the Dangers of Change

RONALD HEIFETZ

MARTY LINSKY

Harvard Business Review Press
Boston, Massachusetts

Library of Congress Cataloging-in-Publication Data

Names: Heifetz, Ronald A. (Ronald Abadian), 1951-author. | Linsky, Martin, author.
Title: Leadership on the line: staying alive through the dangers of leading / Ronald
    A. Heifetz, Marty Linsky.
Description: Boston, Massachusetts: Harvard Business School Press, [2017] |
    Includes bibliographical references and index.
Identifiers: LCCN 2016058719 | ISBN 9781633692831 (hardcover: alk. paper)
Subjects: LCSH: Leadership. | Risk Management. | Life skills.
Classification: LCC HM1261 .H45 2017 | DDC 303.3/4—dc23 LC record available
    at https://lccn.loc.gov/2016058719

ISBN: 978-1-63369-283-1
eISBN: 978-1-63369-284-8

To David and Ariana (Anni), and Alison, Sam,
Max, Rich, Meredith, LeAnna, Guy, and Wit,
with faith that you will step out there
with heart and make a difference to people

Contents

Preface   ix

Acknowledgments   xxiii

Introduction   1

Part One: The Challenge

1 The Heart of Danger   9
2 The Faces of Danger   31

Part Two: The Response

3 Get on the Balcony   51
4 Think Politically   75
5 Orchestrate the Conflict   101
6 Give the Work Back   123
7 Hold Steady   141

Part Three: Body and Soul

8 Manage Your Hungers   163
9 Anchor Yourself   187
10 What's on the Line?   207
11 Sacred Heart   225

Notes   237
Index   243
About the Authors   251

Preface

Adaptability has been an essential ingredient for surviving and thriving for every species of life, from life's beginning on earth.

This has surely been true for human systems trying to meet difficult challenges and flourish in the face of uncertainty and change, for whatever forms that system takes: global networks, a nation, a tribe, a town, a company, a family, or a person.

So if your community, at whatever scale you define it, needs to focus on enhancing one skill set, one capacity, one competency to help ensure going forward successfully, choose adaptability. And, what holds for any human system we think holds for you as an individual as well.

Now More Than Ever

We wrote this book with three goals in mind: (1) to show that productive change must be adaptive to be sustainable; (2) to offer tools and frameworks that lower risk so people can see how to lead and stay alive through the dangers of change; and (3) to encourage people to seize opportunities to exercise leadership that are within reach every day.

While the need for adaptability has always been critical, never has its significance been as front and center as it is today. People everywhere are having to figure out how to adapt to the multiple daunting challenges facing the world: stateless and state-sponsored terrorism, wars, and refugees; the effects of climate change in the violence of storms, flooding of coastal cities, and drought; the dangers of new viral pandemics; population growth that exceeds the carrying capacity of families and economies. The internet and its social media offspring have changed how human beings communicate with each other, how war is fought, and how politics are played. The Great Recession that began in 2008 not only threw the worldwide equity markets into free fall, but led to a recovery that fell unevenly, widening further the income gap.

Politically, the United States elected its first African American president, yet polarizing movements emerged in the world, on both the left and the right, often entering and upending mainstream electoral processes. Elections in democratic settings in Asia, Australia, Europe, South America, and the United States have been won, or nearly won, by politicians with authoritarian inclinations and an appeal promising easy answers and a restoration of order, predictability, and calm. The key word in President Trump's 2016 campaign mantra, "Make America Great Again," was "Again." The desire for restoration, to take one's country back, whether you share that yearning or not, is a pushback against the difficulties and hardship of adapting to new, unfamiliar, often threatening realities.

The constancy, complexity, and depth of the change challenge all of us. On one hand, we face extraordinary new opportunities to thrive individually and collectively. On the other hand, with deep change comes loss, people left behind, long-held values questioned, beloved norms and practices undone, and the security of jobs, familiarity, and predictability gone, simply and suddenly gone.

All of this volatility has surfaced festering challenges in the world order and in the differential experiences of those people who were riding the waves versus those who felt they were drowning in them.

Take population growth. A worldwide consensus on the importance of population policy has unraveled, for reasons that we believe are only partly justifiable, with major impact on poverty, terrorism, sex trafficking, pandemics, mass migrations, and of course, climate change. In many countries around the world, families, school systems, and local economies are overwhelmed by the number of children, rendering young men vulnerable to terrorist and criminal recruiters, and young women to sex predators and traffickers. Climate change seems intractable not only because, as consumers, many people are wedded to old jobs and old patterns of fuel and meat consumption, but also because, as aspirants, particularly in the digital age, huge populations of young poor people worldwide will seek to consume more. No longer will people find happiness in subsistence and isolation. Pandemics, too, are fed by the high density of people living close together. These factors have combined to strain the holding environments of all of our communities and societies, including those in the West, creating the trigger points of drought and floods from home, and migrations, epidemics, and terrorism from abroad. In Syria, for example, a high rural growth rate combined with a long drought prior to 2011 led to a massive movement of farming communities to the cities, and created a ripe context for civil war, brutal repression, the growth of regressive Islamic movements, terrorism, and mass migration.

In leadership terms, these conditions too often generate yearning for authoritative direction, protection, and the return of order. Just as dictatorships in history usually emerge in crisis, the conditions of our times create a political marketplace for certainty and answers. Distressed citizens reward pandering, and politicians oblige. Politicians overpromise to win election and earn distrust because they cannot deliver. Inevitably, amid the adaptive challenges of these decades, people feel that those in authority are letting them down, not meeting their expectations, not hearing their pain, talking at them rather than listening to them. Feeling betrayed and increasingly insecure, many people angrily retreat into narrower identity groups. The strain on solidarity in diversity is palpable around the world.

We need to break this vicious cycle. Citizens need to face the complexity and consequences of their demands, but politicians need to engage citizens more honestly and artfully to lead that process. It's not enough for officeholders to work hard to comprehend the issues if they then shield their constituents from tough choices. Profound change is more honest than grandiose, more incremental than the experience of it, and builds from the enduring values of individual human beings and the orienting values of human communities. We believe it's possible to lead and stay alive, to both win reelection and engage people to own their part of change in an iterative, adaptive process of renewal.

Leadership Traps: The Transformation Dilemma

When we and our colleagues began thirty-five years ago to develop these perspectives on the practice of leadership, initially in Ron's collaboration with Riley Sinder and the seminal book *Leadership Without Easy Answers* and subsequently here in *Leadership on the Line*, the term commonly used to capture the aspirational in leadership thinking was "transformational."

Transformation by itself is problematic as a frame for leadership. First, it encourages self-referential grandiosity—"I have a transformational vision and now I am going to sell it to you." Leadership seen in this light too readily becomes about "me and my vision" rather than the collective work to be done. The transformational mindset does not begin with a diagnostic focus and search process: the crucial step of listening to comprehend the gap between values, capacities, and conditions, before formulating a path forward. Rarely does it encourage the quest for shared purposes; far too often, the self-styled "transformational leader" begins with a solution and then views leadership as a sales problem of inspiration and persuasion.

Second, by itself, the transformational mindset tends to be ahistorical. It tends to start with the change idea, perhaps a "best practice," with little respect for the soil in which it must take root. Even if it is on paper a great idea, the importation of the idea risks uprooting more than it should, disorienting and devaluing people more than is needed, and in the end often generates a cultural immune reaction that rejects or distorts the original idea, regardless of one's good intention. The allergic reaction may happen quickly (Egypt, Yemen, and the Arab Spring), or it may take forty years (the Chinese Revolution) or sixty years (the Russian Revolution).

Third, emphasizing transformational change alone encourages passionate and courageous people to seek big, systemic change, but also risks encouraging them to rush to scale and discount the incremental and transactional day-to-day work of leadership. The world today needs adaptations at every level, from the way families raise children to the way neighbors, consumers, and citizens interact, to the ways we operate across national boundaries and among nation-states. The challenges of the twenty-first century need not a single savior, but everyday leadership from people mobilizing collective creativity on tough problems within their reach from wherever they live.[1]

Sustainable Change Is Adaptive

We believe our times call for deep and widespread change that transforms people's capacity to meet today's challenges and thrive in new ways. We also believe that sustainable, transformative change is more evolutionary than revolutionary, conserving far more cultural DNA than it tosses out. For example, Google's search engine depended on and conserved an already evolved economic and technological infrastructure—the US economic system and the growing market for web-based products, a rich network of tech industries, the ecosystem of Silicon Valley, and many previous engineering solutions, including lessons from the search engines that preceded it. Google's technology transformed our human capacities in a sustainable way because these deep changes took root in established technological, economic, and cultural competencies, institutions, and values, and built from there. And though Google's business model, based on advertising revenues and new data-gathering techniques, transformed the online marketplace, much of it drew on essential lessons and conserved essential capacities that had already evolved over the course of generations in advertising and marketing. To take a historical example, the American Revolution conserved most of the cultural DNA of Great Britain, its language, arts, science, political theory, and the nascent free-market system. A nation built upon values rather than ethnicity, enabling an architecture for diversity, was not only transformative, it was also adaptive. The founders conserved more than they changed.

For transformative change to be sustainable, it not only has to take root in its own culture, but also has to successfully engage its changing environment. It must be adaptive to both internal and external realities. Therefore, leadership needs to start with listening and learning, finding out where people are, valuing what is best in what they already know, value, and do, and build from there. It's dangerous to lead with only a change idea in mind. You need both a healthy respect for the values, competence, and history of people, as well as the changing environment, to build the capacity to respond to new challenges and take advantage of new openings.

Systemic Adaptation: The Colombian Example

Even big change led from the top of a government is the accumulation of countless daily increments and transactions. Over the past decades, Ron has had the privilege of educating and advising several presidents and prime ministers around the world, all of whom had high aspirations for accomplishing significant changes in their societies, and all of whom both succeeded and failed (depending on the issue) based in part upon their ability to think in evolutionary, adaptive terms about the demands of leading deep social change and preparing their peoples accordingly.

President Juan Manuel Santos of Colombia began taking big but incremental steps toward a peace accord with the FARC even before his inauguration in August 2010. He knew the war intimately, having just served as defense minister. He began by building an ecosystem, a holding environment, for peace negotiations. He appointed as foreign minister the previous ambassador to Venezuela so he could establish a working relationship with Venezuelan president Hugo Chávez, who had provided sanctuary to the Colombian guerrillas. Santos needed to persuade Chávez to change course and put pressure on the guerrillas to end the violence and move instead to the negotiating table. Santos also successfully reached out to Cuba, historic supporters of the guerrillas. Raúl Castro too changed course, not only by pressuring the FARC to negotiate, but also by offering to host the negotiations. And Santos brought in the Norwegians, who had hosted the Israeli-Palestinian negotiations and the Oslo Accords, to serve as a neutral host along with the Cubans. These were big moves, but they were also incremental steps.

The negotiation process itself lasted more than five years. President Santos had a first-rate negotiating team, but he also established multiple lines of communication with the FARC to increase his options and maintain control over the process. Daily, he paid attention to the work of his negotiating team, the challenges and opposition of his political colleagues, and the difficult adjustments for various publics, as they each were being challenged to face the host of tough issues placed on the negotiating table and before the country at large. There were endless, big, tough questions, as narrow as the mechanisms for the confiscation of weapons and as broad as policies to tackle the inequity that gave rise to the guerrilla wars in the first place fifty years earlier. Each required detailed, specific analysis and creativity, and significant changes in the heart and minds of everyone, from the negotiators to the average citizen.

That President Santos survived reelection in 2014 and concluded the peace agreement in 2016 is a testament to the detailed, daily, transactional, and dangerous work of nurturing deep societal change.

Of course, the jury is still out. Santos lost the referendum on the peace agreement in October 2016, but adapted quickly, revised the agreement, and rapidly won congressional approval. To secure those gains in his last year in office, President Santos turned the focus of his attention toward the public's reparative work. For most of his time in office, he focused on the negotiation with less time for engaging and building trust with relevant communities across the countryside. Everyone inside the negotiation process went through a deeply emotional change experience over years of intense effort. They were held well by Santos at every step. But the president was less available to hold those who would have to bear the brunt of reconciliation—the families of kidnapped and murdered victims— and those who would have to risk their political, economic, or cultural standing in the new political order. A sustainable peace is not achieved in an agreement; it's only achieved in the adaptive changes in people's lives as they lay their traumatic past to rest, gain new social and economic policy, and build new working political relationships. Peace will remain a work in progress for a generation, with starts and stops requiring highly adaptive leadership not only from Santos and his successors, but also from people leading with and without authority throughout the society. President Santos won the 2016 Nobel Peace Prize because, with courage, stamina, and political artistry, and with an evolutionary mindset and adaptive approach, he did something extraordinary: he gave peace a chance and strengthened the odds of its sustainability.

Adaptation at the Personal Level: The Stages of Life

Adaptive work at the systemic level is equally tough as an individual.

We are certain that somewhere along the way you have had to cope with unanticipated and unwelcome new realities in your personal and/or professional life. The sudden death of a loved one. An unexpected divorce. An election defeat. The loss of a job. A health crisis. A business failure. A romance for which you had high hopes suddenly fell apart. A trusted friend betrayed you.

Add your own examples to this list.

The challenges of adaptation in any of these situations parallel those facing President Santos and the people of Colombia. What do you preserve going forward? What do you lay to rest and leave behind? How do you sustain yourself through the loss? What new behaviors, values, and beliefs do you take up and try on?

For Marty, this has had a special resonance since this book was first published. More particularly, in the past few years, Marty has faced the challenge of adapting to the inexorable process of aging. Advances in health care, dietary guidelines, and the practice of wellness lifestyles has meant that everyone has the possibility of living longer and healthier than did the previous generation. There are two easy, lazy options: (1) Retire like the previous generation did, move to a warmer climate, play golf and bridge, read, travel, hang around with kids and grandkids, and volunteer, give back. Or, (2) keep on doing what you have been doing. There's a lot of systemic pressure to do that. Why not just stay the course, do what you've been doing, what you are valued for, what you do well? The world appreciates it (and pays you for it), and it makes you feel competent and useful. Not bad. Many friends are doing just that.

The adaptive challenge, however, is the opportunity to see this period as a new, next chapter, not just same old, same old, or just fading gloriously off into the equally glorious sunset, but as a whole new period of the journey, needing to be invented, what Mary Catherine Bateson called "active wisdom" in her recent book, *Composing a Further Life*: the challenge of figuring out how to take what you think you have learned and make it available to a wider and different audience, or in a different way, than you have expressed it in the past.

Nevertheless, Marty says that nothing he has ever learned, observed, been told, or experienced has prepared him for this phase of life. As his body deteriorates (and, alas, memory starts to fade), he is constantly facing difficult choices: give in to it, fight it, go with it, or try to fix it. Fixing it was always the preferred option; now not necessarily so. Try to avoid a back operation by giving up running (a central element of his self-identity), going to physical therapy, and doing forty minutes of exercises every day? Hearing aids? Cataract operations? No more long, back-to-back plane flights? No more successive nights of less than seven hours of sleep? Naps? Yikes!

What to give up? What to hold onto? And, of course, how to make best use of whatever time there is left. Emotionally painful prioritization processes. Unlike for humanity as a whole, for Marty the end is known. How, when, and what to do between now and then are not completely within his control, to be sure, but retaining his sense of agency by framing a series of choices, one-by-one, every day, *and* making them through the lens of what is essential and what is expendable has become his new, nearly full-time job.

Our Own Evolution

As teachers and consultants, we saw that the responses to the frameworks and tools we laid out in this book pivoted dramatically after the Great Recession.

Before that, the challenges of adaptation seemed to many people to be a "nice to have," not a "need to have." From 2009 onward, people's perspectives shifted. The capacity to adapt came to be seen as an immediate necessity and, for many individuals and organizations, a difficult and traumatic challenge. This realization led to the decision by the editors at Harvard Business Review Press to republish this book, and to this new preface. HBRP strongly encouraged us not to make substantive changes in this edition. "The book holds up well as it is," we were told. However, they also wanted us to reflect on what we have learned and to suggest in this preface some reconceptualizations you might want to take into account as you explore these pages.

Our ideas about thinking and acting politically (chapter 4) have morphed as readers, students, and clients have pushed us to be more expansive about how to use the ideas at the ground level. Some of this gap we began to address in our subsequent book, *The Practice of Adaptive Leadership*. Acting politically involves much more than having partners, the main thrust of the chapter. Acting politically means customizing interventions, tailoring what you say and what you do to engage each particular target population for your initiative. It means knowing that all people in their professional and personal roles profoundly identify with other people, and therefore are best understood to represent others. People represent people. Respecting those professional and personal loyalties becomes key to finding cooperative options. Acting politically, then, requires deep empathy, understanding the story people are telling themselves and you, even if you think that story is foolish, so that you can meet them where they are, instead of where you are. Operating in this way requires you to know what's at stake for the people they represent, for their "constituents," and to be open to alliances with people and factions whose motivation, interests, values, and agendas might be very, very different and even in some ways contrary to yours.

And we have learned from our work over these years that orchestrating conflict (chapter 5) is really a subset of the broader umbrella idea of creating a holding environment. Orchestrating conflict requires a vessel—bonds that can hold people together against the divisive forces that pull them apart. These bonds are both vertical and horizontal—bonds of trust in authority and lateral bonds of trust called social capital. Wonderful work has been done by our colleagues in politics and sociology, negotiation and diplomacy, on the careful, detailed analysis of the structures and processes that build these holding environments. Leadership requires not only pacing and sequencing the issues themselves to contain division, but also tending to the holding environment itself to strengthen the bonds of trust and shared interest that make the losses of compromise and innovation worth sustaining. You can't cook without a pot to cook in, and leadership is as much about strengthening the pot and controlling the temperature as it is about which ingredients to add when. Many people tell us that they find it difficult and personally well outside their comfort zones to raise and lower the heat (especially to raise the heat), although they may realize that doing so may be essential to getting people to address difficult issues. There are many tools here, some more challenging than others, for raising the heat; but strengthening the holding environment provides crucial leverage.

Similarly, skillful interventions (chapter 6) involve giving the work back, not only tactically, but also strategically. Intervening to make progress on adaptive work requires experimentation, making an ask, and customization. This is a retail business, not a wholesale operation. But you also have to think strategically about capacity and context: both about setting and framing priorities, and about timing, pacing, and sequencing interventions in an arc of change over time.

Finally, we say in these pages (chapters 7, 8, and 9) that "self-knowledge and self-discipline form the foundation for staying alive." Not surprisingly given the risks involved, we have found that people trying to exercise leadership are keenly interested in advice about survival. But we also find that people often undermine themselves by taking pushback, criticism, and attack personally. Self-awareness and discipline are relevant to the task of generating for yourself the freedom to respond with a nondefensive defense when the attack is personal, and with an expanded set of options when it is not. To effectively distinguish role and self, manage your hungers, and anchor yourself, you will want to know how to identify the default settings within you that are shaped by the loyalties you've internalized from your professional and personal life, and sometimes your ancestry; and you will then want to learn how to renegotiate the relevant loyalties that inhibit the freedom to see and respond more creatively to what's really in front of you.

Rereading this book closely, writing this new preface, and making tiny word changes here and there has been a labor of love for us, an opportunity to reflect on our own experience and the dramatic changes in the world since it was first published fifteen years ago. We are humbled by the testimony of so many people that *Leadership on the Line* has continued to be a useful beacon for them in doing the meaningful yet difficult work of leading adaptive change.

For us, this experience has also been an opportunity to reconnect and reinvigorate our professional collaboration and personal friendship, both of which have seen some bumps in the road over the years. Adaptive challenges *are* with us every day. Reading, writing, lecturing, teaching, and consulting on adaptive change with so many people have not necessarily made us experts at doing it ourselves. Like the changes in the world, the need for learning never stops.

Ron Heifetz
Marty Linsky
December 1, 2016

Acknowledgments

This book is the product of our combined half-century of teaching and consulting. It draws on the experiences and insights of students, clients, friends, and professional colleagues, and we owe them our thanks for sharing their stories and lessons, although they bear no responsibility for what we have done with them.

We have been blessed with an extraordinarily attentive and skilled team at the Harvard Business School Press. Individually and collectively they put the lie to the notion that old-time collaborative relationships between authors and editors are passé. This book was first encouraged years ago by Linda Doyle and Carol Franco. The belief of our first editor, Marjorie Williams, in the project was a critical factor in our proceeding at all. Sarah Weaver's copyediting has clarified what we wanted to say by cleaning up the prose and clearing out the underbrush. Amanda Elkin, our manuscript editor, has been a steady and supportive force. But we never would have made it to the finish line without the gentle prodding, great insights, and nurturing encouragement of Jeff Kehoe, our editor. A relatively new parent, Jeff handled us with subtle parenting skills, knowing just when to draw the line and when to let us go. We also want to thank, but unfortunately not by name, the anonymous readers selected by the Press, whose no-holds barred critique was a critical wake-up call for us at a crucial juncture in the process.

There are eight people who played a special role in helping this book come to be. Many of these ideas were first articulated by Ron's longtime collaborator, Riley Sinder, who first intuited the difference between leadership and authority, who cobuilt the framework, and who painstakingly reviewed this manuscript with detailed comments and rewrites at every stage of the process. Sousan Abadian played a special role in taking us through the penultimate manuscript line-by-line and pushing us over the top. Marty's wife, Lynn Staley, brought her designer's eye and editor's judgment to bear at important turning points; she also endured with grace his absence and inattentiveness as the project rumbled toward its close. Kathryn Heifetz, Ron's wife, brought wonderful clarity of logic with words, a more active voice, and human understanding to our new preface. We hired two book doctors along the way. Kelly Rappuchi helped us clarify our essential purposes and better use of Ron's experiences and stories. And Kent Lineback became part of our core team, coming to endless meetings, forcing us to clarify and refine the story line, drafting and redrafting, prodding us to do better—all the while being an unflagging cheerleader for what we were trying to do. We were also blessed with two wonderful faculty assistants at the Kennedy School, Sheila Blake and Kathleen Kaminski. Sheila and Kathleen provided terrific research support, screened out diversionary intrusions so we could work together, and did their best to keep the rest of our lives from spiraling out of control when this project became all-consuming.

We imposed shamelessly on many of our friends and colleagues to read part or all of the manuscript at various stages of its creation. We received extremely detailed and constructive page-by-page feedback from Tom Bennett, Charles Buki, Robyn Champion, Katherine Fulton, Milton Heifetz, and Steven Rothstein. We had generous and very useful advice from David A. Heifetz, Steve Boyd, Ben Cheever, Brent Coffin, Phil Heymann, John Hubner, Barbara Kellerman, John Kotter, Steve Lakis, Larry Moses, Hugh O'Doherty, Sharon Parks, Richard Pascale, Bernie Steinberg, Bill Ury, and Dean Williams.

Finally, this effort began more than a decade ago in the first years of the Leadership Education Project at the Kennedy School. Derek Bok suggested that we write a practical treatment of leadership, in the spirit of Fisher and Ury's *Getting to Yes*, which Marty edited. Sr. Theresa Monroe, a colleague and gifted educator who helped give birth to the Project, devoted mind, heart, and soul to setting this effort on its way. Jenny Gelber, a skilled consultant to the Project, held together with warmth and ingenuity a small team of pioneering graduate students who brainstormed ideas with us and gave us courage. We have not strayed far from those initial purposes.

> *Ron Heifetz*
> *Marty Linsky*
> *Cambridge, Massachusetts*

Leadership on the Line

Introduction

Every day the opportunity for leadership stands before you.

- A father gets drawn into the same old destructive argument at the dinner table, but one day breaks out of the pattern and seeks family counseling.

- An investment banker nearly closes a $100 billion acquisition, but confounds everyone by putting the whole deal at risk when she asks, "Can these companies create synergies fast enough to satisfy the investors, given the current talent and different cultures within each of the businesses?"

- A politician challenges constituents to accept responsibility for locating a prison in their community, rather than chant the same old slogan, "Not in our backyard!"

- A neighbor watches the nice kid down the street getting lost in his teenage years long after his mother dies, and organizes a weekly coffee for parents in the neighborhood in order to provide support for the father and his family.

- You sit through a meeting, watching people avoid the real issues, and decide that you will be the one who puts them on the table.

Each day brings you opportunities to raise important questions, speak to higher values, and surface unresolved conflicts. Every day you have the chance to make a difference in the lives of people around you.

And every day you must decide whether to put your contribution out there, or keep it to yourself to avoid upsetting anyone, and get through another day. You are right to be cautious. Prudence is a virtue. You disturb people when you take unpopular initiatives in your community, put provocative new ideas on the table in your organization, question the gap between colleagues' values and behavior, or ask friends and relatives to face up to tough realities. You risk people's ire and make yourself vulnerable. Exercising leadership can get you into a lot of trouble.

To lead is to live dangerously because when leadership counts, when you lead people through difficult change, you challenge what people hold dear—their daily habits, tools, loyalties, and ways of thinking—with nothing more to offer perhaps than a possibility. Moreover, leadership often means exceeding the authority you are given to tackle the challenge at hand. People push back when you disturb the personal and institutional equilibrium they know. And people resist in all kinds of creative and unexpected ways that can get you taken out of the game: pushed aside, undermined, or eliminated.

It is no wonder that when the myriad opportunities to exercise leadership call, you often hesitate. Anyone who has stepped out on the line, leading part or all of an organization, a community, or a family, knows the personal and professional vulnerabilities. However gentle your style, however careful your strategy, however sure you may be that you are on the right track, leading is risky business.

This book is about taking opportunities to lead, and staying alive. We ask these fundamental questions: Why and how is leadership dangerous? How can you respond to these dangers? And how can you keep your spirit alive when the going gets very tough? We are both straightforward about the hazards of leadership and idealistic about the importance of taking these risks. Many leadership books are all about inspiration, but downplay the perspiration. We respect how tough this work is. We know too many people with scars to show for their efforts. We have scars ourselves and harbor no illusions.

Yet we believe that leadership, while perilous, is an enterprise worthy of the costs. Our communities, organizations, and societies need people, from wherever they work and live, to take up the challenges within reach rather than complain about the lack of leadership from on high, hold off until they receive a "call" to action, or wait for their turn in the top job. This has always been true, but may especially be so now, in the post-September 11, 2001, world of uncertainty and vulnerability.

Meeting these challenges need not entail getting put down or pushed aside, personally or professionally. To adapt a phrase from Johnny Cash, we believe you can "walk the line," step forward, make a difference, take the heat, and survive to delight in the fruits of your labor.

Leadership is worth the risk because the goals extend beyond material gain or personal advancement. By making the lives of people around you better, leadership provides meaning in life. It creates purpose. We believe that every human being has something unique to offer, and that a larger sense of purpose comes from using that gift to help your organizations, families, or communities thrive. The gift might be your knowledge, your experience, your values, your presence, your heart, or your wisdom. Perhaps it's simply your basic curiosity and your willingness to raise unsettling questions.

So, first and foremost, this book is about you, about how to survive and thrive amidst the dangers of leadership. It's also about getting more out of life by putting more into it. We've written it for those of you who play it safe because you can't imagine stepping out or speaking up without getting burned, as well as for the risk-takers among you who know what it's like to get shot down when you challenge people to change. This book is about putting yourself and your ideas on the line, responding effectively to the risks, and living to celebrate the meaning of your efforts.

This book is about our times, too. We live in a period in history when taking on the risks of leadership in your individual world is both more important and more complicated than ever before. Globalization of the economy, the necessary interaction of cultures, and ready access to information and communication through the internet make interdependence palpable. Hierarchical structures with clearly defined roles are giving way to more horizontal organizations with greater flexibility, room for initiative, and corresponding uncertainty. Democratization is spreading throughout organizations as well as countries. All of these movements create new opportunities for you to make a difference.

This book is also about us, Ron and Marty. We have been colleagues and friends for thirty-plus years, working and teaching together; sharing our research and experience; and exploring, testing, and refining our ideas about the demands of leadership in modern life. The more we talk and work together, the more we find our experiences and insights overlap. Ron first draws inferences about how the world works from music and medicine, and Marty from media and politics. What do these four diverse fields have to do with leadership? Music is about moving people, about striking chords that resonate deeply in the hearts of listeners. It provides a language for elusive but central qualities like harmony, resolution, timing, improvisation, creativity, and inspiration. Politics teaches that no one can accomplish anything of significance alone; the more challenging the problem, the more the people who will bear the consequences of its solution must take responsibility for working on it. Psychiatry opens up a greater understanding of the way humans contend with challenges, individually and collectively, and the media make us aware that the way the message is delivered and the identity of the messenger can often seem as important to making progress as the message itself. Perspectives and lessons from these and other disciplines will, we hope, add depth and color.

As consultants, we work with clients from the public, private, and nonprofit sectors. As teachers, we work in and out of the classroom with hundreds of students at the John F. Kennedy School of Government at Harvard University, where each of us has served on the faculty for two decades. From these experiences, we have come to understand that many people operate at the frontiers of leadership in their personal, civic, and professional lives. We've been inspired repeatedly by those who take responsibility for mobilizing people to seize new opportunities and tackle tough problems. From the stories of our students and clients around the world, we have distilled and captured lessons that we now offer, not as brand-new ideas, but as guides to help you name, organize, and make sense out of your experience.

A number of the ideas in this book were first introduced in Ron's earlier book, *Leadership Without Easy Answers*; and indeed, this book grew out of the last section entitled "Staying Alive." In our subsequent teaching and consulting, people have found this issue compelling, calling for much fuller consideration. *Leadership Without Easy Answers* was intended as a theoretical framework for understanding leadership and authority in the context of adaptive change; *Leadership on the Line* is very different in voice and character. We wanted this second book to be more focused, more practical, and more personal. We hope this book will be accessible, eminently usable, and inspiring in your life and work.

Leadership on the Line builds upon our years of working with people from many nations and walks of life: from workers, managers, and activists; presidents of countries and multinational corporations; homemakers and parents working outside the home; generals and admirals as well as lieutenants and privates; senior and junior executives within businesses and governments; teachers and principals; and trustees and clergy.

None of these people sat content on the sidelines day after day. They take pride in their successes, but most carry wounds from the times they gave voice to a point of view that disturbed people. They all wanted their lives and their work to matter.

In part one of the book, we discuss why leadership is so dangerous and how people get taken out of the game.

In part two, we offer a series of action ideas designed to reduce the risk of getting pushed aside.

In part three, we discuss ways that people contribute to their own demise. We offer ideas about critical, though often neglected, aspects of exercising leadership: how to manage your personal vulnerabilities, care for yourself, and sustain your spirit.

Leadership opportunities beckon daily. We hope these lessons will help you put yourself on the line and stay alive, not only in your job, but also in your family and community, and in your heart and soul.

PART ONE

The Challenge

1

The Heart of Danger

Maggie Brooke grew up on a small Native American reservation in which nearly everyone older than twelve drank alcohol. After sobering up in her twenties, she spent more than a decade leading her people toward health. Now a grandmother in her forties and a tribal elder, Maggie counsels a steady stream of visitors in her home throughout the day. One evening, she told her visitor about Lois, the woman who first inspired her to try to do something about the alcohol dependency among her people.

"Twenty years ago I used to baby-sit for Lois, who lived in a neighboring band within our tribe. Once a week I'd go the few miles to her community and take care of Lois's little ones. But after about two months, I started to wonder, 'What could Lois possibly be doing every Tuesday night? There's not much to do around here in these villages.' So one evening after Lois left to go to the meeting lodge, I packed up the children and went over to the lodge to find out what she was doing. We looked through a window into the lodge and saw a big circle of chairs, all neatly in place, with Lois sitting in a chair all by herself. The chairs in the circle were empty.

"I was really curious, you know, so when Lois came home that evening, I asked her, 'Lois, what are you doing every Tuesday night?'

And she said, 'I thought I told you weeks ago, I've been holding AA (Alcoholics Anonymous) meetings.' So I asked her back, 'What do you mean you're holding meetings? I went over there tonight with the children and looked through the window. We watched you sitting there in that circle of chairs, all alone.'

"Lois got quiet—'I wasn't alone,' she said. 'I was there with the spirits and the ancestors; and one day, our people will come.'"

Lois never gave up. "Every week Lois set up those chairs neatly in a circle, and for two hours, she just sat there," Maggie recalled. "No one came to those meetings for a long time, and even after three years, there were only a few people in the room. But ten years later, the room was filled with people. The community began turning around. People began ridding themselves of alcohol. I felt so inspired by Lois that I couldn't sit still watching us poison ourselves."

Lois and then Maggie worked on becoming sober themselves, and then challenged their friends, families, and neighbors to change and renew their lives, too. Leading these communities required extraordinary self-examination, perseverance, and courage. Their native history was full of people, some of them with goodwill, who had forced tribes to give up familiar and reliable ways, and now these communities were being asked to change again, with no reason to think that things would get much better. Lois and Maggie were asking people to face the trade-offs between the numbing solace of alcohol and the hard work of renewing their daily lives. There would be no progress until they had put alcohol dependency behind them. But people found it extremely difficult to give up their way of coping, particularly for some intangible idea about the future. They had fought back before when others had made them change their ways, and they fought Lois and Maggie.

The two women were mocked and marginalized. They spent years feeling out of place in their own communities, unwelcome at parties and gatherings where alcohol flowed, so ostracized that even holidays became lonely, solitary events. Indeed, for long stretches of time they spent weekends off the reservation to find people they

could talk to. They had put themselves at risk, as well as key relationships with neighbors, friends, and family. Eventually, they succeeded and survived. But for a long time, they could not know.
They could have lost everything.[1]

Leadership Is Dangerous

In the early 1990s, Yitzhak Rabin, then prime minister of Israel,
had been moving the country toward an accommodation with the
Palestinians. Slowly but surely Rabin was bringing a majority of
Israelis along with him. But he also had deeply disturbed the right
wing in Israel, particularly the religious right, by his success in
getting the community to wrestle with the difficult and painful
trade-offs between long-term peace and territory. The right wing
refused to face the reality that they would have to give up land they
considered sacred for peace. They tried to debate the issue, but they
were losing the argument. So they began to make Rabin himself the
issue, rather than his policies. The result was Rabin's assassination,
a tragedy, as well as a terrible setback for his initiatives. His successor, Benyamin Netanyahu, retreated, unwilling to push the Israeli
people to face the costs of peace. Indeed, the period before Rabin's
death marked a high point in the willingness of the Israeli people to
decide, among deeply held values, which were most precious and
which could be left behind.

Assassinations are extreme examples of what people will do to
silence the voices of frustrating realities. Asking an entire community to change its ways, as Lois and Maggie succeeded in doing and
Yitzhak Rabin sacrificed himself in attempting, is dangerous. If
leadership were about giving people good news, the job would be
easy. If Lois had been gathering people every week to distribute
money or to sing their praises, the chairs would not have stayed
empty for so long. If Rabin had promised peace with no loss of
land, he might have survived. People do not resist change, per se.
People resist loss.

You appear dangerous to people when you question their values, beliefs, or habits of a lifetime. You place yourself on the line when you tell people what they need to hear rather than what they want to hear. Although you may see with clarity and passion a promising future of progress and gain, people will see with equal passion the losses you are asking them to sustain.

Think about the times you have had something important to say and have pulled back, when you have tried and failed, or succeeded but were bruised along the way. Or when you have watched the trials and successes of other people. The hope of leadership lies in the capacity to deliver disturbing news and raise difficult questions in a way that people can absorb, prodding them to take up the message rather than ignore it or kill the messenger.

As a doctor, Ron faced this challenge every day. Every patient looks to the doctor, hoping for a painless remedy; and every day doctors have to tell people that their health depends on enduring the pains of change—in giving up their favorite foods, taking time out of each overextended day for exercise, taking medications that have side effects, or breaking an addiction to cigarettes, alcohol, or work. Ron saw a few doctors who were artists of the profession as well as technical experts. They had learned how to engage patients and their families in reshaping their values, attitudes, and long-standing habits. But this was demanding and risky. Discussions can backfire if they seem unfeeling or abrupt, and angry patients can find a variety of ways to damage a doctor's reputation. Ron saw many more doctors give little more than lip service to this part of their job, all the while complaining about *patient noncompliance*—a term doctors use to describe people's resistance to taking medicine and advice. In frustration, they would say to themselves, "Why do people avoid facing reality and resist following my instructions?" But then they would take the easy road, playing it safe by pandering to the desire for a technical fix, avoiding the difficult conversations rather than disturbing people in an attempt to change the ways they lived.

Lois, Maggie, and Rabin had to engage people in facing a hard reality. Just as patients hope to receive a doctor's fast and painless cure, some Native Americans might place all their hopes on a new casino or look for a technical explanation for their pains (a genetic predisposition to alcoholism). And most every Israeli would prefer to have peace without giving up any of their ancient homeland. In each case—the patient, the Native American community, the Israeli people—people must face the challenge of adapting to a tough reality, and the adaptation requires giving up an important value or a current way of life. Leadership becomes dangerous, then, when it must confront people with loss. Rabin, Lois, Maggie, and the best doctors mobilize change by challenging people to answer a core but painful question: Of all that we value, what's really most precious and what's expendable?

The Perils of Adaptive Change

Leadership would be a safe undertaking if your organizations and communities only faced problems for which they already knew the solutions. Every day, people have problems for which they do, in fact, have the necessary know-how and procedures. We call these technical problems. But there is a whole host of problems that are not amenable to authoritative expertise or standard operating procedures. They cannot be solved by someone who provides answers from on high. We call these adaptive challenges because they require experiments, new discoveries, and adjustments from numerous places in the organization or community. Without learning new ways—changing attitudes, values, and behaviors—people cannot make the adaptive leap necessary to thrive in the new environment. The sustainability of change depends on having the people with the problem internalize the change itself.

People cannot see at the beginning of the adaptive process that the new situation will be any better than the current condition. What they do see clearly is the potential for loss. People frequently avoid painful adjustments in their lives if they can postpone them, place the burden on somebody else, or call someone to the rescue.

When fears and passions run high, people can become desperate as they look to authorities for the answers. This dynamic renders adaptive contexts inherently dangerous.

When people look to authorities for easy answers to adaptive challenges, they end up with dysfunction. They expect the person in charge to know what to do, and under the weight of that responsibility, those in authority frequently end up faking it or disappointing people, or they get spit out of the system in the belief that a new "leader" will solve the problem. In fact, there's a proportionate relationship between risk and adaptive change: The deeper the change and the greater the amount of new learning required, the more resistance there will be and, thus, the greater the danger to those who lead. For this reason, people often try to avoid the dangers, either consciously or subconsciously, by treating an adaptive challenge as if it were a technical one. This is why we see so much more routine management than leadership in our society.

The table "Distinguishing Technical from Adaptive Challenges" captures the difference between the technical work of routine management and the adaptive work of leadership.

Indeed, the single most common source of leadership failure we've been able to identify—in politics, community life, business, or the nonprofit sector—is that people, especially those in positions of authority, treat adaptive challenges like technical problems.

In times of distress, when everyone looks to authorities to provide direction, protection, and order, this is an easy diagnostic mistake to make. In the face of adaptive pressures, people don't want questions; they want answers. They don't want to be told that they

Distinguishing Technical from Adaptive Challenges

	What's the Work?	Who Does the Work?
Technical	Apply current know-how	Authorities
Adaptive	Learn new ways	The people with the problem

will have to sustain losses; rather, they want to know how you're going to protect them from the pains of change. And of course you want to fulfill their needs and expectations, not bear the brunt of their frustration and anger at the bad news you're giving.

In mobilizing adaptive work, you have to engage people in adjusting their unrealistic expectations, rather than try to satisfy them as if the situation were amenable primarily to a technical remedy. You have to counteract their exaggerated dependency and promote their resourcefulness. This takes an extraordinary level of presence, time, and artful communication, but it may also take more time and trust than you have.

This was the box Ecuador's president Jamil Mahuad found himself in early in January 2000, when he faced the prospect of mass demonstrations, with thousands of indigenous Ecuadorians mobilizing to throw him out of office. His popularity had fallen from 70 percent approval to 15 percent in less than a year. With the country in the midst of a catastrophic and rapid economic meltdown, on the eve of the demonstrations Mahuad said he felt trapped. "I've lost my connection with the people."

One year before, he had been a hero, a peacemaker. In his first months in office, he ended a war with Peru that had lasted more than two hundred years, signing a peace treaty with great excitement in the air. But his heroic accomplishments were to be washed away within less than four months by the effects of numerous natural and economic disasters: El Niño storms, which devastated 16 percent of Ecuador's gross domestic product, the financial crisis that swept through East Asia and then Latin America, high inflation, crushing foreign debt, bankrupt banks, the lowest oil prices since Ecuador had started to export oil, and a political culture that had brought down four presidents in eight years. On January 21, 2000, a coalition of military officers and indigenous demonstrators forced Mahuad out of office, another casualty of the country's ongoing crisis.

Mahuad described the contrast between being mayor of Quito and president of the entire country. As mayor, the people welcomed him openly as he walked daily around town. During his walks, he could often get people to cooperate to solve their own problems, or he could apply a little pressure and resources to help out. As mayor, he had the advantage that people looked for local solutions to local problems, and worked with him. He was in touch with them and they with him.

However, when he became president and had responsibility for the national economic crisis, the people wanted him to find remedies for which other regions and localities would pay the costs. The people did not want him to tell them they had to change. He made several trips abroad to plead for help from the International Monetary Fund, World Bank, and U.S. Treasury. He consulted many worthy economic experts at home, in Latin America generally, in the United States, and in Europe. He came to see that any practical solution would require each region and sector of his society to endure considerable pain, at least in the short run.

Mahuad said afterward, "I felt like a doctor in an emergency ward on a Saturday night. And the patient came in with a badly damaged and gangrenous leg. And, from my medical experience, I had to amputate the patient's leg to save the patient's life. The family said, 'You don't have to amputate.' I insisted on amputation to save the patient's life, but I lost the confidence of the family. The family held me responsible for the patient's problem."

As president, he grew increasingly distant from his various publics as he faced rising hostility and focused most of his attention on finding the right economic policy to reverse the downturn. Yet his trips to Washington yielded no assistance. Countless conversations with policy experts prompted a variety of prescriptions, but no clear way out of the quagmire. Meanwhile, poor people in the villages found the price of food rising beyond their reach. Many flocked to the cities, selling their wares on the streets. As inflation soared, the unions became furious at the lost value of paychecks. The business sector lost faith, sending their money north to the United States and hastening the insolvency of the banks.

Mahuad made bold moves in response to the crisis. Ecuador would cut government salaries, reduce conscription into the army, cancel orders for the purchase of military equipment, default on its loans, freeze bank balances to stop the run on the banks and the draining of foreign currency reserves, and finally, convert its currency to the dollar.

Yet the adaptive challenge was enormous. Even under the rosiest scenarios, there would be further job loss, more rising prices, and increased uncertainty before people would feel the benefits of an economic turnaround. The most brilliant policy solution, coupled with a rise in the price of oil, would not have stopped the ongoing disruption caused by opening the economy to a more competitive world.

Although Mahuad worked tirelessly to halt the falling economy, ironically, the public felt that he had disengaged. They were right in one sense: He had disengaged from them. To use his metaphor, he had performed the amputation because it was the best of the available options, but he did not prepare the family for what they would have to endure. Many surgeons could have done the amputation, but only Mahuad, as president, could have helped the family face their situation. Spending most of his time working through the issues and options with technical experts and trying every means available to persuade foreign creditors for assistance, Mahuad paid less attention to his political colleagues and to the people on the streets and in the villages. In retrospect, he might have let his technical experts in the ministries do all of the technical work so that he could focus heavily on the political and adaptive work. Instead, looking back at his weekly calendar, Mahuad realized he had spent more than 65 percent of his time working in a technical problem-solving mode and less than 35 percent of his time working with the politicians and public groups with direct stakes in the situation. Rather than using every day as an opportunity to be a visible champion to his people—to provide hope and to explain the process and pains of modernization in a globalizing economy—he devoted most of his time to searching for the right policy solution and then attempting to get the people to be reasonable in accepting the necessary technical fixes. Although he recognized the adaptive challenges, he hoped to find a short-term remedy that would give him time to deal with them.[2]

Clearly, the odds were badly stacked against him. But when you focus your energy primarily on the technical aspects of complex challenges, you do opt for short-term rewards. Sometimes by doing so you might strategically buy some time to deal with the adaptive elements. But you might use up precious time and find yourself, like Mahuad, running out of it anyway. In a far less demanding crisis, you may make people happy for a while, but over time you risk your credibility and perhaps your job. Reality may catch up with you as people discover that they are unprepared for the world in which they now live. And though they ought to blame themselves for sticking their heads in the sand and pressuring you to sanction their behavior, it's much more likely they'll blame you.

When you are in a position of authority, there are also strong internal pressures to focus on the technical aspects of problems. Most of us take pride in our ability to answer the tough questions that are thrown our way. We get rewarded for bearing people's uncertainty and want to be seen in a competent, heroic light. We like the feeling of stepping up to the plate and having the crowds cheer us on. Yet raising questions that go to the core of people's habits goes unrewarded, at least for a while. You get booed instead of cheered. In fact, it may be a long time before you hear any applause—if ever. They may throw tomatoes. They may shoot bullets. Leadership takes the capacity to stomach hostility so that you can stay connected to people, lest you disengage from them and exacerbate the danger.

There is nothing trivial about solving technical problems. Medical personnel save lives every day in the emergency room through their authoritative expertise because they have the right procedures, the right norms, and the right knowledge. Through our managerial know-how, we produce an economy full of products and services, many of them crucial to our daily lives. What makes a problem technical is not that it is trivial; but simply that its solution already lies within the organization's repertoire. In contrast, adaptive pressures force the organization to change, lest it decline.

In the twenty-first century, people and organizations face adaptive pressures every day, in their individual lives and at all levels of society; and each leadership opportunity to respond to these challenges also carries with it attendant risks. For example, when your car breaks down, you go to a mechanic. Most of the time, the mechanic can fix it. However, if the car breaks down because of the way members of the family use it, the problem will probably happen again. The mechanic might be able to get the car on the road once more. But by continuing to deal with it as a purely technical problem a mechanic can solve, the family may end up avoiding the underlying issues demanding adaptive work, such as how to persuade the mother to stop drinking and driving, or the grandfather to give up his driver's license, or the teenagers to be more cautious. No doubt, any family member would find it difficult and risky to step forward and lead the prickly conversations with the mother, grandfather, or even the teenage driver.

The terrorism of September 11, 2001, brought home to the United States an adaptive challenge that has been festering for a very long time. With the unthinkable destruction of the World Trade Center, Americans felt a new vulnerability. In response, the initial tendency of the U.S. government was to reduce terrorism to a technical problem of security systems, military and police operations, and criminal justice. But terrorism represents an adaptive challenge to our civil liberties, our mindset of invulnerability, and our capacity to narrow the divide between Christian West and Muslim East that began with the Crusades one thousand years ago. Should we trust government officials with information that we consider private, in the interest of our collective security? Can we accept the undeniable reality that we live in an interdependent world in which safety must primarily be found in the health of our relationships with very different cultures? Can we refashion the religious arrogance that leads people to equate their faith in God with the singular belief that they know God's truth better than anyone else, and that their mission then is to capture the market for people's souls? Nearly everyone in the United States has the opportunity to exercise leadership in this adaptive context, yet there will be personal dangers in raising the more difficult questions, some of which, like religious triumphalism, go to the root of religious loyalty and dogma.

Going Beyond Your Authority

People rarely elect or hire anyone to disturb their jobs or their lives. People expect politicians and managers to use their authority to provide them with the right answers, not to confront them with disturbing questions and difficult choices. That's why the initial challenge, and risk, of exercising leadership is to go beyond your authority—to put your credibility and position on the line in order to get people to tackle the problems at hand. Without the willingness to challenge people's expectations of you, there is no way you can escape being dominated by the social system and its inherent limits.

Generally, people will not authorize someone to make them face what they do not want to face. Instead, people hire someone to provide protection and ensure stability, someone with solutions that require a minimum of disruption. But adaptive work creates risk, conflict, and instability because addressing the issues underlying adaptive problems may involve upending deep and entrenched norms. Thus, leadership requires disturbing people—but at a rate they can absorb.

Typically, a company faces adaptive pressures when new market conditions threaten the company's business. For example, in the last decade of the twentieth century, innovators in IBM attempted to get the company to wake up to the real threats from small computers running what soon came to be called the "internet." And the innovators in IBM repeatedly found themselves in Lois's position when she tried to get her community to face up to alcoholism. Their efforts illustrate the perseverance required of leadership until a successful adaptation can take hold.

As an established corporate giant, IBM in 1994 was a master of technical problem solving. The corporation embodied technical proficiency and served as the official technology sponsor of the 1994 Winter Olympics. IBM kept track of the many winter sports competitors, competition areas, timings, and standings that were scattered over a wide expanse in Norway.[3]

IBM understandably wanted to protect its position in the technical areas in which IBM managers excelled. When the sports standings were reported on television, viewers saw the IBM logo on their screens. This was smart problem solving within the business areas that IBM managers understood well: sports, television, and marketing. Corporate buyers of IBM mainframe systems who watched the Olympics on television probably appreciated the appearance of the IBM logo.

But the markets were changing and business was migrating to the internet. The companies that did not adapt fast enough would fail. Some dark clouds were hovering over IBM's technological successes in the Olympics. The corporation had suffered $15 billion in losses over the prior three years, reflecting problems in many of their product lines. The financial setbacks made people at IBM vulnerable and even more risk averse than usual. Moreover, they were culturally and emotionally unprepared to make the big leap to the internet world.[4] The underlying value structure of the organization as a whole was characterized by a smug parochialism coupled with a resistance to early entry into new markets. Nothing less than the IBM culture and underlying corporate values had to change in order to succeed in the internet environment.

Watching the Olympics at home near his office at Cornell University's Theory Center, a young IBM Corporation engineer named David Grossman discovered that an enterprising website had intercepted the IBM feed to the television networks, diverted the information to the internet, and was displaying IBM's tabulations under the Sun Microsystems, Inc., logo. Grossman was shocked. "And IBM didn't have a clue . . ." he recalled.

As he soon discovered, the problem, like many tough problems, contained both technical and adaptive elements. After his effort to get managers to understand the technical parts of the problem, IBM attorneys sent Sun Microsystems a letter demanding that Sun stop displaying the IBM data on the Sun site. That effort to protect IBM's work product was resolved with IBM's existing legal and technical expertise.

At the same time, as Grossman pushed IBM managers to deal with the business that the internet would continue to grab from IBM, he uncovered values and lifetime habits that were unrealistic and dysfunctional in the internet age. These beliefs about how the business world worked kept IBM from dealing with the reality of the new market challenge. The internet provided an entirely new channel for marketing products and a vehicle for a raft of potential new products and services, such as consulting services to existing clients on internet applications and new internet-friendly software. The speed of change was faster than any of the senior managers had ever witnessed in their long careers. It was as if IBM were depending on continued strong sales of first-rate buggy whips while the automobile was right around the corner. The company was so behind the curve that Grossman could not even find a way to use IBM's primitive email system to send the IBM marketing staff in Norway the screen shots from Sun's website as he watched the piracy during the Winter Games.

Luckily, some IBM managers grasped enough of the reality of the problem to come to Grossman's aid when he made his arguments. In particular, John Patrick, who had managed the marketing of the IBM ThinkPad laptop, proceeded to secure for Grossman and other innovators the attention they would need to shift the outmoded values and habits in the IBM corporate culture.

Grossman and Patrick led a struggle inside the company that lasted for five years. Just prior to the new millennium, IBM managers emerged as a team with revamped values, more flexible beliefs, and new behavior patterns designed to make IBM a proactive force in an internet world.

The change was profound and deep. IBM had a reputation for being a bureaucratic dinosaur. But by 1999, Lou Gerstner, CEO of IBM, could trumpet hard figures on the five-year IBM restructuring to Wall Street investors. Gerstner could show that IBM was a highly profitable internet company, with internal operations, business processes, and customer responses that compared favorably with even the most innovative of internet corporations. Approximately one-quarter of its $82 billion in revenues was now Internet related.[5] The demonstration of the culture change in IBM was so convincing that IBM's stock shot up twenty points.[6]

Rather than frame the internet as a technical challenge for IBM's experts, Grossman and Patrick presented it as a cultural and values problem that IBM had neglected when it broke into smaller, more manageable departments. CEO Gerstner described the work this way: "We discovered what every large company has. When you bring your company to the web, you expose all the inefficiency that comes from decentralized organizations."[7]

As middle managers, Grossman and Patrick had the authority to direct only those few who reported to them. And even then, they could not order their employees to act against company policy. They each also reported to a boss. Both Grossman and Patrick went beyond their authority when progress required it. Patrick said, "If you don't occasionally exceed your formal authority, you are not pushing the envelope."[8]

As a lowly engineer, Grossman went around the chain of command, taking the risk of being obnoxious and putting himself on the line in danger of ridicule. Once, he barged into the Armonk, New York, IBM corporate headquarters, alone but for a UNIX computer under his arm, to introduce the senior executive in marketing, Abby Kohnstamm, to the internet. In the same vein, Patrick saw at an early internet trade show how much difference it made to have the biggest space in the display. So he committed IBM for the biggest display space in the next year's show, even though it was not his job to make that decision alone. However, if he had waited for the IBM bureaucracy to set aside the money and give him the authorization, the display space auction would have closed and the opportunity would have been missed.

To act outside the narrow confines of your job description when progress requires it lies close to the heart of leadership, and to its danger. Your initiative in breaking the boundaries of your authorization might pay off for your organization or community. In retrospect, it might even be recognized as crucial for success. Along the way, however, you will face resistance and possibly the pain of disciplinary action or other rebukes from senior authority for breaking the rules. You will be characterized as being out of place, out of turn, or too big for your britches.

The toughest problems that groups and communities face are hard precisely because the group or community will not authorize anyone to push them to address those problems. To the contrary, the rules, organizational culture and norms, standard operating procedures, and economic incentives regularly discourage people from facing the hardest questions and making the most difficult choices.

In the 1990s, when New York City mayor Rudolph Giuliani and his police chief, William Bratton, forcefully went after the crime problem in New York City, they were doing exactly what many in the community wanted them to do, and what they were implicitly authorized to do. They were expected to relentlessly crack down on crime without forcing the community to accept any trade-offs the police might have to make in terms of police brutality and people's civil liberties. Like many communities, most people in New York City wanted the crime problem to be solved without having to compromise other values. Going with the grain of public expectations—their informal authorization—Giuliani and Bratton brought down the crime rate. Giuliani was rewarded when a satisfied public reelected him in 1997 by a landslide.

However, just before his reelection, on the night of April 9, 1997, some police officers brutalized Abner Louima with a toilet plunger. The incident came to light very quickly, and the ensuing controversy began to focus the broader community on some of the difficult trade-offs they had heretofore been reluctant to make. The issue of racial profiling by police had already been percolating as a signal that an erosion of civil liberties was the price to pay for the reduction in crime. Then, a year and a half later, a young, unarmed West African immigrant, Amadou Diallo, was shot forty-one times by four white police officers in a search for a rape suspect that went terribly wrong. Although the four officers in the Diallo incident were acquitted, the incident raised further questions about what had been the social and human costs of the otherwise successful crackdown on crime.

Leadership is not the same as authority. It would have been an exercise of leadership, and not just authority, had Giuliani gone public with the question: "How zealous should the police be, at the expense of individual liberty and increased brutality?" Had the public, and Bratton's police department, been forced to deal with that trade-off, Giuliani would surely have been attacked by the press, the public, and the police department. However, this also might have provoked people to take responsibility for their choices as citizens. Moreover, it might have led to creative thinking and new options—solutions that other police departments across America were finding during those very same years, producing dramatic reductions in crime without such high costs.[9] Giuliani and Bratton were not authorized to make their constituencies own the issue and resolve those trade-offs.

Of course, exceeding your authority is not, in and of itself, leadership. You may be courageous and you may have vision, but these qualities may have nothing to do with getting people to grapple with hard realities. For example, Colonel Oliver North went beyond his authority in the Iran-Contra affair. Transferring money from Iran arms sales to buy Contra weapons may or may not have had approval from the White House, but it was certainly beyond the authority he had from the Congress. Yet, rather than get U.S. policymakers to tackle the problems posed by Iran and Nicaragua, he tried to engineer secret fixes behind their backs. He failed to lead because he took Congress and the White House off the hook of having to grapple with the issues and make unpopular choices.

Rosa Parks, an elderly black woman, also went beyond her authority when she refused to move to the back of a bus in Montgomery, Alabama, in 1955. What distinguishes her from North, however, and made her behavior an act of leadership, was that she and other civil rights leaders used the incident to *focus* public attention and responsibility on the issue of civil rights, not to avoid it. Her action provoked an outcry of protest that catalyzed the civil rights movement of the 1960s. Congress, the White House, and the American people were provoked to engage the issues, confront deep-seated loyalties, and make new choices.

At the Heart of Danger Is Loss

Frequently, people who seek to exercise leadership are amazed that their organizations and communities resist. Why should people oppose you when you are helping them change habits, attitudes, and values that only hold them back, when you are doing something good for them?

Ron recalls serving as a medical intern at the King's County Hospital emergency room in Brooklyn, New York, and working with women who had been battered by their boyfriends or husbands. He would ask in various ways, "Why not leave the guy? Surely life can be better for you." And in a variety of ways they would respond, "Well, my boyfriend gets this way sometimes when he's drinking, but when he's sober he loves me so much. I've never known anyone love me more sweetly than he does, except when he's going crazy. What would I do alone?"

To persuade people to give up the love they know for a love they've never experienced means convincing them to take a leap of faith in themselves and in life. They must experience the loss of a relationship that, despite its problems, provides satisfaction and familiarity, and they will suffer the discomfort of sustained uncertainty about what will replace it. In breaking with the past, there will be historical losses to contend with, too, particularly the feelings of disloyalty to the sources of the values that kept the relationship together. For example, acknowledging the damage from abusive parents earlier in life also means experiencing disloyalty to them. It's hard to sift through and salvage what's valuable from those primary relationships and leave the chaff behind. Even doing that success-fully will be experienced somewhat as a disloyalty to those relation-ships. Moreover, change challenges a person's sense of competence. A battered woman experiences some competence in coping with her familiar setting; starting anew means going through a sustained period in which she experiences a loss of that competence as she retools her life.

Habits, values, and attitudes, even dysfunctional ones, are part of one's identity. To change the way people see and do things is to chal-lenge how they define themselves.

Marty experienced this when he got divorced. He had two young children. He had always told himself that he was deeply committed to their welfare as well as to his own self-actualization. But then he had to choose between the two; he could no longer say truthfully that he was equally committed to both values. His self-identity changed.

People's definitions of themselves often involve roles and priori-ties that others might perceive as self-destructive or as barriers to progress. For some young people, to be a woman is to be a teenage mother. To be a cool man is to take drugs or father a child. For some, to honor one's family is to be a terrorist. For some rich people, to be somebody is to belong to an exclusive club. For some politicians, satisfaction comes from making constituents happy, even if what they need is to be shaken out of their complacency. To give up those conceptions of self may trigger feelings of considerable loss.

Habits are hard to give up because they give stability. They are predictable. In going through the pains of adaptive change, there is no guarantee that the result will be an improvement. Smokers understand this. They know that the odds of getting cancer are uncertain, while they know for sure that an enormous source of relaxation and satisfaction will be lost when the cigarettes are gone.

But perhaps the deepest influence is that habits, values, and attitudes come from somewhere, and to abandon them means to be disloyal to their origin. Indeed, our deeply held loyalties serve as a keystone in the structure of our identities. Loyalty is a double-edged sword. On one hand, it represents loving attachments—to family, team, community, organization, religion—and staying true to these attachments is a great virtue. On the other hand, our loyalties and attachments also represent our bondage and limitations. Intuitively, people play it safe rather than put at risk the love, esteem, and approval of people or institutions they care about. The experience of disloyalty to our deeper attachments is often so painfully unacceptable that we avoid wrestling with them altogether, or do so by acting out. Witness the turmoil of teenagers trying to grow up and decide what to take from home and what to leave behind.

Refashioning loyalties is some of the toughest work in life. Perhaps one of the most difficult challenges facing the U.S. civil rights movement in the 1960s was that progress required lots of decent people to abandon attitudes, habits, and values that had been handed down to them by their loving parents and grandparents. To abandon those values felt like abandoning their family.

People hold on to ideas as a way of holding on to the person who taught them the ideas. An acquaintance of ours, an African-American woman, once talked to us about her persistent difficulty respecting her friends who saw themselves in a subordinate role because they lived in a society where the mainstream cultural values were white and male. She said that her late father had always told her that she was not subordinate to anyone—that she should never, ever think of herself that way. If she did so now, she added, she would desecrate the memory of her beloved parent.

Another friend told us that her mother had always counseled that "you can get more done with sugar than vinegar." She now believes that for most of her professional life she held on to that attitude—to her detriment, and despite much contrary evidence—out of loyalty to her mom.

Some of our most deeply held values and ideas come from people we love—a relative, a favored teacher, or a mentor. To discard some part of their teaching may feel like we are diminishing the relationship. But if the first of our two friends were to sift through her father's wisdom, she might discover that he saw and encouraged only two options: sacrifice your self-respect and defer, or never answer to anybody. With further reflection, and if she's lucky to have some help, she might see a third option: One can maintain one's pride and self-worth when taking subordinate roles in authority relationships; also, there may be a host of ways to challenge authorities respectfully and pursue objectives effectively from below.

Our former student Sylvia now understands this disloyalty issue very well. She was part of the group of people who put the first public service announcements on television promoting the use of condoms to protect against AIDS and venereal disease. The ads produced a firestorm of protest from people who believed that they promoted free and irresponsible sex, particularly among young people. Sylvia received death threats. But the protesters' anger also triggered something in her. At the time, she, too, had teenagers. The values of the protesters were the values that had been handed down to her and that she, in turn, espoused to her own children. She was brought up to believe in responsible sex, in the sanctity of sexual relationships, in people honoring each other by their fidelity. And she knew that handing out condoms was in a way a short-term technical fix for a much bigger adaptive problem about relationships between men and women, about sexual mores, and about individual responsibility. As Sylvia pushed ahead with the condom campaign, the protesters forced her to experience her own disloyalty to her old values. Upon seeing the television ads, Sylvia's mother felt embarrassed and her children were confused. Sylvia had to engage in a series of charged and uncomfortable conversations as she clarified her priorities and reconstructed some of the expectations and deep understandings in her relationships with her mother and children. She had made some decisions about which values were more important to her, but getting to the other side of feeling disloyal to her loved ones was a painful process as she moved toward a more deliberate integration of herself.

. . .

The dangers of exercising leadership derive from the nature of the problems for which leadership is necessary. Adaptive change stimulates resistance because it challenges people's habits, beliefs, and values. It asks them to take a loss, experience uncertainty, and even express disloyalty to people and cultures. Because adaptive change forces people to question and perhaps redefine aspects of their identity, it also challenges their sense of competence. Loss, disloyalty, and feeling incompetent: That's a lot to ask. No wonder people resist.

Since the resistance is designed to get you to back away, the various forms may be hard to recognize. You may not see the trap until it is too late. Recognizing these dangers, then, becomes of paramount importance.

2

The Faces of Danger

The dangers of leadership take many forms. Although each organization and culture has its preferred ways to restore equilibrium when someone upsets the balance, we've noticed four basic forms, with countless ingenious variations. When exercising leadership, you risk getting marginalized, diverted, attacked, or seduced. Regardless of the form, however, the point is the same. When people resist adaptive work, their goal is to shut down those who exercise leadership in order to preserve what they have.

Organizations are clever about this. Each of these forms has its subtleties. What makes them effective is that they are not obvious. So, people trying to exercise leadership are often pushed aside by surprise. For example, betrayal often comes from places and people you don't expect. Some individuals may not even realize that they are being used to betray you. We know from personal experience that when you are caught up in the action, carrying a cause you believe in, it can be difficult to see the patterns. Over and over again we have heard stories of people exercising leadership who never saw the danger coming until it was too late to respond.

Marginalization

Getting marginalized sometimes takes literal form. In the 1970s, at the old U.S. Department of Health, Education, and Welfare (HEW), Marty knew a high-ranking, respected, long-time employee named Seth, who began aggressively questioning a new plan designed to fundamentally change the way that HEW delivered social services. The reform was the brainchild and the most important initiative of Seth's boss, the HEW secretary. Seth argued sincerely, but provocatively and repeatedly, raising doubts about the value of something close to the heart of the chief. No one wanted to hear his questions.

One day Seth came into work and found his desk moved into a corridor. His senior colleagues had given most of his responsibilities to others. He believed in his initiatives and questions, and his martyrdom initially appealed to him, but not for long. He soon left the agency and his disturbing questions were no longer heard.

Most of the time organizations marginalize people less directly. An African-American man tells of his frustration at being part of a management team but finding his input limited on any issue other than race. A woman, promoted through the civilian side into a senior management role in an organization dominated by military personnel, notices that her colleagues listen to her only when the topic of discussion concerns information technology, her particular field of expertise. Unlike the rest of the senior managers— all men—her views are not taken seriously when she strays beyond her defined field of competence.

Many women have told us that in male-dominated organizations they were encouraged, and even told they were hired, to carry the gender issue for the whole organization. But they learned painfully that "tokenism" is a very tricky role to play effectively, and costs dearly. When a person or a small group of people embodies an issue and carries it prominently within the organization as a token, then the organization as a whole never has to take on the issue. It can feign the virtue of diversity, but avoid the challenge diverse views pose to its way of doing business. The women therefore were unable to move the issue into the heart of the organization. More-over, when they raised a different perspective on whatever task was at hand, people would roll their eyes and say to themselves, "There she goes again." Singing the gender song so regularly gave the other members of the group a fake excuse not to listen on any other subject.

A good example can be found in a mid-1990s diversity initiative of the New England Aquarium.[1] The Aquarium opened in 1969, at the leading edge of the revitalization of Boston's waterfront. An instant hit, it quickly attracted about a million visitors annu-ally, well in excess of the 600,000-person capacity that its plan-ners had designed. But beginning in the mid-1980s, the board of trustees and the senior staff began to be concerned that members of Boston's minority communities were consistently underrep-resented among the institution's visitors, employees, and volun-teers. Various initiatives directed at people of color during the next decade had not made any noticeable difference. In 1992, a cultural diversity committee of the trustees developed a strategy to attract minority youths as volunteers, which served as the hiring pool for new paid employees. Additions to the Aquarium's mission state-ment in 1992 reflected a new priority on increased diversity in its staff and visitors.

The most visible effort toward meeting this new priority was the establishment of a summer intern program for minority interns in the Aquarium's education department. Unlike the regular sum-mer interns, these interns were to be paid. The funds came primar-ily from outside sources that supported summer jobs for students whose families met federal poverty guidelines.

As is often the case, this problem had both a technical aspect ("How can we get more people of color into the Aquarium?") and an adaptive aspect ("Which of our values are keeping people of color away from our door, and are we willing to change them?"). The nature, design, and location of this program were strong sig-nals that the trustees wanted to address only the technical piece.

There was little advance planning for the seven high school stu-dents who showed up for the new intern program in the summer of 1992. Deemed a modest success, the Aquarium expanded the program to thirty interns the following summer. But the second year did not go as well. The resulting space crunch created tensions with other volunteers, particularly with the other high school and college interns who resented that the minority interns were being paid for doing the same work they were doing for free. The minority interns had been selected by the funding agencies and had not expressed any particular interest in the Aquarium or its work. The staff had issues concerning their behavior, attendance, attitude, and even dress. Although these problems were not unique to the new volunteers, because the group had distinguishing characteristics, they were more visible.

Late in the summer of 1993 the Aquarium hired into the education department Glenn Williams, an African American, to take lead responsibility for programs involving inner-city youth. Williams was older than the other educators in the department, the only African American, and, unlike most of his colleagues, without academic training in relevant fields. By the end of 1994, Williams had raised enough outside money to develop two additional programs for inner-city youth to complement the summer jobs program. As Williams's program expanded, so did the tensions with the rest of the Aquarium staff, in his education department and elsewhere, whose cooperation he needed if the programs were to be integrated into the institution. As long as he kept the program small and did not interfere with anything else, it was okay.

Brick walls could not have done a better job of marginalizing the diversity issue at the Aquarium. The minority interns never fit in, and the program failed. Although the trustees earnestly wanted to share their vision of a great Aquarium with people of color, they were not particularly interested in changing the Aquarium itself— its operations, culture, and ways of doing business—to attract minority visitors. Williams, frustrated, eventually left the Aquarium. From his perch at the lower end of the authority structure, he could not redesign the whole institution's diversity response. He had tried, but his complaints had not been addressed. The institution from the top down really did not want to face the implications of the deep changes that would have to be undertaken throughout the Aquarium to make it accessible in every way to lower economic constituencies and communities of color. Williams had not seen the problems earlier because he believed in the diversity goal, he trusted the supportive and well-intentioned words of the higher-ups, and he was committed to the kids in the internship and other programs. The programs themselves were fine, but the role they were playing in the overall organization served to marginalize the issue, not resolve it.

We sometimes collude unwittingly with our marginalizers. A thirty-five-year-old well-established synagogue appointed a young rabbi to be its head rabbi. The retiring rabbi had led the congregation for thirty-two of those thirty-five years.

At first, everything seemed just perfect for the young man. His predecessor said all of the right things, both publicly and privately. He promised to let go. He said he supported the many modernizing changes the new rabbi had talked about instituting during his many interviews for the job. But the new rabbi began to notice some unsettling patterns. When he went to a congregant's house for dinner, his predecessor ate there as well, usually seated next to him. Frequently, people having weddings, bar and bat mitzvahs, and funerals would ask the senior man to share the responsibilities for performing the ceremonies. More important, when he asked his predecessor for advice and counsel on specific changes he wanted to make in the liturgy or ritual, he received a polite but less than enthusiastic response, which was similar to what he heard from senior members of the congregation. So, he would hold off.

He continued to respond to the elder man with great respect, always deferring, agreeing to the joint activities, postponing changes, and generally, from his point of view, demonstrating a willingness to wait until the path forward was clear. He even passed on speaking engagements that came to the synagogue. He continued to attribute the prolonged transition to an understandable sensitivity to the former rabbi's feelings.

After a while, however, the new rabbi realized that he had unwittingly cooperated with a broad effort to suspend the uncertain future and retain the more familiar and comfortable past represented by the rabbi who had led the congregation for so long. Both the older rabbi and the congregation wanted to avoid as long as possible the hard work of facing the change and the challenges that would inevitably follow the retirement of the elder and the institution of a new spiritual leader for the synagogue. The younger man colluded with the rest of the community in delaying the pain of transition.

Eventually the young man saw the dynamics and his role in it. But by then the congregation had so undermined his authority and credibility that he saw no way to succeed in the role. People in the faction that had pushed hard for hiring him were disillusioned with his go-slow approach. And those who were most resistant to change were invigorated by their success in holding on to what they had. Despairing, the young rabbi resigned.

Marginalization often comes in more seductive forms. For example, it may come in the guise of telling you that you are special, *sui generis,* that you alone represent some important and highly valued idea, with the effect of keeping both you and the idea in a little box. First, the role of "special person" keeps you from playing a meaningful part on other issues. You are kept from being a generalist. Second, after a while you are devalued even on your own issue, because it's all people hear you talking about. Third, as with other forms of marginalization like tokenism, the organization can sing its own praises for welcoming unusual people without investigating the relevance and implications of their work to the central mission of the enterprise. If only you can do what you do, then the organization doesn't have to develop and institutionalize your innovation.

In several of these examples, the people exercising leadership and getting marginalized did not hold senior positions of authority in their organizations. Marginalization, however, can happen to anybody, including those on top. Authority figures can be sidelined, particularly when they allow themselves to become so identified with an issue that they become the issue.

President Lyndon Johnson took the Vietnam War personally. Understandably, he did not want to be the first U.S. president to preside over a defeat. He also did not want his secretary of defense, Robert McNamara, to take the heat for the war, and by 1966, anti-war activists were calling it "McNamara's War." So Johnson took the heat himself, and soon the war protesters began to chant, "Hey, ho, LBJ must go." That was probably the most polite of the slogans they yelled at him. Naively, the protesters substituted defeating Johnson for a much harder problem, namely, getting Congress and the public to choose between extracting the country from Vietnam and accepting defeat, or making the huge financial and human sacrifice that might have enabled the country to win the war. Initially, Johnson did not see the danger of taking on himself so much responsibility for escalating the war and letting Congress and the public off the hook for these tough choices. Indeed, he began to take the war as personally as the activists who targeted him. Eventually, however, he realized that the personalization of the war both impeded debate about the conflict and made him ineffective in advancing his extraordinary domestic agenda. By joining the orchestra, he had given up his baton. To his credit, he decided to step down from the presidency rather than seek reelection in 1968.[2]

Personalization tends toward marginalization. Embodying an issue may be a necessary though risky strategy, particularly for people leading without authority. However, for people in senior authority positions, embodying the issue can be even more perilous. Authorities commonly have to represent a variety of constituents. They rarely can afford to embody one issue. They need to keep their hands free so they can orchestrate conflicts, rather than become the object of conflict. And, as we will discuss later, embodying an issue in your authority role ties your survival, not just your success, to that of the issue. That's a dangerous platform on which to stand.

Diversion

Another time-honored way to push people aside is to divert them.

There are many ways in which communities and organizations will consciously or subconsciously try to make you lose focus. They do this sometimes by broadening your agenda, sometimes by overwhelming it, but always with a seemingly logical reason for disrupting your game plan.

Opponents of the Vietnam War enticed Martin Luther King, Jr., into expanding his agenda from civil rights to the war. Of course, they had a rationale for his doing so. Widening his agenda appealed not only to King's moral convictions, but also perhaps to his own self-importance and prowess, fueled legitimately by the enormous progress made on civil rights. But as hard as the civil rights struggle had been in the South, some of the hardest issues—namely, ending racial intolerance in the North—were yet to be addressed. Diverting King's attention to the Vietnam War had the dual effect of generating even greater solidarity with northern liberals who felt moral antiwar outrage, without challenging them personally. He might have strained those relationships had he brought the civil rights movement to their communities, schools, law firms, and corporations. Their lives would have been disrupted, their values questioned, and their behaviors and practices scrutinized. They would have been on television either defending their way of life or denouncing it in front of their friends and neighbors.

King turned his attention to opposing the Vietnam War with terrible results. His core constituents, Southern black people, were not with him. They knew that too much work still lay ahead in the South as well as in the North. Not only did King achieve little success on the Vietnam War issue, but by losing his focus, he became less available to lead the movement beyond establishing the foundations of equality, like voting rights. Facing complex issues in northern cities and ghettos, the movement bogged down.

Some people are promoted or given new, glamorous responsibilities as a way of sidetracking their agenda. Whenever you get an unexpected promotion, or when some fun or important tasks are added to your current role, pause and ask yourself: Do I represent some disquieting issue from which the organization is moving to divert me, and itself, from addressing? We know a cantankerous newspaper columnist who found herself promoted to an editor's position as much to silence her provocative writing as to make use of her editing skills. We also know a primary school principal in the poorest community in her Missouri school district whose extraordinary success with students and parents generated sufficient disturbance among some teachers (whom she rode pretty hard) that the school superintendent promoted her to district headquarters to serve as a consultant. He even touted his ingenuity in finding a way to get her out of the primary school she had spent twenty years working to transform, with the goal of restoring "order and calm" to his school system. Corporate management will sometimes calm the waters by promoting union rabble-rousers into exempt positions, in the hope that the next generation of union leadership will be more cooperative.

People in top authority positions can easily be diverted by getting lost in other people's demands and programmatic details. Our friend Elizabeth was about to achieve a long-time ambition to become head of the state human services agency with a multibillion-dollar budget, thousands of employees, and the well-being of hundreds of thousands of people under her charge. She yearned for the job because, having watched the agency for years, she had a long list of initiatives and reforms that she thought would make a difference. She understood that she was going to upset some people wedded to the current system, but with courage and strength, she felt confident that she could see change through. She did not, however, take stock of two important dynamics.

First, she knew her various constituencies both inside and outside the agency disagreed deeply among themselves on the size, scope, and delivery systems for various health and welfare programs. But she did not realize that they agreed on one thing, namely, that Elizabeth should focus on their collective set of issues, whatever they were, rather than on her own or anyone else's. And second, she didn't understand that they could squash her agenda more easily by overwhelming her with demands and details than by fighting her head-on.

As she was about to take the job, Marty suggested that they have lunch in six months to see how she was progressing on the list of things she wanted to accomplish. Then she charged off into the fray. The lunch date came. Elizabeth looked frustrated.

"What happened?" Marty asked. "It's the most amazing thing," she replied. "I've never been so busy. My appointment calendar is full, and each meeting is important. Many are contentious. I am working more hours than I ever did before. I'm exhausted at the end of every day. I take work home on the weekend. But I have barely begun to work on my agenda. I finally realized that since I've been in the job, I've only seen a hundred or so people. It's as if they all got together, whatever their differences, and agreed to keep me so busy with their lists, that I would never get to anything on my list!"

Known as a workaholic, Elizabeth is extremely conscientious. She takes pride in answering her phone calls and staying in touch with her constituencies, even those who disagree with her. She enjoys intense policy debates. The folks in the human services world knew that.

She was right. They *had* gotten together, albeit not in a literal sense. Warren Bennis calls it the Unconscious Conspiracy to take you off your game plan.[3] Diversion by inbox-stuffing kept Elizabeth's eyes off the ball. It kept her immersed in the perspectives, problems, and infighting that had bedeviled others for years. The technique worked; it was much more effective than if folks had tried to battle her directly on her own issues.

Attack

Attacking you personally is another tried-and-true method of neutralizing your message. Whatever the form of the attack, if the attackers can turn the subject of the conversation from the issue you are advancing to your character or style, or even to the attack itself, it will have succeeded in submerging the issue. Attention, the currency of leadership, gets wasted. If you can't draw people's attention to the issues that matter, then how can you lead them in the right direction or mobilize any progress?

You have probably been attacked in one form or another. Perhaps you've been criticized for your style of communication: too abrasive or too gentle, too aggressive or too quiet, too conflictive or too conciliatory, too cold or too warm. In any case, we doubt that anyone ever criticizes your character or your style when you're giving them good news or passing out big checks. For the most part, people criticize you when they don't like the message. But rather than focus on the content of your message, taking issue with its merits, they frequently find it more effective to discredit you. Of course, you may be giving them opportunities to do so; surely every one of us can continue to improve our style and our self-discipline. The point is not that you are blameless, but that the blame is largely misplaced in order to draw attention away from the message itself.

The most obvious form of a diverting attack is physical. You might remember the protests at the World Trade Organization (WTO) meeting in Seattle, Washington, in the fall of 1999. The protesters were interested in raising issues about WTO policies and their impacts on poor people, on jobs in the United States, and on the environment. The local law enforcement officials were interested in protecting the security of the delegates and their meeting. The WTO delegates were interested in keeping the debate focused on their concerns and not on the protesters' agenda. Whether intentional or not, the physical contact between the police and the protesters had the effect of making the fight, not the issues, the focus of public attention. The squabbles between protesters and police took the protesters' agenda out of the news.

People become easily diverted by physical attack. It's full of drama. It hurts. Some people are repulsed by it; some are drawn to it in a macabre kind of way. Whatever the reaction, the spectacle of violence is effective in moving people away from any underlying, deeply troubling issues. For example, an angry outburst that turns physical in a family immediately replaces the primary issues with the issue of the violence itself. The violent person loses legitimacy for his or her perspective and unwittingly colludes with the offended parties in sabotaging the discussion of his or her views.

In the 2000 presidential election, an unplanned personal attack created diversionary news. In an aside to his running mate Dick Cheney, George W. Bush used a vulgarity to describe Adam Clymer, a longtime *New York Times* political reporter. Bush had not realized that the microphones were on, and he felt embarrassed when his remark was overheard. The press attacked Bush, using the incident to raise issues about his character. No one bothered to analyze whether Bush was on to something, whether Clymer's articles had been fair and responsible or had been biased in favor of the Democratic nominee. And Bush, by making it personal, unwittingly served up the distraction and diminished his capacity to raise the issue of journalistic bias.

Assassinations, like those of Yitzhak Rabin and Anwar Sadat, are the most extreme examples of a silencing attack as a way of stopping the voices of difficult realities. Both assassinations set back the cause of peace in the Middle East, delaying the day when people would have to experience loss of land and disloyalty to their ancestors, in order to thrive in today's interdependent world.

Fortunately, your opponents, those people most disturbed by your message, are far more likely to use verbal rather than physical attacks. The attacks may go after your character, your competence, or your family, or may simply distort and misrepresent your views. They will come in whatever form your opponents think will work. Through trial and error, they will find your Achilles' heel. They will come at you wherever you are most vulnerable.

In politics, people frequently finger-point at character to deflect attention from the issues. For much of Bill Clinton's eight years in the White House, his ideological opponents came after him not on the issues but on his character. They found an obvious Clinton vulnerability. As you know, he provided them with ammunition. The personal attacks on him succeeded considerably in diverting him from his policy agenda. It's quite interesting that the conservatives were not threatened by all of his agenda. Quite to the contrary, Clinton threatened them because some of his agenda was theirs. Clinton was stealing their issues, such as welfare reform and the balanced budget, and if he succeeded, his leverage to promote the detested aspects of his agenda would increase substantially.

The function of attacking Clinton on character was no different than the function of attacking Clarence Thomas on character during his hearings for confirmation to the U.S. Supreme Court. Opponents went after him personally because they had great difficulty defeating his nomination on the issues. Thomas did not fit the mold of an easy-to-oppose conservative judicial nominee. He was an African American with not much of a paper trail documenting his judicial philosophy or political ideology. He was no easy target like G. Harrold Carswell, the intellectually, professionally, and judicially undistinguished southern conservative whom Richard Nixon nominated to the Supreme Court in 1970. He was not even as vulnerable as Robert Bork, Ronald Reagan's unsuccessful 1987 nominee, who had written extensively and whose published views were anathema to many members of the U.S. Senate. But like Clinton, Thomas had somehow made himself vulnerable to attacks on his character, particularly the sexual harassment charges from Anita Hill and others.

Attacks may take the form of misrepresentation. Early in his tenure, President Bill Clinton nominated Lani Guinier to be assistant attorney general for civil rights. She enjoyed a reputation as a brilliant law school professor, a trusted friend of Bill and Hillary Clinton, and a creative thinker. She believed strongly in government action to ensure individual rights, and she would likely have made the Civil Rights Division a visible and aggressive activist agency. However, a search of her writings found a law review article in which she analyzed the issue of political representation.[4] In fact, her notion of proportional representation was not a new or crazy idea. In political theory, her argument had both respectability and a long history, similar to arguments about the principles upon which voting district lines should be drawn. Moreover, the argument that drew attack represented only one thought in an article full of ideas, and it appeared in one law review article by a woman who had written several. But focusing on it provided an opportunity for her opponents to label her the "Quota Queen."

The misrepresentation placed Clinton in a tough position. He could have taken on the difficult task of trying to explain that the clever, memorable, and politically unacceptable label "Quota Queen" was a distortion, and then draw the focus back to the real issue—the difficult challenges she would indeed represent as an activist on civil rights. Or, he could accede to the misrepresentation and then either tough it out and defend her, or let her go. He chose the easiest route and let her go. His opponents had reason to know that's what he would choose because he had already backed away from other nominees and issues when the heat became uncomfortable. But by doing so once again, he gave his opponents more reason to believe that continued misrepresentations and character attacks would indeed serve their purposes.

It is difficult to resist responding to misrepresentation and personal attack. We don't want to minimize how hard it is to keep your composure when people say awful things about you. It hurts. It does damage. Anyone who's been there knows that pain. Exercising leadership often risks having to bear such scars.

Later, in part two of this book, we explore many ways to respond to misrepresentation and attack. But first you have to recognize the effort for what it often is, a way to divert your attention from an issue that is more troubling to people. Fundamentally, the dynamic is no different in a family than on the national stage. When your teenager in an angry outburst calls you names, in your best moments you know you ought to stop and ask, "What's this really about?" Perhaps your son can't stand having to depend on you, once again, to drive him places. Or he might be just testing to see if you really care for him enough to stick to the curfew you have imposed. It may be a great deal more productive, though challenging, to negotiate with him over the issues of responsibility and dependency than to get into another personal fight. But it is not easy to do.

When the Manchester, New Hampshire, *Union Leader* attacked Senator Edmund Muskie's wife during the 1972 presidential campaign, describing her in negative and demeaning language, he took it personally and responded accordingly, shedding what appeared to be a tear in her defense and making the same diagnostic mistake. His opponents were trying to derail his campaign and undermine the power of his stands on the issues. They didn't care about his wife one way or the other. Once Muskie withdrew from the campaign, she became a nonissue. By responding to the misrepresentation personally, Muskie colluded with the attacker in distracting the public from the real target.

Seduction

Many forms of bringing you down have a seductive dimension. We use the word *seduction,* a politically charged word, as a way of naming the process by which you lose your sense of purpose altogether, and therefore get taken out of action by an initiative likely to succeed because it has a special appeal to you. In general, people are seduced when their guard is down, when their defense mechanisms have been lowered by the nature of the approach.

We are not talking about neurotic needs only. People are diverted by initiatives that meet normal, human interests, too. One of the everyday forms of seduction, for example, is the desire for the approval of your own faction, your own supporters.

An old aphorism attributed to the late Speaker of the House of Representatives, Tip O'Neill, advises, "Always dance with the one who brought you." It's about loyalty to your own people. But that advice, appealing as it is, carries with it a significant risk.

When you are trying to create significant change, to move a community, the people in your own faction in that community will have to compromise along the way. Often, the toughest part of your job is managing *their* disappointed expectations. They may well support change, but they also want you to ensure that the change will come with minimal sacrifice on their part. Tacitly, or perhaps explicitly, your own people will instruct you to get the job done by having the people from the other factions make the tough trade-offs.

Disappointing your own core supporters, your deepest allies on your issue, creates hardships for you and for them. Yet you make yourself vulnerable when you too strongly give in to the understandable desire to enjoy their continuing approval, rather than disappoint them. Over and over again we have seen people take on difficult issues, only to be pushed by their own faction so far out on a limb that they lose credibility in the larger community.

Several years before the signing of the Good Friday peace agreement in Ireland, Marty facilitated a gathering of representatives from all but the most militant of the political parties and factions in Northern Ireland. Tentativeness and tension filled the room. Many of the participants had never been in the same space with their most hated opponents. Some of the participants would not talk to others. They refused to pose for a group picture.

They began to discuss a conflict resolution case set in a very different time and place. They conversed slowly, with care and caution. They moved on to the question of how the protagonist in the case had managed his own employees and the difficulty of bringing them along. Suddenly, the talk in the room intensified. The Northern Ireland antagonists began to talk with each other without Marty's intervention. They found common ground in the difficulty they were all having managing their own people.

They realized that they faced a shared dilemma. They understood that the way to peace meant giving something up, but each of their factions wanted to be represented by someone who promised not to yield anything. If the representatives tried to educate their own people on the need to bear some loss, they would be challenged by a potential successor who promised to hold the hard line. Beyond this tactical challenge to their authority, they sought and desired the approval and support of their own people as they entered difficult conversations with their opponents. The applause of their own factions gave them courage. It made them feel important and valued, and it gave them confidence that the risks they took were worth it. And yet the need for that applause and the desire to keep it ringing in their ears compromised their capacity to think purposefully about the larger change.

Negotiators describe a related dynamic called "the constituency problem." Every labor negotiator knows it well: the experience of being yanked back into the previous posture by workers who have not gone through the same compromising and learning process that the primary negotiators have endured (often lasting many long nights). Unprepared for giving up on any of their goals, they boo and hiss the "compromiser," branding him disloyal to the cause.

Marty experienced this himself in 1992, when he joined the administration of Massachusetts governor William Weld as chief secretary, responsible for personnel and politics. He enjoyed a reputation for being more liberal than most of the senior staff in the governor's office. He felt not the slightest embarrassment. To the contrary, he was comfortable with his beliefs and even assumed that Weld hired him, in part, to broaden the range of viewpoints the governor heard on a regular basis. Most of Marty's friends outside of the government held more liberal views than he did; they were happy to see him get a good job, but skeptical that he took a job in a Republican administration that had been doing a lot of budget slashing in its first year.

The liberal interest groups, such as the advocates for gay rights and women's rights, applauded his appointment. They saw him as their conduit into the conversations in the governor's office. And Marty enjoyed the role and their approval, too much perhaps. The advocates knew, and constantly told him, that they would not know what to do or how to be heard within the governor's office if he were not there.

Marty began to rely on their flattery, to enjoy being indispensable to them, so much so that he never noticed what was gradually happening. The advocates pushed him to do more and go further, which appeared to him to be the price for their continuing approval. Instead of pushing back on the advocates to depend less on him and broaden their base of support and leverage, Marty opted for the special status he needed to feel significant in his role.

As a result, his voice within the councils of the governor's office narrowed and his tone sounded more shrill as he pressed the issues harder. His effectiveness seeped away, day by day. He was seduced by his own desire to "do the right thing" and, more important, to have the support of people whose values he shared. But the costs weighed heavy. Confined more and more to being the carrier of unpopular causes, he slowly but inexorably became less successful in moving them along, and increasingly was cut out of the conversation on other issues.

Although the advocates surely did not intend to undermine him, by conditioning their approval on his increasingly strident advocacy of their interests, they forced him to choose between their continuing loyalty and his diminishing success in the wider community.

· · ·

Seduction, marginalization, diversion, and attack all serve a function. They reduce the disequilibrium that would be generated were people to address the issues that are taken off the table. They serve to maintain the familiar, restore order, and protect people from the pains of adaptive work. It would be wonderful if adaptive work did not involve hard transitions, adjustments, and loss in people's lives. Because it does, it usually produces resistance. Being aware of the likelihood of receiving opposition in some form is critical to managing it when it arrives. Leadership, then, requires not only reverence for the pains of change and recognition of the manifestations of danger, but also the skill to respond.

PART TWO

The Response

3

Get on the Balcony

Few practical ideas are more obvious or more critical than the need to get perspective in the midst of action. Any military officer, for example, knows the importance of maintaining the capacity for reflection, even in the "fog of war." Great athletes can at once play the game and observe it as a whole—as Walt Whitman described it, "being both in and out of the game." Jesuits call it "contemplation in action." Hindus and Buddhists call it "karma yoga," or mindfulness. We call this skill "getting off the dance floor and going to the balcony," an image that captures the mental activity of stepping back in the midst of action and asking, "What's really going on here?"[1]

Why do so many of the world's forms of spiritual and organizational life recommend this mental exercise? Because few tasks strain our abilities more than putting this idea into practice. We all get swept up in the action, particularly when it becomes intense or personal and we need most to pause. Self-reflection does not come naturally. It's much easier to adopt an established belief than create one's own. Most people instinctively follow a dominant trend in an organization or community, without critical evaluation of its merits. The herd instinct is strong. And a stampede not only tramples those who don't keep pace, it also makes it hard to see another direction—until the dust settles.

For example, we were recently at a business meeting in which a woman named Amanda made a provocative comment, questioning whether everyone in the room was pulling their weight during a challenging restructuring of the firm. Her comment didn't seem to go anywhere. Then some time later Brian, a man a bit senior to her in the organization, offered what amounted to the same comment. Suddenly, the group engaged around the idea and the conversation moved, or at least lurched, in the direction Amanda had originally hoped. Brian walked away feeling influential, and Amanda felt invisible and frustrated.

Groups often devalue someone by ignoring them, by rendering them invisible—a form of marginalization. Surely this has happened to you at least once or twice. Women tell us this happens often to them.

Amanda would have had a tough time getting on the balcony. She wondered why she had been ignored, but mostly she felt trampled and angered, diminishing her capacity to distance herself from the situation. She was totally engaged on the dance floor: preoccupied by the fear of being ineffective, reacting to having been brushed aside, and unable to get an overview and see what was really going on.

Typically only a few people see these dynamics as they happen. Swept up in the action of the meeting, most never notice. They simply play their parts. The observational challenge is to see the subtleties that normally go right by us. Seeing the whole picture requires standing back and watching even as you take part in the action being observed. But taking a balcony perspective is tough to do when you're engaged on the dance floor, being pushed and pulled by the flow of events and also engaged in some of the pushing and pulling yourself.

The most difficult part to notice is what you do yourself, whether you play Amanda's or Brian's part. So you might imagine looking down on the room from a sky camera and seeing yourself as merely another player in the game.

The balcony metaphor captures this idea. Let's say you are dancing in a big ballroom with a balcony up above. A band plays and people swirl all around you to the music, filling up your view. Most of your attention focuses on your dance partner, and you reserve whatever is left to make sure that you don't collide with dancers close by. You let yourself get carried away by the music, your partner, and the moment. When someone later asks you about the dance, you exclaim, "The band played great, and the place surged with dancers."

But if you had gone up to the balcony and looked down on the dance floor, you might have seen a very different picture. You would have noticed all sorts of patterns. For example, you might have observed that when slow music played, only some people danced; when the tempo increased, others stepped onto the floor; and some people never seemed to dance at all. Indeed, the dancers all clustered at one end of the floor, as far away from the band as possible. On returning home, you might have reported that participation was sporadic, the band played too loud, and you only danced to fast music.

Achieving a balcony perspective means taking yourself out of the dance, in your mind, even if only for a moment. The only way you can gain both a clearer view of reality and some perspective on the bigger picture is by distancing yourself from the fray. Otherwise, you are likely to misperceive the situation and make the wrong diagnosis, leading you to misguided decisions about whether and how to intervene.

If you want to affect what is happening, you must return to the dance floor. Staying on the balcony in a safe observer role is as much a prescription for ineffectuality as never achieving that perspective in the first place. The process must be iterative, not static. The challenge is to move back and forth between the dance floor and the balcony, making interventions, observing their impact in real time, and then returning to the action. The goal is to come as close as you can to being in both places simultaneously, as if you had one eye looking from the dance floor and one eye looking down from the balcony, watching all the action, including your own. This is a critical point: When you observe from the balcony you must see yourself as well as the other participants. Perhaps this is the hardest task of all—to see yourself objectively.

To see yourself from the outside as merely one among the many dancers, you have to watch the system and the patterns, looking at yourself as part of the overall pattern. You must set aside your special knowledge of your intentions and inner feelings, and notice that part of yourself that others would see if *they* were looking down from the balcony.

Moving from participant to observer and back again is a skill you can learn. When you are sitting in a meeting, practice switching roles, watching what is happening while it is happening, even as you are part of what's happening. When you make an intervention, resist the instinct to stay perched on the edge of your seat waiting to defend or explain what you said. Simple techniques, such as pushing your chair a few inches away from the meeting table after you speak, may provide some literal as well as metaphorical distance to help you detach just enough to become an observer. Don't jump to a familiar conclusion. Open yourself up to other possibilities. See who says what; watch the body language. Watch the relationships and see how people's attention to one another varies: supporting, thwarting, or listening.

Of course, the observer's perch can be used to analyze not only small group meetings, but also large political and organizational processes. For example, in the early 1960s, the founder of modern Singapore, Lee Kuan Yew, was intrigued by the perspectives of his anticolonial comrades, such as India's Jawaharlal Nehru, who viewed Western imperialism and capitalism as one and the same thing. Lee left home and traveled widely to see firsthand the progress these other founders had made as they guided their new nations. But what he saw disturbed him. By tying their anticolonialism to anticapitalism, many founding fathers were impeding economic progress in their countries and preventing a decent standard of living for their people. By stepping back and testing the conventional wisdom of his contemporaries in other emerging nations, Lee gained not only freedom from those views, but also a more accurate and complete picture of reality, which then became the basis for his leadership. Unlike most fighters for independence, he embraced free markets. Between 1965 and 2000, Singapore went from being a poor and racially divided city to an integrated community with one of the world's most competitive economies. None of Lee's contemporaries, who were stuck in ideologies based on reactions to colonial trauma and who demonized export-driven free-market economies, achieved anything remotely similar.[2]

Lee got on the balcony by getting out of town. He shifted his perspective from the Singapore dance floor to the regional and international balcony.

Any one of a number of questions will help you get beyond your own blind spots. The most basic question is always the best place to start: What's going on here? Beyond that question, we suggest four diagnostic tasks to safeguard against the more common traps that snare people.

1. Distinguish technical from adaptive challenges.

2. Find out where people are.

3. Listen to the song beneath the words.

4. Read the behavior of authority figures for clues.

Distinguish Technical from Adaptive Challenges

There are many possible interpretations for the Amanda/Brian incident. Why was Amanda rendered invisible?

Style. Perhaps Amanda spoke in a manner different from the style preferred by the group. For example, she might have spoken with such unexpected conviction and power that everyone tuned out. Demonstrating too much aggressive self-assurance with people who have a high regard for humility could have reduced her credibility.

Track Record. Amanda's and Brian's roles and reputations might have influenced the way they were heard. Brian may have demonstrated more consistent insight and competence over time. He might have had a proven track record on the subject.

Ripeness. Possibly, the issue had not "ripened" when Amanda put it on the table. Amanda may have been thinking faster than the rest of the group so that, at the time she spoke, the group lacked enough familiarity with the issue to deal with it. It can take time for other people to catch up to a new idea. By the time Brian made substantially the same comment, Amanda's insight was "ripe," and people were ready to take it up.

Status. Brian might have slightly more formal authority in the organization than Amanda. Brian might also be an important person in the community, to whom people tend to listen on a wide range of subjects. In most cultures, people pay more attention to those at the top of the hierarchy, whether or not that attention is warranted. The impact of both formal and informal hierarchies is extremely powerful.

Prejudice. Some interpretations of the Amanda/Brian incident cut directly to deeply held values and norms within the group. The group may not take women's views as seriously as those of men. If prejudice is a group phenomenon, you may see it only from the balcony and not observe bias by any individual. Similarly, if Amanda is quite a bit younger than Brian, the group may be prejudiced, perhaps unconsciously, against young people. Or, her political leanings might make people uncomfortable, whereas Brian shares the group's prevailing political views. Amanda may remind people of a problem in the society, and the group may unconsciously ignore her business suggestions as part of a larger pattern of ignoring the social issue that she brings to mind. These explanations turn on the group's tolerance for "the other," that is, for any aspect of the non-majority culture Amanda might embody.

Some of these interpretations—style, track record, and ripeness—suggest problems that Amanda can correct herself. A modest adjustment to her intervention style, greater selectivity in choosing when to speak up, or laying a better foundation for her perspective would be enough to forestall a recurrence. With these interpretations, her invisibility represents a technical problem on which she can take corrective action without disturbing anyone.

But the last two interpretations—status and prejudice—go to the heart of how the group, and the individuals within it, see themselves. Speaking to these issues will threaten the group's stability and civility and disrupt the agenda. The group will likely resist if she suggests that it discounts the views of people with lower status, rather than weigh everyone's views on the merits, or that its behavior is racist, sexist, ageist, or prejudicial in any way.

Typically, the group will strongly prefer the technical interpretation, particularly one in which the "problem" lies with an individual rather than the group as a whole. This allows for a simple, straightforward solution, one that does not require any hard work or adaptation on the group's part.

Amanda might have tested which interpretation was more accurate by watching reactions to the comments of others who had less status or represented a minority voice. She could have observed whether the pattern of response to her contributions continued even after she applied technical fixes to her style, timing, and track record. If Amanda gets to the balcony, collects information, listens carefully, and questions her usual mindset, she may find that her invisibility provides a clue, not to an individual issue, but to a group issue. She may find that she's "carrying the ball" for her team on this adaptive challenge, and being chased down the field accordingly.[3]

Of course, being rendered invisible doesn't *feel* like being chased down the field with the fans cheering. On the contrary, you feel ignored, diminished, or worse, stupid. That's the point! After investigating the personal, technical reasons for being neutralized and correcting for them, you may well find that you are continuing to be ignored precisely because you have so much to say. In Amanda's case, she may be carrying the adaptive challenge of valuing diverse perspectives for her whole team, *without being asked or authorized to do so*. By ignoring that challenge, the team loses a voice that may prove crucial to its future success in situations when it needs her particular perspective.

Most problems come bundled with both technical and adaptive aspects. Before making an intervention, you need to distinguish between them in order to decide which to tackle first and with what strategy.

Our friend Ken worked for AT&T, where he had concerns about the impact of a departmental reorganization plan. Coming from an engineering background, he readily saw some technical flaws in the plan. He believed that it failed to put the right people in touch with each other, replacing one set of silos with a new set. But Ken realized that silos represented an adaptive issue: People in the corporation tended to fortify their own silos and resisted taking responsibility for the broader view.

After working his way through the system, he finally got fifteen minutes on the vice president's schedule, an unusual event for someone at his level, two layers below top management. He worked hard to get the appointment, and he knew he would be exceeding his authority if he raised the deeper, systemic issue. He worried that the VP might react badly. So he had to choose: He could raise either the technical or the adaptive issue, or both; but if both, in what order? When he finally had his fifteen minutes, Ken began by commenting on the technical aspects of the problem. The vice president politely heard him out, without comment. He kept talking and the fifteen minutes ran out. Ken quickly but belatedly realized his mistake. The VP wanted those technical questions to be resolved below his pay grade. Ken allowed himself to be silenced by the pressures he felt, and served up to the VP the easier of the two interpretations.

Once Ken distinguished the technical and adaptive aspects of the problem, he began to feel the internal and external pressures to stick to the technical issues and avoid the more troubling adaptive concerns. The organization would prefer an easy, nondisruptive interpretation. Often, organizations will try to treat adaptive issues as technical ones in order to diffuse them. The technical face of the issue was comfortable and familiar to Ken, and well within his scope of authority.

These pressures are all to the good if they lead you to challenge without arrogance. On the other hand, the silencing itself is a clue. Had Ken been able to get to the balcony right before the meeting, he might have read his own hesitancy as an indication that, in fact, he was really on to something quite challenging. He might then have taken action to lay the foundation for this challenge as he moved up the chain of command. (We'll discuss how to do this later.) After all, what's the point of getting time with the vice president if you're not going to identify the problems that are worth his attention?

Budget crises provide a good, general illustration of the pressures toward technical interpretations. Typically, a budget crisis in the public or private sector stimulates an effort to find more money. The people in authority might squeeze expenses here, postpone some expenditures there, or do some short-term borrowing. Those solutions deal with the problem as a technical issue. But very often the source of the crisis is a clash of values, a difference in priorities. Finding more money temporarily smoothes over the conflict, but does not resolve it. Solving the underlying problem would require the factions with competing priorities to acknowledge the gaps between them and work through the differences. It would require strategic trade-offs, and losses. The result might well deeply disappoint some people, perhaps many. "Balancing the budget" might in fact mean refashioning the organization's agenda and changing the way it conducts business. Thus, the task of leadership would be to mobilize people to adapt to a world with different constraints and opportunities than they had imagined.

How do you know whether the challenge is primarily technical or primarily adaptive? You can never be certain, but there are some useful diagnostic clues. First, you know you're dealing with something more than a technical issue when people's hearts and minds need to change, and not just their preferences or routine behaviors. In an adaptive challenge, people have to learn new ways and choose between what appear to be contradictory values. Cultures must distinguish what is essential from what is expendable as they struggle to move forward.

In South Africa in the 1990s, Marty witnessed teachers struggle in the face of the obvious reality that their students' hearts and minds needed to undergo a huge transformation. For several years during the transition to a democratic government, Marty worked with professors in a wide range of South African universities to develop new courses, new programs, and, most important, new teaching methods. The teachers all knew they had to adapt, from whatever group in the old South Africa they came. But they had to be pushed hard to face up to the profoundly difficult work of changing their beliefs in order to continue to be relevant to their students in the new South Africa. Accustomed to lecturing in front of classrooms full of homogeneous groups of students with a narrow range of clearly defined career options, professors now had to face heterogeneous groups of students with open-ended futures who brought to the classroom varied and conflicting values, perspectives, and experiences from the days of apartheid and the long struggle to end it. The personal qualities required for progress in the new South Africa would be different from those required in the past. Hierarchically determined roles would give way to fluidity and flexibility. Delivering dry, technical lectures and modeling an authoritarian approach to problem-solving discussions failed to serve students whose future paths were no longer so clearly predetermined by race, class, and ethnicity. All of this presented an adaptive challenge for South Africa and for the professors.

Second, you can distinguish technical problems from adaptive challenges by a process of exclusion. If you throw all the technical fixes you can imagine at the problem and the problem persists, it's a pretty clear signal that an underlying adaptive challenge still needs to be addressed.

Third, the persistence of conflict usually indicates that people have not yet made the adjustments and accepted the losses that accompany adaptive change.

Fourth, crisis is a good indicator of adaptive issues that have festered. Crises represent danger because the stakes are high, time appears short, and the uncertainties are great. Yet they also represent opportunities if they are used to galvanize attention on the unresolved issues.

Like all problems, sudden crises tend to include both technical and adaptive parts. But in a crisis, the level of disequilibrium is very high. Consequently, you will face a lot of pressure, both external and internal, to see the crisis as a technical problem, with straightforward solutions that can quickly restore the balance. Indeed, most people in authority squander the opportunity of crisis because all eyes are turned to them to restore order, even if it means ignoring the adaptive issues and focusing on only the technical fixes. When facing a budget crisis, for example, many organizations opt for the salami cutter as a way to cut expenses (take an equal 10 percent from each division), rather than face the more difficult strategic questions.

In 1991, when Saddam Hussein invaded Kuwait, former President George H. W. Bush was able to rally a large and diverse coalition around the technical problem of pushing the Iraqi troops back into their own land. When a cry arose to go further, to eliminate Saddam Hussein, his military, and his capacity to create havoc around the world, Bush held back. Wiping out Hussein instead of just pushing him back into his geographical box represented an adaptive challenge that would have threatened the alliance. Finishing the job would have meant the humiliation and likely death of thousands of Iraqi troops—shown every night on television sets in the homes of everyday Arab people in the Arab coalition countries. The authorities of those nations would have had the daunting challenge of helping their own people adapt to an uncomfortable new reality: that it was in their interest to tolerate and even support the killing of thousands of Arab soldiers by Westerners. Keeping the coalition together through an invasion of Iraq also would have required the Western partners to make a major adaptation. For them, the price of a continuing alliance with the East would have been some serious soul-searching and an acknowledgment that the old fears of Western dominance of the Muslim world were warranted, given the history of colonial and missionary activity going back to the Crusades. Accepting responsibility for that old pattern of behavior and its consequences would have been its own daunting challenge, especially for the European partners in the coalition.

In the short term, you may want to deal with the technical aspects first, as Bush did in pursuing the war. However, many crises manifest issues that have been festering for a long time. Saddam Hussein represented not only an evil individual, but also the more fundamental and unresolved conflict between the Christian West and the Islamic East. To have joined that issue, President George H. W. Bush would have put his fragile coalition at risk and unleashed forces beyond his control. In the short term, perhaps he could see no alternative but to stick with the technical issue, and speak of a New World Order primarily as an abstraction. But an unresolved issue does not go away just because it disappears from view, as we have been reminded since that time in upheavals in countries and terrorism in cities around the world.

Find Out Where People Are

Getting people in a community or organization to address a deeply felt issue is difficult and risky. If people have avoided a problem for a long time, it should not be surprising that they try to silence you when you push them to face it. Both your survival and your success depend on your skill at reaching a true understanding of the varying perspectives among the factions. Learn from them their stakes and fears.

As social workers say, "Start where people are." Beyond the capacity to listen, this requires curiosity, especially when you think you already know someone's problem and what needs to be done. Their view is likely to be different from yours, and if you don't take their perspective as the starting point, you are liable to be dismissed as irrelevant, insensitive, or presumptuous.

This is particularly difficult in a crisis. In Ecuador, Jamil Mahuad was so focused on providing a short-term remedy that he delayed connecting with the general population, largely poor and vulnerable. They were frightened about the failing economy and angry about unending inequities. By not finding out where *they* were focused, he put himself at risk—no matter how good his policies may have been.

A Jesuit friend of ours held a series of discussions for a group of government officials about spirituality in the workplace. They were supposed to talk about religion in public policymaking as well as more personal issues, such as how to manage their own spirituality in their professional roles, and how to manage an organization in which people have very different views of religion and its relationship to work. Many of them felt deeply threatened by aspects of the issue, but had never had the opportunity to discuss their concerns in a public conversation with colleagues. They were looking forward to the sessions with a mixture of eagerness and anxiety.

Our friend began in his usual fashion. Seamlessly, he laid out a series of ideas and frameworks about the relationship between religion and the state. Then he took questions. They asked. He answered. He performed smoothly, but there was palpable unease in the room. The relationship between church and state interested them, but the problem that really troubled them was what to do with their own spirituality at work, and how to manage diverse feelings about the place of religion at the office. Impressive as he was, our friend had missed the core of their concerns.

A month later he had the opportunity to give the same series of talks to a similar group. This time he put aside his well-practiced and impressive presentation. He started by simply asking them what they wanted to talk about. They raised the issues. They set the agenda. Working off their ideas, he engaged them in an intense conversation over several hours. The sessions had a huge impact. He caused people to rethink long-held views. The conversations gave some of them the courage to change their own behavior toward coworkers who had very different spiritual orientations than their own. He succeeded where he had failed before because he had stepped back and started where *they* were instead of where *he* was.

When Lee Kuan Yew first became prime minister of Singapore, he took precious time from his daily schedule to painstakingly learn Mandarin, the local dialect, and improve his Malay. After more than three years of effort, he arrived at a crucial crossroads for Singapore in which the communists had a significant chance for victory in the elections. Lee's capacity to listen to and speak with the people in their own languages proved decisive. It gave him the credibility to successfully challenge postcolonial ideology when he asked people to embrace the free market economic policies of their former British masters.[4] If Lee could take years to learn the languages of his constituents, then surely we can take time simply to listen before we intervene.

Listen to the Song Beneath the Words

Observing from the balcony is the critical first step in exercising— and safeguarding—leadership. Despite a detached perspective, though, the observation itself must be close and careful. Once you find out where people are coming from, you can connect with them and engage them in change. But hearing their stories is not the same as taking what they say at face value. People naturally, even unconsciously, defend their habits and ways of thinking and attempt to avoid difficult value choices. Thus, after hearing their stories, you need to take the provocative step of making an interpretation that gets below the surface. You have to listen to the song beneath the words. In small ways, we do this every day. For example, if you ask someone how he is doing, and he says "OK," you can hear a big difference between a bright accent on the "K" and a sad emphasis on the "O."

Leaders are rarely neutralized for personal reasons, even though an attack may be framed in personal terms. The role you play or the issue you carry generates the reaction. When the players chase you down the field in a soccer match, they are not after you personally. They want you because you control the ball. Even though people yell her name and block her way, a fine soccer player would never think of taking it personally. Taking a "balcony" perspective, she sees the game on the field as a whole and immediately adjusts her behavior to take account of the patterns she sees. Great players in any sport can do this.

When the game is highly structured and the goal is clear, interpreting events on the playing field is a matter of technical expertise. But in organizational life, the various players compete by different rules and hold different visions of what it means to score a goal. Successful players in communities and groups need to understand a much more complex reality than do their counterparts on the soccer field. Interpretation, then, becomes at least as challenging as getting to the balcony for a bird's-eye view. In political and organizational life, no one finds it easy in the midst of action to step back and interrogate reality. Some people may be better at it than others, but no one has the "playbook."

Think back to Amanda. If you were at that meeting and had observed the dynamic by which Amanda became invisible and Brian received the credit, you would have to decide whether and then how to intervene. You would determine the course of action based on how you understood the significance of the marginalization. Once you observed it, you would have to interpret it in order to decide what to do.

Beware of making interpretations immediately and aloud, since this can provoke strong reactions. Interpreting other people's intentions is best done first inside one's own head, or with a trusted confidant. Interpreting behavior means looking at more than just the way people present themselves. Understandably, then, if you propose alternative explanations for people's behavior—alternatives to the messages they want you to adopt—they may get upset. Making an interpretation is a necessary step. Whether and how you voice it, however, must depend on the culture and adaptability of your audience.

Miles Mahoney, an economic development specialist, took on the job of heading a large state agency in Massachusetts that suffered a reputation for ineffectiveness. The governor appointed Mahoney because he liked his passion and his commitment to strengthening the state's role in large housing and economic development projects, although these were not the governor's top priorities.

Mahoney's office would have to approve development plans for funding. And Mahoney picked a doozy for his first project. The plan envisioned a huge development in downtown Boston, in an area that needed development but was not in such bad shape that it fell into a category called "blighted." The city of Boston and its mayor supported the project with great enthusiasm, as did the major newspaper, the unions, and most of the business community. The city chose a developer for the project—a new partnership created by two young real estate entrepreneurs who were friendly with the mayor but had never before tackled anything of this size and scope.

The law required Mahoney to examine the suitability of the project, the developers, and the plan. He could exercise considerable discretion, and the findings relied on judgments about the facts. Mahoney and his staff believed strongly that the project failed to meet the statutory requirements in several respects, including the fact that much of the proposed area was not blighted. Mahoney saw this as the opportunity to demonstrate the state's willingness to use its muscle to do what was in the public interest. He decided to reject it.

He went to the governor's key advisors to explain his position and to seek their support. They listened to him and said: "Go ahead and kill it, Miles. But kill it quickly. You have no idea how heavy those people are who are going to jump on you."

Mahoney heard what he wanted to hear: The governor would support his killing the project. But he missed the song behind the words.

The two most important clues in the advice he received were the words "quickly" and "you." What the governor's people were really saying could only be understood by listening beyond the explicit message.

Mahoney failed to hear the very different, almost inconsistent, message communicated with more subtlety. The governor would support Mahoney's rejection, but only if it happened so fast that the issue did not linger and affect the governor's more important initiatives. Governors' agendas are much wider and more dynamic than those of department heads. The governor could promise to stand behind Mahoney, but only for a short period of time, because he knew that his own attention would shift as new crises arose and new initiatives came on line. If the issue lingered and caused continuing trouble, the responsibility would be Mahoney's alone. The governor would not indefinitely expend his own political capital to make Mahoney's rejection stick.

Because Mahoney heard only the literal message, he moved ahead. Interpreting the governor to be more committed than he actually was, Mahoney turned down the project, sending its supporters into full battle mode. Six months later, Mahoney lost his job and his successor approved the project.

Read the Authority Figure for Clues

Miles Mahoney failed to listen to the song beneath the governor's words, but even if he had heard it, he might well have interpreted it as the governor's personal point of view. When you seek to instigate significant change within an organization or community, focus on the words and behavior of the authority figure; they provide a critical signal about the impact of your action on the organization as a whole.

The senior authority will reflect what you are stirring up in the community. He or she will consider and react to the responses of the factions in the organization. Look through the authority figure as you would look through a window into a house, understanding that what you are seeing is really in the rooms behind the glass. The trap is thinking that the authority figure is operating independently and expressing a personal point of view. In fact, that person is trying to manage all the various factions, and what you observe is a response to the pressures he or she is experiencing.

In reading an authority figure, you must not only look for shifts of view on relevant issues, but also assess where the authority stands on the ruckus you have created. In general, no one in an organizational system will be more tuned to the levels of distress than the person in charge, because an essential part of that job is to control any disequilibrium and restore order. In other words, authority figures sit at the nodes of a social system and are sensitive to any disturbances. They not only act as indicators of social stability, but will act to restore equilibrium if change efforts go too far.

Paula, a bright ambitious lawyer, had a strong interest in politics and public service. She achieved success as a prosecutor and then as a senior manager in an executive branch agency in the government of her home state. While taking a year off to get her master's degree in public administration, she continued to nurture her political contacts, particularly with the state's governor. She completed research projects, organized constituencies, and raised money on his behalf.

When Paula finished her graduate studies, the governor appointed her to head a small and troubled state agency charged with investigating wrongdoing in the state's welfare program. The unit had been criticized in press exposés that accurately described an organization fraught with dysfunction, although not guilty of prosecutable corruption.

The governor encouraged Paula to "go in there and clean the place up." At the time of the appointment, the governor also appointed another outsider to be her deputy. Together they thought they would carry out their mandate to reform the agency.

Paula charged ahead, throwing herself into the job as she always did. She didn't mind working long hours; she was totally committed to the task. She also loved being the head of the agency, enjoying the accoutrements of the position, which included a state car and a large office. But as she pushed for change, she began to feel resistance, both from above and below. Along with the State Police and other law enforcement–related agencies, Paula's agency was located in the Department of Public Safety. The culture in the agency reflected the values of the larger department: a police-oriented, hierarchical, almost paramilitary, don't-rock-the-boat bureaucracy. She was seen as a civilian change agent, forcing people to work harder than they were accustomed to working and to adopt new procedures and work conditions. Some people inside the agency and many of those in the umbrella department began to resent her, especially when her successes were reported in the media.

When she experienced resistance from the bureaucrats above and below, she created an alliance with the head of the union representing some of her employees. She confided in her deputy, who shared her agenda, and who had creatively designed and managed some of her early programmatic and media successes. However, she distrusted others in the organization.

Gradually, but noticeably, she became the target of leaks and internal criticism. Her relationship with the union head had turned into a personal friendship. She began to hear reports of gossip that it was sexual as well.

Although she was still getting reinforcement and reassurance from the governor's office, he himself became less accessible. She knew how busy he was so she didn't take it personally, and she took the staff's reassurance as a signal to keep moving forward.

She continued in this unstable and stressful situation for some time. Then the press ran a story about the union head's unexplained job absences, with the implication that she was aware of the situation, if not approving of it as well. A short time later, the governor's office began to drop hints to Paula that she consider other jobs. She left soon afterwards, accepting a general counsel's job in an obscure state agency. Not long after that, she was out of government altogether.

Like all people in authority, the governor responded to a wide range of interests from both within and outside the government. He distanced himself from her as a reaction to the distress she generated in the system. He did not want to oppose her reforms, but he also felt the pressure to reduce the upheaval in the department. If she had read his behavior as a signal of how much turmoil she had stirred up, rather than just as a function of her relationship with him, she might have been able to pull back, let things calm down, regroup, and move forward again.

Politics influence executive behavior in business as well as government. For example, Daniel heads the training program for a financial conglomerate that dominates the fast-moving financial services industry in the mid-Atlantic states. There was a sense in the company that despite their success, they were in danger of being swamped by bigger corporations and displaced at the niche level by boutique firms offering a narrower range of products but greater customization and personal service. The CEO encouraged Daniel to develop training programs that would challenge people and prepare senior management for turbulent paradigm-shifting times ahead.

He took the CEO at her word and created training that pushed people far outside their comfort zones. He made them examine their own habits and question glib assumptions about their capacity for exercising leadership. He put them through training that tested them physically and emotionally as much as it did intellectually. He challenged them with the idea that unless they changed their tried-and-true habits, they might not be with the organization as it dramatically expanded and reached for a new level. He experienced some negative feedback, but the CEO continued to back him.

Daniel never noticed, however, that she complimented him less frequently in public and did not mention his training program in the annual report. Apparently, she couldn't help but react to the criticisms of him from some in the first cohort of trainees. What he did notice, finally, was that his training budget got cut for the following year. When he raised the issue with the CEO, she said that it was part of a broader cut aimed at holding down the costs of "non-revenue-producing activities." Once again, on the individual level she still saw herself as fully supportive. But when at last Daniel began to read her behavior as a reflection of the distress his work had been generating throughout the organization, he realized that he had pushed too fast, too far, creating so much tension that the CEO needed to restore stability by trimming his sails.

He was never again able to get the more dramatic training off the ground. His initiative failed in part because he, like Paula, had not read the authority figure sensitively and systemically, in order to assess the tolerance for the level of discomfort he was creating in the community as a whole.

In times of adaptive stress, groups exert pressure on people in authority to solve the problems that seem to be causing it. Consequently, the behaviors of authority figures provide critical clues to the organization's level of distress and its customary methods for restoring equilibrium.

For example, in a rapidly growing twenty-year-old company we know well, the new CEO, Jerrold Petrey, quickly began to focus on the budget as the central issue facing the organization. Although the budget problem was quite real, it more deeply reflected the organization's unwillingness or inability to resolve fundamental questions and disputes about its identity, purpose, and priorities. There were two major factions in the company, each believing that it represented both the core values and the potential for future success. One faction wanted the company to deepen its commitment to its main product line. The product dominated the market and was responsible for the company's early success. The other faction wanted to diversify and build on the early success by introducing new products to existing satisfied customers. Rather than resolve the deep, fundamental issues, however, the company tried to do everything without exciting anyone, and growth began to flatten out.

Petrey's focus on the budget as a technical problem in cost containment exemplified how the community continued to avoid resolving its internal contradictions. Senior management would be let off the hook entirely, while lower levels of administrative staff, as well as frontline employees, would be squeezed.

The more passion Petrey put into dealing with the budget as a technical issue, the more apparent it should have become that the underlying problems were someplace else. Watching people in authority, like Petrey, can provide signals as to both the level of anxiety and the cause of anxiety in the system as a whole.

When the authority figure in an organization or community, even a large community such as a nation, behaves in an unusual way, it is always tempting to personalize the interpretation of his or her behavior. For example, you might think that the boss was simply a rigid person, or you might wonder if something is happening in your boss's private life to cause the behavior. But we suggest it is just as likely, if not more likely, that the conduct you observe is a response to pressures the authority figure is feeling from key constituents, like senior management in Petrey's case. When you are seeking to exercise leadership within an organization, observe the authority figure closely. What clues does his or her behavior offer about what is going on in the social system in response to your initiative and other adaptive pressures?

People in authority, like Petrey, Daniel's boss, and the Governor, want to think of themselves as supporters of innovation, as modern managers who "empower" their subordinates, rather than as political creatures limited by the resistance of factions wedded to the old order. So they often continue to pay lip service to those in the trenches who are tackling tough issues, long after they have begun to respond to the pressures on them to curb the action.

Watch them closely and interpret their behavior as a reflection of what is going on in the system. You might retreat, engage, or try to outflank the opposition. In any case, a cooling attitude from your authority figure indicates the resistance of the larger organization to your initiative, and therefore provides an essential clue for leading and staying alive.

.   .   .

Leadership is an improvisational art. You may have an overarching vision, clear, orienting values, and even a strategic plan, but what you actually do from moment to moment cannot be scripted. To be effective, you must respond to what is happening. Going back to our metaphor, you have to move back and forth from the balcony to the dance floor, over and over again throughout the day, week, month, and year. You take action, step back and assess the results of the action, reassess the plan, then go to the dance floor and make the next move. You have to maintain a diagnostic mindset on a changing reality.

As General Dwight D. Eisenhower described after leading the successful D-Day invasion on the beaches of Normandy, the first thing he had to do when the troops hit the beach was throw out the plan. On the other hand, he said they never would have gotten onto the beach without a plan. A plan is no more than today's best guess. Tomorrow you discover the unanticipated effects of today's actions and adjust to those unexpected events.

Sustaining your leadership, then, requires first and foremost the capacity to see what is happening to you and your initiative, as it is happening. This takes discipline and flexibility, and it is hard to do. You are immersed in the action, responding to what is right there in front of you. And when you do get some distance, you still have the challenge of accurately reading and interpreting what you now observe. You need to hear what people are saying, but not accept their words at face value. Groups want you to take their viewpoint. People want you to understand their motivation and the explanation of their behavior in their own terms. Creating alternative interpretations, listening to the song beneath the words, is inherently provocative, but necessary if you are going to address the real stakes, fears, and conflicts.

Pay very close attention to senior authority figures. Read their words and behaviors as signals for the effects you are stimulating in the group as a whole. See through them to the constituencies pulling them in a variety of directions. Don't just personalize what you see. Read authorities to gauge the pace and manner to push forward.

4

Think Politically

One of the distinguishing qualities of successful people who lead in any field is the emphasis they place on personal relationships. This is certainly true for those in elective office, for whom personal relationships are as vital as air is to breathing. For political people, the merits of a cause and the strategy used to move it forward are relevant but not controlling. The critical resource is access, and so the greatest care is given to creating and nurturing networks of people whom they can call on, work with, and engage in addressing the issue at hand. Able politicians know well, from hard experience, that in everyday personal and professional life, the nature and quality of the connections human beings have with each other is more important than almost any other factor in determining results.

There are six essential aspects of thinking politically in the exercise of leadership: one for dealing with people who are with you on the issue; one for managing those who are in opposition; and four for working with those who are uncommitted but wary—the people you are trying to move.

Find Partners

Finding partners is sometimes easier said than done. Both your own faction and other camps will happily watch you take on the challenge alone. Your own group wants to see how secure the footing is before they follow. Why should they risk their necks? And if you disrupt the status quo too much, other factions can push you aside more easily if you are by yourself.

Indeed, there can be internal pressures, inside of you, that resist joining forces. Partners might push their own ideas, compromising your own; connecting with them takes time, slowing you down; and working with a group might dilute your centrality—a drawback if it is important that you get credit, or if you want to reassure yourself and others of your competence.

Our friend Jack is trying to create a new organization for research and training built around a set of ideas about management. He has secured enough funding to get the program off the ground and to underwrite a core set of initiatives for several years. The word has gotten around, and so Jack spends a lot of time wading through offers of help and proposals. Emails, letters, and calls come in every day from associates and colleagues who want to be part of the new enterprise. He feels torn. He knows that he cannot do it alone, but he is certain that some of these people will undermine the clarity of his vision, delay his progress, and divert him from his core purposes. He wants to create an organization that is flexible and open, but he does not want to dilute the power of his ideas, which he has been formulating for twenty years.

M. Douglas Ivester also experienced those internal drives to do it alone. He was born in 1948, the son of a factory foreman in a small town in Georgia. He became an accountant and began a career at Coca-Cola as its outside auditor, joining the company full-time in 1979. A prodigious worker, he would come into the office at 7:00 A.M. every day of the week, including Sundays. He climbed rapidly up the organizational ladder on the financial side by solving any and all financial problems thrown at him, no matter how complex. He always managed to pull a rabbit out of his hat. In 1985, at age 37, he was appointed chief financial officer. He continued to shine in the role, developing creative financial and accounting moves and methods that increased Coke's bottom line and market share. He increased his visibility and experience within the company by moving to the operations side, where he studied management and hired tutors to fill in the gaps in his own training. But his habits did not change: working long hours and attending to the most minute of details ("8-day-a-week work ethic" was how *Time* magazine described it[1]).When legendary Coca-Cola CEO Roberto Goizueta died of lung cancer in October 1997, it took the board of directors only fifteen minutes to appoint Ivester, by then the chief operating officer, to succeed him.

As CEO, Ivester operated with the same passion and commitment. No problem was too small for his attention. Coca-Cola board member Warren Buffett tells the story of casually mentioning to Ivester that Buffett's grandson's favorite pizza parlor served Pepsi, only to find that it had been replaced by Coke on his next visit.

Ivester took the idea of going it alone to an extreme. He resisted the board's importuning to hire a deputy to fill the role he had occupied under Goizueta. He reduced his direct reports from sixteen to six, in the process demoting the highest-ranking African American in the company, a former city council president in Atlanta, Coca-Cola's headquarters city. He made decisions about investments, personnel, and media relations that were consistent with a single-minded strategy for ever-increasing growth and market share. But his moves did not take into account the sometimes countervailing interests of the company's "extended family" of bottlers, politicians in countries where Coke wanted to expand, or even customers. For example, he discussed with the press the development of a new dispensing machine that could be programmed to change prices—that is, increase them—on warm days when demand would rise. He didn't consider how badly this might play with consumers. And when Belgian schoolchildren became ill after drinking Coke products, Ivester decided to wait for more information before flying there to apologize. By the time he arrived it was too late. Coke's reputation had taken a severe blow just at the time when the company was trying to convince European regulators to approve acquisitions that were being opposed by Pepsi and other beverage companies.

After only two years into the job, Ivester had one by one alienated key constituencies, including his own board of directors. And while he was trying to do it all by himself, Coca-Cola's bottom line was not improving. He continued to insist to the board that if they would just leave him alone, he could make the right decisions—do it all, as he had always done, by working long hours and attacking every problem with his own intellect and energy. The board disagreed and forced him to resign in December 1999, barely into the third year of his tenure.

This unconscious dynamic is really a systemic reality in the modern world. As obvious as it was to Jack and to Douglas Ivester that it would be impossible to do it alone, there were real and formidable incentives inside and around each of them pushing them to be out there by themselves.

It's not a good idea. Partners provide protection, and they create alliances for you with factions other than your own. They strengthen both you and your initiatives. With partners, you are not simply relying on the logical power of your arguments and evidence, you are building political power as well. Furthermore, the content of your ideas will improve if you take into account the validity of other viewpoints—especially if you can incorporate the views of those who differ markedly from you. This is especially critical when you are advancing a difficult issue or confronting a conflict of values.

Finding the right partners can be tough. Why? Partnering on an issue means giving up some autonomy, causing both you and your potential partners some degree of reluctance about getting together. Moreover, developing trust takes the time and the perseverance to move productively through conflicts. But without working together, your efforts incur greater risk.

Sara lived in the Midwest and enjoyed considerable professional success designing newspapers and magazines. Then a large, successful daily newspaper in the Northeast hired her to completely

redesign the product and make design a factor in decisions throughout the organization—an undertaking that would alter the paper's
culture, not merely its appearance. The editor of the paper spon-
sored her recruitment and hiring. He understood that the visual age
had arrived. He knew that if he were to succeed not only in having the paper grow and prosper, but also in becoming a nationally
respected journalistic institution, he had to modernize its look.

But the idea of a major redesign clashed with the culture of the
company and threatened reporters and editors. To them, designers made the newspaper "pretty," which, in turn, made it fluffy and
soft. They feared that they would lose copy space to pictures, illus-
trations, and, worst of all, to plain, empty white space, all in the
interests of aesthetics and spoon-feeding readers. There would be
protocols for page layouts, the size of headlines, the choice of type-
faces, and the use of captions. The front pages of the various sec-
tions would have to be laid out earlier than before. Editorial staff
felt the new design scheme would hinder the freewheeling, seat-
of-the-pants tradition that was central to daily newspapering. The
relatively unfettered discretion of the writers and editors would be
forever compromised.

Sara and the editor were under no illusions. They knew this
would be a rough journey. They understood that he would have to
support her and act as a lightning rod for the criticism that would
surely come her way. Without his help, she could never bring about
a deep, value-laden change in the way people at the newspaper
understood their work.

Sara also knew that even with his backing, people who did not
believe in her efforts would attack any vulnerability she revealed.
Although she did not want to stay at the same paper forever, she
did want to leave behind a permanent improvement. If she did
not plan carefully, people at the paper would easily undo whatever progress she achieved. She had to find a way to ensure that her
work could not be rolled back once she left the scene.

Sara understood that the editor's partnership was necessary but
not sufficient. He would back her unless, or until, the heat became

so intense that he risked losing his own authority. She knew that the temperature level he could tolerate would in part be a function of the additional support she gained for her initiatives. So she set out to find more partners, identifying and wooing the very small number of senior people in the organization who shared her view that design mattered. She kept them informed, and a few of them became reliable allies.

In addition, and perhaps more important, she resisted the temptation to try to retrain existing employees, particularly the layout team, to become designers. Instead, she recruited from the outside. She hired as quickly as possible and as many new people as the editor would permit, going after the best and brightest graphic designers she could find. Eventually she built a solid cadre of design acolytes who were totally committed to design and did not have to overcome the cultural baggage of a previous history at the paper.

Sara survived for several years and was undeniably successful. Before leaving, she had woven design deeply into the fabric of the organization. Now, nearly everyone at the paper accepts the idea that part of the daily publishing challenge is making the paper look good. Designers work routinely and collaboratively, if not always amicably, with reporters and editors. After her departure, Sara's detractors could not turn back the clock on the changes she had made. She left behind not only a very different-looking newspaper but also a different culture: a group of young designers thoroughly integrated into the organization and determined to keep the momentum going.

Her partners, both in the design department and those few on the news side, saw her through some difficult moments, kept her afloat for a long period, and ensured that her accomplishments would stick after she left. She could not have done it alone.

During her tenure, Sara operated from a position with very little formal authority, certainly not enough to accomplish the culture change that she desired. Her partners—her design-supporting allies—gave her some running room, some informal authority to tread into new territory. But even people with great authority and a powerful vision need partners when they are trying to bring about deep change in a community.

Robert Moses, sometimes called the greatest builder of public works since the Medici family, took on the challenge of changing the face of New York City in the 1930s. He envisioned creating a system of large parks, parkways, beaches, and bridges, all coordinated, connected, and designed to meet the needs and desires of New York's growing middle class. He developed enormous formal authority. During the course of his career, he accumulated a huge power base, holding several gubernatorial and mayoral appointments. He promoted his ideas with such oratorical skill and persuasion that his political overseers granted him more and more power. The state legislature gave him eminent domain authority and discretion over a large, steady stream of revenue from bridge tolls.

Nevertheless, Moses understood that with all of his power and resources, he could not create sustained revolutionary change without key partners. He had plenty of opposition. Other people and other interests wanted to get their hands on the huge sums of money he controlled. There were competing ideas for parks. People whose homes or businesses stood in the way of his plans fought him at every turn. He offended someone with every idea he proposed.

For his first big initiative, Moses created a public beach on Long Island—what became Jones Beach. He carved this out of property owned and occupied by well-connected and wealthy families on a handful of big estates. Most of those folks opposed him, albeit unsuccessfully, horrified by the idea of making their private preserve accessible to thousands of "ordinary" people. Many simply lost their property when Moses came along, armed with his power of eminent domain.

When Moses moved into Manhattan and the Bronx, he met stiffer resistance. The people whose homes and businesses he wanted to seize fought him bitterly. They were shrewder opponents than the Long Island landed gentry, and more numerous. The tight-knit communities he disrupted organized themselves to challenge him. And the advocates for other interests—education, social services, and the like—fought his projects with the clout of their well-established groups. Collectively they posed a considerably greater threat to Moses' vision, even though individually they were not as rich or powerful as the big property owners on Long Island.

Moses possessed far more formal power in his community than Sara did in hers. Nevertheless, he, too, understood that even with all his legal authority and all his money, he could not see his ideas through to completion by himself, supported only by his own factions: his employees, contractors, and those who shared his vision.

He expended enormous effort in finding additional partners. He explained his vision to the newspapers. He used whatever means were at his disposal to create alliances with key political figures. He formed relationships with midlevel people in other agencies who bought into his vision; they, in turn, provided him with inside information so he could counter efforts to derail his projects. He knew the attacks were coming; well-intentioned people with very different visions wanted to stop him. He did not aspire to be popular. Even some of his partners did not like him personally, but they believed in what he was trying to do.

Like Sara, Moses understood that whatever formal power he had, he needed the partnership of senior authority figures in order to survive and succeed. For Sara it was her editor. For Moses, it was the governor of New York and the mayor of New York City. Neither of them could have accomplished anything of lasting significance without these partnerships.

They both understood another essential idea: Partners who are members of the faction for whom the change is most difficult can make a huge difference. From the start, Sara had a few people in the newsroom who valued design. Moses had allies in other agencies of city and state government. These partners not only provided key intelligence and enabled each of them to monitor what was happening in pockets of resistance, but they were much more effective advocates and useful lightning rods within their own camps than Sara or Moses could ever have been.

Finding real partners—people both inside and outside your organization who share the same goals—takes considerable time and energy. However, making the effort pays off. Successful CEOs such as Jack Welch, formerly of General Electric, and Leslie Wexner of The Limited have referred to themselves as the chief personnel officers for their corporations, recognizing that getting the right people on the team is their number one priority and responsibility. But they also understand that partnerships are not unlimited, unconditional, or universal.

A natural ally agrees with you on your issue and is willing to fight for it, but the alliance doesn't mean your partner will abandon all other commitments. No doubt your ally enjoys many relationships and identifies as a loyal member of other groups. Think of that as good news. After all, allies from other factions within or outside the organization help enormously by working within their faction on the issues you care about. Creating change requires you to move beyond your own cohort, beyond your own constituents, your "true believers." In order to use your allies effectively, you need to be aware of those other commitments. If you forget about them or their influence on your partner, you risk undermining your effectiveness and destroying the alliance.

Tom Edwards and Bill Monahan worked in different parts of a manufacturing company in the Northwest. Tom worked in information technology, and in Bill, who worked in sales, he had found a reliable ally for moving the company kicking and screaming into the world of high-speed IT. Bill not only worked the IT adaptation within his own group, but he gave Tom credibility on the issue company-wide.

Tom and Bill were also good friends, and their families socialized with one another. One evening, over dinner, Tom shared with Bill his strategy for getting the senior management team to approve the purchase of a new information management system at a meeting the next day. In the long run, the new system would save the company millions of dollars, but in the short run implementation required a difficult and painful transition in which some folks, including some people in sales, would probably lose their jobs.

Tom sensed some coolness in Bill after he laid out his plan, and asked whether something bothered him. "I wish you hadn't told me," Bill said. "I need to protect my people on this one and now you've given me some important information as to how I can do that before tomorrow's meeting."

In the end, Tom did not lose the alliance because Bill had openly shared his conflicting loyalties. They had a solid relationship where neither person held back, and they could talk things through in long, and at times difficult, conversations. But more often in such cases, an ally like Bill would just listen and go home, and then toss and turn all night wondering what to do. To whom should he be disloyal? In the end, he might be tempted by the easier option of staying loyal to his sales group and, in their interest, abandon Tom. All the while, a person in Tom's shoes might show up at the meeting thinking he had done his groundwork, only to find that his ally had done some preparation, too, and was taking action to derail the project.

This happens all the time. Have you ever gone to a meeting and realized that there was a "pre-meeting" that did not include you? The pre-meeting allowed those attending to minimize their internal conflict at the real meeting, present a united front, and isolate you.

It's a mistake to go it alone. By doing the same kind of home-work, you can increase the possibility that both you and your ideas stay alive. Make the next meeting one for which it is you who have made the advance phone calls, tested the waters, refined your approach, and lined up supporters. But in the process, find out what you are asking of your potential partners. Know their existing alliances and loyalties so that you realize how far you are asking them to stretch if they are to collaborate with you.

Keep the Opposition Close

As the executive director of a local nonprofit organization, Pete developed and maintained shelters for homeless and physically disabled people in an upper middle class suburb in southern Connecticut. He had achieved a record of remarkable success. He carefully planned each project from concept through land acquisition and implementation. He operated with political sensitivity. As a result, he acquired broad support from elected and appointed officials in town government.

Now he moved forward in a slightly new direction. He organized to create a home for mentally ill residents of the town, so that they could choose an option other than a remote hospital-type facility or living on the streets. The potential residents were stable people, but they could not afford to rent or buy in the high-income community. Pete's organization already owned the land he had targeted, a lot on a main highway next to a McDonald's restaurant that backed up to a residential area. A halfway house, which had been operating without incident for over fifteen years, occupied part of the lot.

Pete went to the elected executive of the town and received support for an application for a grant from the U.S. Department of Housing and Urban Development to build eight units of permanent housing on the site. He had to jump over only one more administrative hurdle: approval from the town planning and zoning commission.

Pete did most of his background work. He sought and received strong support from the fancy, locally owned clothing store across the highway. He worked with the bureaucrats in town hall. The chair of the Planning and Zoning Board told mutual friends that she favored the project. The architectural competition produced a creative design showing how affordable housing could be built cheaply, but attractively, on the site. Pete notified the neighbors, as the law required him to do, sending them a letter to let them know the plans.

The Planning and Zoning Board met monthly. Pete prepared for the February meeting, when the project made it onto the agenda. But the board had to reschedule the discussion for March because the public notice for the hearing came out late, and the community had not been given the necessary two weeks advance warning.

Only two nearby residents appeared at the February meeting, and they were obviously unhappy with the plan. Pete had resisted having a neighborhood meeting because he knew it would be unpleasant. He said he hated those "angry neighbor" meetings. But between February and March he grudgingly met with the two folks who showed up in February. He remembers their leaving "very disgruntled. They felt we were undermining their property values and endangering their children." They would return in March.

At the March meeting, the two February opponents had morphed into an angry group of forty. When it was their turn to speak, they opposed the project forcefully and vociferously. As Pete recalls, "They said their kids would no longer be safe going to McDonald's, that we were lowering their property values and destroying their only investment, and that the neighborhood was already a dumping ground. We were called irresponsible. One talked about a schizophrenic uncle who embarrassed the family by taking off his clothes in public."

The Planning and Zoning Board rejected the project by a vote of 5–2. Now, belatedly, Pete began to meet with the neighbors. Emboldened by the board's decision, the residents at those meetings lambasted the project, with as much vitriol as there had been at the March meeting, and as much pain for Pete. Logic, outside experts, and local political and civic support did not count for much at those gatherings. Finally, after several of those unhappy events, Pete withdrew the proposal and his organization went away to look for another site.

Looking back on these events, Pete saw his big mistake: his early neglect of the neighborhood residents. Yet Pete had reacted in a way that was human and understandable. He thought he had enough power and support to push his way through and he shuddered at the prospect of subjecting himself to difficult, contentious, time-consuming meetings with people who did not share his vision.

From all the support he had lined up, he enjoyed, in his words, "a false sense of invulnerability. The voices I listened to said this is the right thing to do and the right place to do it." He not only ignored the warning signals in February, but he also dismissed the arguments of the few members of his own board who had expressed reservations.

To survive and succeed in exercising leadership, you must work as closely with your opponents as you do with your supporters. Most of us cringe at spending time with and especially taking abuse from people who do not share our vision or passion. Too often we take the easy road, ignoring our opponents and concentrating on building an affirmative coalition. But rather than simply recognize your own anxiety and plow ahead, as Pete did, you need to read this anxiety both as a vulnerability on your part and as a signal about the threat you represent to the opposing factions. These are clues to the resistance you will face, made worse if you do not engage with your opposition.

Michael Pertchuk failed to understand this when he moved from an advocacy position on Capitol Hill to a policymaking and regulatory position as chair of the Federal Trade Commission (FTC).

Pertchuk had arrived at the FTC as something of a hero with the consumer activist community based on his work in the U.S. Senate as the chief counsel for the Senate Commerce Committee. On Capitol Hill, he innovated continuously, bringing new policies and programs at a rapid rate and seeing many of them enacted into law. He earned the complete confidence of Senator Warren Magnuson (D-WA), his chairman, who benefited enormously in political support, publicity, and prestige from Pertchuk's popular consumer initiatives.

At the FTC, Pertchuk continued to see himself in an advocacy role. His consumer constituency expected that and wanted it. So he searched around for a new issue to champion. Soon he found one, dubbed "KidVid"—the control of advertising on children's television programs.

Recent studies had shown the impact on impressionable minds of the heavy dose of ads scheduled for the Saturday morning cartoon shows. Pertchuk moved ahead, proposing sweeping new regulations. He chose an issue and attacked it the same way he had done when he served on Capitol Hill.

In his congressional staff role, all Pertchuk had to do was count the votes. And he usually had the votes for whatever he put on the agenda. Moderate and liberal Democrats controlled the Congress at that time and they voted for popular, consumer-oriented laws with great enthusiasm. When he had enough votes to pass legislation, he moved ahead. He ignored people on the other side. He spent his time thinking up new ideas, not garnering support.

That strategy had worked well in the legislative branch, so he transferred it wholesale to his new role. He avoided any contact with the business community, whose products were being advertised. He knew they would undoubtedly reject his idea. He even steered clear of the television industry, which not only had a direct stake in the policy, but also were going to cover it and comment on it. "What could they add," he must have reasoned, "except a lot of trouble."

He was right that they would likely react with hostility. Leaving them out or bringing them in was not going to change that. But by leaving them out, Pertchuk helped doom KidVid himself. He lost contact with key, relevant opposition. Pertchuk's proposed policy would choke off the manufacturers' main channel for getting to their primary customers—the kids. The advertising community would lose the revenue from creating the ads. And of course network and cable television companies depended on advertising revenue for their profits. On KidVid, Pertchuk was dancing with all of these groups whether he faced them or not.

He careened forward, proposing an outright ban on advertising during children's television programs. The consumer groups loved the idea and cheered him on. With his collusion, Pertchuk's core constituency pushed him further out on a limb than he ever should have gone.

The press and the business community, particularly, responded with the vehemence he had predicted. Respected people spoke out and said the legislation overreached, that it went way beyond what the problem required. To many observers, a legal ban disregarded the rights of free speech and ignored the consequences on the future funding of children's programs. Pertchuk behaved as if he were still Magnuson's idea-generator, rather than the head of a regulatory agency. Even members of Congress who admired him had expected him to be more even-handed in this new role. With considerable fanfare, Congress dismissed Pertchuk's proposal without a serious examination. The FTC sustained damage to its credibility in the eyes of legislators and lawyers as well as businesspeople, who might have been sympathetic to another proposal but fought the whole issue because Pertchuk's plan went too far. Within a year, the children's television initiative died definitively. Pertchuk lost legitimacy and found himself on the downside of his tenure in the job.

People who oppose what you are trying to accomplish are usually those with the most to lose by your success. In contrast, your allies have the least to lose. For opponents to turn around will cost them dearly in terms of disloyalty to their own roots and constituency; for your allies to come along may cost nothing. For that reason, your opponents deserve more of your attention, as a matter of compassion, as well as a tactic of strategy and survival.

Keeping your opposition close connects you with your diagnostic job, too. If it is crucial to know where people are, then the people most critical to understand are those likely to be most upset by your agenda.

While relationships with allies and opponents are essential, it's also true that the people who determine your success are often those in the middle, who resist your initiative merely because it will disrupt their lives and make their futures uncertain. Beyond the security of familiarity, they have little substantive stake in the status quo—but don't underestimate the power of doing what's familiar.

As you attend to your allies and opposition in advancing your issue, do not forget the uncommitted and wary people in the middle—the people you want to move. You need to ensure that their general resistance to change doesn't morph into a mobilization to push you aside. What follows are four steps you can take that are specifically focused on gaining their trust.

Accept Responsibility for Your Piece of the Mess

When you belong to the organization or community that you are trying to lead, you are part of the problem. This is particularly true when you have been a member of the group for some time, as in a family. Taking the initiative to address the issue does not relieve you of your share of responsibility. If you have been in a senior role for a while and there's a problem, it is almost certain that you had some part in creating it and are part of the reason it has not yet been addressed. Even if you are new, or outside the organization, you need to identify those behaviors you practice or values you embody that could stifle the very change you want to advance. In short, you need to identify and accept responsibility for your contributions to the current situation, even as you try to move your people to a different, better place.

In our teaching, training, and consulting, we often ask people to write or deliver orally a short version of a leadership challenge they are currently facing in their professional, personal, or civic lives. Over the years, we have read and heard literally thousands of such challenges. Most often in the first iteration of the story the author is nowhere to be found. The storyteller implicitly says, "I have no options. If only other people would shape up, I could make progress here."

When you are too quick to lay blame on others, whether inside or outside the community, you create risks for yourself. Obviously, you risk misdiagnosing the situation. But you also risk making yourself a target by denying that you are part of the problem and that you, too, need to change. After all, if you are pointing your finger at them, pushing them to do something they don't want to do, the easiest option for them is to get rid of you. The dynamic becomes you versus them. But if you are with them, facing the problem together and each accepting some share of responsibility for it, then you are not as vulnerable to attack.

Leslie Wexner, founder and CEO of The Limited, faced that challenge in the early 1990s, when his company began "spinning," as he recalls. "We were working hard but going nowhere." He had taken the corporation to great heights, going from four employees to 175,000, but his strategy was no longer producing growth.[2] After a terrific fourth quarter in 1992, the company experienced two down years.

Wexner hired a consultant, a Harvard Business School professor named Len Schlesinger, to take a very deep look at the company's problems and to assess what it would take to turn things around.

The consultant returned with three messages. First, strengthen the brands; that made sense to Wexner. Second, Wexner would have to fire a significant portion of the corporation's workforce, perhaps as many as one third of his people. But Wexner had run the company as a family since its inception in 1963. He had never been in the habit of firing people. He thought this part heretical.

The third message cut even deeper. Schlesinger told Wexner that he was part of the problem. The company could make a transition with him or without him, the consultant said, but if the former, he would have to take responsibility. He would have to make substantial, significant changes in his own beliefs and behaviors. Without that, the remaining employees, the shareholders, and the company's corporate board would be able to successfully resist the needed transformation.

Wexner found the message difficult to hear. He had started the company in 1963 with a loan of $5,000 from his aunt. That was enough to open one women's clothing store in a suburban shopping mall in Columbus, Ohio. His goal then was to earn a salary of $15,000 a year and have enough left over to buy a new car every few years. First-year sales were $165,000. From that point on, he had enjoyed nearly thirty years of significant annual growth, and his one store had burgeoned into a retailing colossus. He was accustomed to accepting plaudits for success, not for throwing overboard values and practices that had been near the heart of his self-image. Besides, he was fifty-eight years old, and questioned his capacity to admit error and to mend his own ways.

Wexner uses a metaphor to describe the feeling: "I was an athlete trained to be a baseball player. And one day someone taps me on the shoulder and says 'football.' And I say, 'No, I'm a baseball player.' And he says, 'football.' And I say, 'I don't know how to play football. I'm not 6'4" and I don't weigh 300 pounds.' But if no one values baseball anymore, the baseball player will be out of business. So, I looked into the mirror and said, 'Schlemiel, nobody wants to watch baseball. Make the transformation to football.'"

He believed in Schlesinger and so, painfully, he began to accept his piece of the mess. He committed himself to a personal as well as a corporate makeover. He hired an executive coach to help him learn new ways and to stay on track. People in the company as well as shareholders and lenders noticed. They saw the changes he was making and began to understand that he was on their side, facing up to difficult issues, taking responsibility and risks, and facing an uncertain future. He embodied his message, and thereby avoided becoming a target for attack for most of the long turnaround period. His personal commitment helped to sway the vast uncommitted.

Wexner changed, survived, and thrived. So did The Limited. Between 1996 and 2001, the corporation increased sales by 50 percent and its operating margin by 4 percent, with 1,000 fewer stores, and a reduced workforce of 124,000 employees.

Acknowledge Their Loss

Remember that when you ask people to do adaptive work, you are asking a lot. You may be asking them to choose between two values, both of which are important to the way they understand themselves. Any person who has been divorced with children understands how difficult this is. Most of us shudder at the prospect of having to choose between our own happiness and what's best for our children. We might try to convince ourselves that we are serving the children's happiness by ending a dysfunctional or unsatisfying marriage, but usually the children would not agree and neither would many of the experts.

You may be asking people to close the distance between their espoused values and their actual behavior. Martin Luther King, Jr., challenged Americans in that way during the civil rights movement. The abhorrent treatment he and his allies received in marches and demonstrations dramatized the gap between the traditional American values of freedom, fairness, and tolerance and the reality of life for African Americans. He forced many of us, self-satisfied that we were good people living in a good country, to come face-to-face with the gulf between our values and behavior; once we did that, we had to act. The pain of ignoring our own hypocrisy hurt us more than giving up the status quo. The country changed.

Of course, this takes time. Confronting the gaps between our values and behavior—the internal contradictions in our lives and communities—requires going through a period of loss. Adaptive work often demands some disloyalty to our roots. To tell someone that he should stop being prejudiced is really to tell him that some of the lessons of his loving grandfather were wrong. To tell a Christian missionary that, in the name of love, she may be doing damage to a native community, calls into question the meaning of mission itself. To suggest to her that, in an age of global interdependence, we can no longer afford to have religious communities compete for divine truth and souls, calls into question the interpretation of scripture lovingly bestowed upon her by family and teachers.

Asking people to leave behind something they have lived with for years or for generations practically invites them to get rid of you. Sometimes leaders are taken out simply because they do not appreciate the sacrifice they are asking from others. To them, the change does not seem like much of a sacrifice, so they have difficulty imagining that it seems that way to others. Yet the status quo may not look so terrible to those immersed in it, and may look pretty good when compared to a future that is unknown. Exercising leadership involves helping organizations and communities figure out what, and whom, they are willing to let go. Of all the values honored by the community, which of them can be sacrificed in the interest of progress?

People are willing to make sacrifices if they see the reason why. Young men and women go to war with the blessings of their parents to protect values even more precious than life itself. So it becomes critically important to communicate, in every way possible, the reason to sacrifice—why people need to sustain losses and reconstruct their loyalties. People need to know that the stakes are worth it.

But beyond clarifying the values at stake and the greater purposes worth the pain, you also need to name and acknowledge the loss itself. It's not enough to point to a hopeful future. People need to know that you know what you are asking them to give up on the way to creating a better future. Make explicit your realization that the change you are asking them to make is difficult, and that what you are asking them to give up has real value. Grieve with them, and memorialize the loss. This might be done with a series of simple statements, but often requires something more tangible and public to convince people that you truly understand.

When the terrorists attacked on September 11, 2001, they generated extraordinary disruption and loss to the United States in general and to New York City in particular. People in New York were forced, not only to grieve losses, but to face a new reality: their own vulnerability. Mayor Rudolph Giuliani seemed immediately to grasp people's struggle to adapt. He spoke clearly, passionately, and repeatedly, giving voice to people's pain. Over and over again, he urged people to resume their pre–September 11 activities, to go to work, use the city's parks, and patronize restaurants and theatres, even though everyone's natural response was to hunker down and stay out of harm's way. But as people began to heed his advice, he also let them know that he realized what he was asking them to do. He asked them to give up their heightened need to maintain a sense of their own personal security on behalf of larger values: not giving in to the terrorists, and rebuilding New York City. Giuliani went even further. He modeled the behavior he was asking of others by putting himself in harm's way, going to Ground Zero over and over again, barely escaping being injured himself on September 11 when the towers fell. Sometimes, modeling the behavior you are asking of others presents itself as an even more powerful way than just words to acknowledge their loss.

Model the Behavior

Avram was the CEO of a highly successful chemical factory in Israel. One day an explosion occurred on the line, tragically killing two of his employees. He swung into action, taking care of the families of the deceased workers and investigating the cause of the disaster. He quickly pinpointed the source of the problem and took steps to ensure that it could not happen again.

But whatever he did seemed not enough. Many of his best workers feared coming back to work. Many who did return performed ineffectively because they were tentative and frightened. They had lost confidence in the safety of the factory, and nothing he said reassured them sufficiently to return to the location where their colleagues had died or to work at their previous level of productivity. Their trauma was palpable, and productivity declined. The future of the company looked very much in doubt.

Reluctantly, Avram came to a decision. He resigned as CEO and took a job on the line, right at the spot where the explosion had taken place. Slowly, workers began to return and production began to creep upward. The company eventually turned a corner. Ten years later, it had become one of the largest in Israel, much more profitable than it had been before the accident.

The CEO had realized that he was asking his employees to do something that looked safe to him but dangerous to them. Because he and they saw the reality differently, it was hard at first for him to appreciate the magnitude of his request. A trained scientist with an equity interest in the company, he was convinced that he had made the plant safe. But no amount of logic or evidence would have assuaged the employees' fears. He had to let them know that he appreciated the risk he was asking them to take, even if he believed their concerns were unwarranted. He had to acknowledge the loss he was asking them to accept, in this case the loss of a sense of personal safety. Because their fears were so deep, verbal acknowledgment would not suffice. He had to model the behavior.

In 1972, soon after leaving his position as the young managing editor of the *Washington Post* and unsure he had a future in journalism, a demoralized Gene Patterson received a call from Nelson Poynter, the owner of the *St. Petersburg Times*.[3] Poynter offered him the job of editor, with the assumption that he would succeed Poynter as the person responsible for the entire company, which included several other media holdings. Patterson and Poynter had been acquainted with each other for many years; they met and talked at newspaper conventions, and respected each other's work. Patterson was interested in running a newspaper and had been a longtime reader and admirer of the *Times*. Poynter was looking for someone to take his already-respected newspaper to another level. He wanted it to be not only a good regional newspaper, but also a beacon of the best in journalism and a force for making St. Petersburg, Florida, what he termed "the best place in the world to live." Both editors wanted the newspaper to enhance its reputation for good writing by becoming fearless, hard-hitting, and more independent of the city's established elite, becoming more of a voice for the powerless than the powerful.

Poynter and Patterson knew that to achieve these aims, they would have to generate significant value-laden changes in the way reporters and other *Times* employees thought about themselves and their roles, as well as in their readers' views of the newspaper.

There could be no sacred cows. Bad news about the community would not be soft-pedaled. Advertisers would be subject to as much journalistic scrutiny as any other organization that wielded power and influence. Investigations would be a steady part of the newspaper's offerings, and prominent organizations and individuals would not be spared if they deserved to be criticized. The news and editorial staffs would not hesitate to use the power of the newspaper to promote progress as they saw it. This meant reporters and others who worked at the newspaper would be subject to intense pressure and controversy.

On July 4, 1976, four years after Patterson arrived, he went to a party at the home of his good friend Wilbur Landrey, the foreign editor of the *Times*. On his way home, Patterson pulled up to a red light and scraped the car next to him. A policeman was called to the scene and charged Patterson with driving under the influence of alcohol. Patterson called Bob Haiman, the veteran *Times* newsman who had just been appointed executive editor, and insisted that a story be run on his arrest.

As Haiman recalls the conversation, he tried to talk Patterson out of it.[4] But Patterson was adamant. "We have to have a story," Haiman remembers him saying. "I said, 'Well OK, Gene.' Then he said, 'Have a reporter get the details from the Police Department. I want you to put this story on page 1.' I argued with him again. 'Most DUI arrests not involving injuries are not even reported any more. Even if it was the city manager we wouldn't do a very big story at all and it would probably be inside the local section.' Patterson was willing to let me talk but he was not about to have his mind changed on this."

Patterson knew that if he wanted the folks who worked for the paper to emulate and adapt to the highest journalistic standards and aspirations, then he and Poynter would have to display those standards, even when it hurt. They both knew that there would be resistance to the changed standards. They also recognized that Patterson—the new editor and an outsider—would be more vulnerable to negative counter-reactions from employees and resistance from community leaders than Poynter, who was increasingly detached from day-to-day operations. The drunk-driving situation gave Patterson the chance to model the behavior he expected of others. He knew this was a unique opportunity in which his commitments would be tested. No matter how embarrassing and uncomfortable, Patterson needed to ensure that the paper treated him the way it would treat any equally prominent person. Otherwise, he and Poynter would have had no hope of moving the organization and the community to embrace a different kind of journalism, journalism that was going to cause some discomfort and controversy in a city that had grown accustomed to putting the best face on its news. Patterson's arrest was on page 1.

The saga quickly became part of the folklore at the *Times* and in St. Petersburg, and remains so to this day. By all accounts Patterson's insistence on the coverage made it easier for people at the newspaper and in the community to move forward into a more honest and vital, albeit contentious, relationship.

The modeling in these cases was more than symbolic. People were taking real risks in doing what they were asking others to do. But even symbolic modeling can have substantial impact. When Lee Iacocca reduced his own salary to $1 during Chrysler's troubles, no one worried that Iacocca would go without dinner. But the fact that he was willing to make a personal economic sacrifice helped motivate employees to do likewise as part of the company's turnaround plan.

Accept Casualties

An adaptive change that is beneficial to the organization as a whole may clearly and tangibly hurt some of those who had benefited from the world being left behind. Wexner's change process at The Limited left many people bruised, their jobs lost and once-secure careers now uncertain. Few people enjoy hurting or making life difficult for old friends and colleagues.

If people simply cannot adapt, the reality is that they will be left behind. They become casualties. This is virtually inevitable when organizations and communities go through significant change. Some people simply cannot or will not go along. You have to choose between keeping them and making progress. For people who find taking casualties extremely painful, almost too painful to endure, this part of leadership presents a special dilemma. But it often goes with the territory.

Accepting casualties signals your commitment. If you signal that you are unwilling to take casualties, you present an invitation to the people who are uncommitted to push your perspectives aside. Without the pinch of reality, why should they make sacrifices and change their ways of doing business? Your ability to accept the harsh reality of losses sends a clear message about your courage and commitment to seeing the adaptive challenge through.

A few years ago Marty consulted with a company that did technical work for the defense industry. The organization had enjoyed a long and successful run, but the fall of the Berlin Wall in 1989 ushered in a new era. The Cold War was over. The new CEO realized that the competition for contracts was getting tougher, that they could no longer rely on their reputation and have the work come to them. He began to think about changing the business, becoming more aggressive and adding to their product line. For many of the long-term and most respected employees, this was hard to accept.

At the CEO's direction, the senior management team went off to a two-day retreat to chart their future direction. Most of them came around, accepting the harsh reality that in order to survive they had to give up some of what they knew and loved. At the end of the retreat, the CEO held a climactic meeting. He wanted an endorsement of the new plan, and he asked each of the participants whether they were with the program. One by one, they each said yes, some with great reluctance. The number-three person in the organization sat near the end of the row. He had worked in the organization longer than anyone else present. The room was quiet as everyone waited. He said nothing. Slowly he got up and left the room. He packed his bags, went back and cleaned out his office, and left his letter of resignation on the CEO's desk. He became a casualty, and the willingness of the CEO to accept his resignation demonstrated to the rest of his team his commitment to change.

People seeking to exercise leadership can be thwarted because, in their unwillingness to take casualties, they give people mixed signals. Surely we would all prefer to bring everyone along, and we admirably hold up this ideal. Unfortunately, casualties are often a necessary by-product of adaptive work.

. . .

The lone warrior myth of leadership is a sure route to heroic suicide. Though you may feel alone at times with either creative ideas or the burden of final decision-making authority, psychological attachments to operating solo will get you into trouble. You need partners. Nobody is smart enough or fast enough to engage alone the political complexity of an organization or community when it is facing and reacting to adaptive pressures.

Relating to people is central to leading and staying alive. If you are not naturally a political person, then find partners who have that ability to be intensely conscious of the importance of relationships in getting challenging work done. Let them help you develop allies. Then, beyond developing your base of support, let them help you relate to your opposition, those people who feel that they have the most to lose with your initiative. You need to be close to them to know what they are thinking and feeling, and to demonstrate that you are aware of their difficulty. Moreover, your efforts to gain trust must extend beyond your allies and opposition, to those folks who are uncommitted. You will have to find appropriate ways to own up to your piece of the mess and acknowledge the risks and losses people may have to sustain. Sometimes you can demonstrate your awareness by modeling the risk or the loss itself. But sometimes your commitments will be tested by your willingness to let people go. Without the heart to engage in sometimes costly conflict you can lose the whole organization.

Orchestrate the Conflict

When you tackle a tough issue in any group, rest assured there will be conflict, either palpable or latent. That's what makes a tough issue tough. For good reason, most people have a natural aversion to conflict in their families, communities, and organizations. You may need to put up with it on occasion, but your default mindset, like ours, is probably to limit conflict as much as possible. Indeed, many organizations are downright allergic to conflict, seeing it primarily as a source of danger, which it certainly can be. Conflicts can generate casualties. But deep conflicts, at their root, consist of differences in fervently held beliefs, and differences in perspective are the engine of human progress.

No one learns only by staring in the mirror. We all learn—and are sometimes transformed—by encountering differences that challenge our own experience and assumptions. Adaptive work, from biology to human culture, requires engagement with something in the environment lying outside our perceived boundaries. Yet, people are passionate about their own values and perspectives, which means they often view outsiders as a threat to those values. When that is the case, the texture of the engagement can move quickly from polite exchange to intense argument and disruptive conflict.

Thus, the challenge of leadership when trying to generate adaptive change is to work with differences, passions, and conflicts in a way that diminishes their destructive potential and constructively harnesses their energy.

Orchestrating conflict may be easier to do when you are in an authority role because people expect those in authority to manage the process. However, the four ideas we suggest in this chapter are also options for people who seek to enact change but are not in senior positions of authority: First, create a holding environment for the work; second, control the temperature; third, set the pace; and fourth, show them the future.

Create a Holding Environment

When you exercise leadership, you need a holding environment to contain and adjust the heat generated by addressing difficult issues or wide value differences. A holding environment is a space formed by a network of relationships that bond people together and enable them to tackle tough, sometimes divisive questions without flying apart. Creating a holding environment enables you to direct creative energy toward working conflicts and containing passions that could easily boil over.[1]

A holding environment will look and feel quite different in different contexts. It may be a protected physical space you create by hiring an outside facilitator and taking a work group off-site to work through a particularly volatile and sensitive conflict. It may be the lateral bonds of shared language and common history that bind people together through trying times. It can be characterized in some settings by vertical bonds of deep trust in an institution and its authority structure, like the military or the Catholic Church. It may be characterized by a clear set of rules and processes that give minority voices the confidence that they will be heard without having to disrupt the proceedings to gain attention. A holding environment is a place where there is enough cohesion to offset the centrifugal forces that arise when people do adaptive work. In a holding environment, with structural, procedural, or virtual boundaries, people feel safe enough to address problems that are difficult, not only because they strain ingenuity, but also because they strain relationships.

But no matter how strong the vertical and lateral bonds of trust and the history of collaboration, no holding environment can withstand endless strain before it buckles. All social relationships have limits; therefore, one of the great challenges of leadership in any community or organization is keeping stress at a productive level. Managing conflict (and your own safety) requires you to monitor your group's tolerance for taking heat.

The design of the holding environment, then, is a major strategic challenge—it must be sound, or else you risk the success of the change effort as well as your own authority. In 1994, Ruud Koedijk, chairman of the partnership KPMG Netherlands, created a series of structures for engaging the firm in a major change to its way of doing business. Although this audit, consulting, and tax partnership was the industry leader and highly profitable, growth opportunities in the segments it served were limited. Audit margins were being squeezed as the market became more saturated, and competition in the consulting business was increasing as well. Koedijk knew that the firm needed to move into more profitable growth areas, but he did not know what those opportunities were and how KPMG might meet them. He and his board of directors engaged a consulting firm headed by Donald Laurie to help them analyze trends and discontinuities, understand core competencies, assess competitive position, and map potential opportunities.

Although Koedijk and his board were confident that they had the tools to plan the strategy, they were considerably less sure that they and their organization could implement it. KPMG had tried to introduce change in the past and found it difficult, probably due to the partnership structure, which inhibited change in two ways: the manner in which partners treated each other and the dynamics that the partnership set up with the nonpartner members of the firm. A culture study revealed that directors generally provided people with little room to use their creativity or perform tasks beyond day-to-day work activities. Were they capable of the changes in beliefs, values, and behaviors that a new strategy might require?

KPMG was less a partnership than a collection of small fiefdoms in which each partner was a king. Success was defined in terms of billable hours and individual unit profitability, not factors such as innovation and employee development. As one partner described, "If the bottom line was correct, you were a 'good fellow.'" As a result, one partner would not trespass on another partner's turf, and learning from each other was a rare event. Conflict was camouflaged: If partners wanted to resist firmwide change, they did not kill the issue directly but silently, through inaction. They even coined the phrase "Say yes, do no" to describe this behavior. For younger people, the atmosphere was sometimes oppressive. They answered to the partner in charge, and found that assuring him that no mistakes were taking place paved the road to success. There was little curiosity and a lot of checking for mistakes.

Koedijk realized that adaptive work had to be done throughout the firm if KPMG were to change direction and enter new businesses. First, he gathered his partners together in a large meeting and provided a coherent context: the history of KPMG, the current business reality, and the business issues they could expect to face in the future. He then asked them how they would go about changing as a company. He asked for their perspectives on the issues. By launching the strategic initiative through genuine dialogue rather than edict, he built trust within the partner ranks. Based on this trust and his own personal credibility, Koedijk got the partners to agree to release a hundred partners and professionals from their day-to-day responsibilities to work on the strategic challenges. They would devote 60 percent of their time to this project for nearly four months.

Koedijk and his colleagues established a Strategic Integration Team (SIT) of twelve senior partners to work with the hundred professionals from different levels and disciplines. Engaging people below the partner ranks in a key strategic initiative was unheard of, and from the start signaled a new approach to work: Many of these people's opinions had never before been sought or valued by authority figures in the firm. Divided into fourteen task forces, these people were to work in three areas—gauging future trends and discontinuities, defining core competencies, and grappling with the value shifts and adaptive challenges facing the organization. Hennie Both, the director of marketing and communications, signed on as project manager.

As the learning process got underway, it became evident that the SIT and the participants embodied everything, both good and bad, about the culture. It did not take long before every member of these task forces came to see that the culture was built around strong respect for the individual at the expense of effective teamwork. For example, each individual brought his or her own deeply held beliefs and way of working to every discussion: They were far more inclined to assert their favorite solution to a problem than listen to a competing perspective. People didn't work well with those from other units. At the same time, they avoided conflict; they would not discuss these problems. A number of the task forces became dysfunctional and were unable to continue their strategy work.

To manage the dysfunction, Hennie Both developed a session in which each task force could discuss its effectiveness as a team. Hennie helped them see these differences by getting them to describe the culture they desired and map it against the current team profile. The top three characteristics of their desired culture were the opportunity for self-fulfillment, a caring and human environment, and trusting relations with colleagues. Their top descriptors of the current culture were: We develop opposing views, we are perfectionist, and we try to avoid conflict. This gap defined a clear adaptive challenge, and paying attention to it was a step forward.

Each of the members was asked to identify the value they added to the strategy effort as well as their *individual* adaptive challenge. What attitudes, behaviors, or habits did they need to change; what specific actions would they take and with whom? They then broke into self-selected groups of three people and served as consultants to each other. This required them to confide in each other and to listen with deeper understanding.

Managing the holding environment as the participants worked through tough adaptive issues was a constant preoccupation of Koedijk, the board, and Hennie Both. They arranged for a separate floor so the group of one hundred could work with its own support staff, unfettered by traditional rules and regulations. It surprised some clients to see managers wandering through the KPMG offices in Bermuda shorts and T-shirts that summer. They established a norm that any individual from any group could walk into any session of another team and contribute to the work. Also, people agreed that ideas were more important than hierarchy and that junior people could challenge senior colleagues; soon the most respected people were those with the most curious minds and interesting questions. The conditions for a different operating culture were being established.

Hennie Both and Ruud Koedijk maintained high energy within the holding environment of the task force structure. They gave broad assignments with limited instructions to groups accustomed to working on fixed, well-defined assignments. The heat rose further when people who thought they were accustomed to working in teams realized that their experience had really prepared them only for sharing routine tasks with people "like them" from their own units.

Koedijk and Both protected the holding environment for their change initiative by creating a task force culture that was kept separate from the organization. People could make mistakes and live with conflict that formerly would have been suppressed in their units. For example, at one point when the heat rose significantly, all one hundred were brought together to meet the management board and voice their concerns in an Oprah Winfrey–style meeting. The board sat in the center of an auditorium, surrounded by the questioning participants.

They held frequent two- and three-day "off-sites" when it was necessary to draw collective closure to parts of the work. These events always included socialization to strengthen lateral bonds, a key source of cohesion. "Playtime" could range from long bike rides to highly entertaining laser gun games at local amusement centers. In one spontaneous moment at KPMG offices, a discussion of the power of people who were mobilized toward a common goal led to a walk outside, where the group used their leverage to move a seemingly unmovable concrete block.

Attitudes and behaviors changed—curiosity became valued more than obedience. People no longer deferred to the senior authority figure in the room—genuine dialogue neutralized hierarchical power in the battle over ideas. The emphasis on each individual representing his or her pet solution gave way to understanding other perspectives. A confidence emerged in the ability of people in different units to work together and reach solutions.

None of this would have happened without a strong vessel of the right design, allowing those leading the effort to keep everyone at just the right temperature, influencing each other in the progress toward a more creative organization. In the end, KPMG Netherlands began to migrate from audit to assurance; from operations consulting to strategy consulting, shaping the vision and ambition of their clients; and from teaching traditional skills to their clients to creating adaptive organizations. Indeed, the task forces identified new business opportunities worth $50–$60 million.[2]

Control the Temperature

Changing the status quo generates tension and produces heat by surfacing hidden conflicts and challenging organizational culture. It's a deep and natural human impulse to seek order and calm, and organizations and communities can tolerate only so much stress before recoiling.

If you try to stimulate deep change within an organization, you have to control the temperature. There are really two tasks here. The first is to raise the heat enough that people sit up, pay attention, and deal with the real threats and challenges facing them. Without stress, there is less stimulus for people to tolerate difficult change. The second is to lower the temperature when necessary to reduce a counterproductive level of tension. Any community can take only so much pressure before it becomes either immobilized or spins out of control. The heat must stay within a tolerable range—not so high that people demand it be turned off completely, and not so low that they are lulled into inaction. We call this span the productive range of stress. (See the figure "Technical Problem or Adaptive Challenge?")

Of course, you can't expect the group to tolerate more stress than you can stand yourself. When you develop your own capacity for taking heat, you raise the tolerance level of the organization or community. But if you lose your poise and turn down the flame, people will take that as a cue that the passions generated cannot be contained. The stress will appear intolerable. In political campaigns, people often look to the candidate to set the standard for the

---

Technical Problem or Adaptive Challenge?

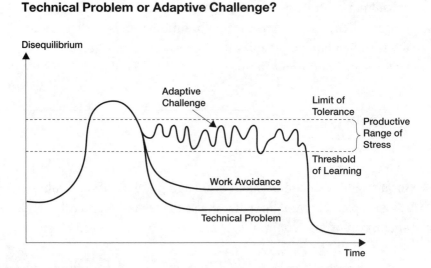

Source: Ronald A. Heifetz and Donald C. Laurie, "Mobilizing Adaptive Work: Beyond Visionary Leadership," in Jay A. Conger, Gretchen M. Spreitzer, and Edward E. Lawler III, eds., *The Leader's Change Handbook: An Essential Guide to Setting Direction and Taking Action* (New York: John Wiley & Sons, 1998).

tolerance of stress. If the candidate blows, it's unlikely that anyone else on the staff will be able to focus on the campaign. The same is true when you are in an authority role in any realm: as project manager, coach or captain of a team, or lead investor in a high-risk venture. There is tremendous pressure on you to control your own natural emotional responses, which may be entirely appropriate and normal to express, except within the role you are trying to play.

People expect the boss to control the temperature, but those without formal authority can do some of this work as well. If you are leading without or beyond your authority, you must assess how far ahead of people you are and then adjust how hard and fast to push for change. As we suggested in chapter 3, one way you make that assessment is to carefully monitor the response of the authority figure to your actions. If the authority figure starts to act precipitously to calm things down—for example, by firing "the troublemakers" or taking action to squelch deviant voices— it probably indicates that you have pushed too hard. The level of social disequilibrium is too high.

You can constructively raise the temperature and the tension in two ways. First, bring attention to the hard issues, and keep it focused there. Second, let people feel the weight of responsibility for tackling those issues. Conflicts will surface within the relevant group as contrary points of view are heard.

By contrast, there are many ways to reduce the heat, since organizations are more practiced at cooling things down than intentionally heating them up. Any method for reducing the heat may also be used as an indirect way of increasing the upper limits of tolerance for it within the organization. To reduce heat you can start on the technical problems, deferring adaptive challenges until people are "warmed up." A little progress on a partial, relatively easy problem may reduce anxiety enough that the tougher issues can then be tackled. Negotiators commonly use this tactic: Strengthen the relationships—the holding environment—by creating shared successes. You can provide structure to the problem-solving process, by breaking down the problem into its parts, creating working groups with clear role assignments, setting time parameters, establishing decision rules, and structuring reporting relationships. You can frame the problem in a less threatening way, or speak to people's fears. You can temporarily bear more of the responsibility yourself. You can use humor or find an excuse for a break, even a party, to provide a temporary release. People may then be able to return to the tough questions. You can separate the conflicting parties and issues, pacing and sequencing the rate at which people challenge one another. Finally, you can speak to transcendent values so that people can be reminded of the import of their efforts and sacrifices. (See "How to Control the Heat.")

Be mindful that the organization will almost always, reflexively, want you to turn down the heat. Therefore, you need to take the temperature of the group constantly, trying to keep it high enough to motivate people, but not so high that it paralyzes them. When people come to you to describe the stress you are causing, it might be a sign that you have touched a nerve and are doing good work.

When the heat hits the ceiling and the system appears on the verge of melting down, you need to cool things off. History provides some striking examples in which people in authority believed that the level of chaos, tension, and anxiety in the community had risen too high to constructively mobilize people to act on difficult issues. As a result, they first acted to reduce the anxiety to a tolerable level, and then made sure enough urgency remained to stimulate engagement and change.

Franklin D. Roosevelt came to power in 1933 amidst the deepening crisis of the Great Depression. After more than three years of economic collapse, with millions unemployed and the nation's banks approaching insolvency, the country had reached a very high level of anxiety and, in many regions, outright despair. The United States faced adaptive work of a magnitude that strained even its boisterous confidence and ingenuity.

The unprecedented level of distress reached during this national crisis, and the resulting conflict and disorientation, called forth all sorts of distorted schemes to calm the country and restore a firm footing, from the demagogic initiatives of Father Coughlin to the

---

HOW TO CONTROL THE HEAT

Raise the Temperature

1. Draw attention to the tough questions.
2. Give people more responsibility than they are comfortable with.
3. Bring conflicts to the surface.
4. Protect gadflies and oddballs.

Lower the Temperature

1. Speak to people's anger, fear, and disorientation.
2. Take action. Structure the problem-solving process—break the problem into parts, and create time frames, decision rules, and clear role assignments.
3. Slow down the process. Pace and sequence the issues and who you bring to the table.
4. Be visible and present—shoulder responsibility and provide confidence.
5. Orient people—reconnect people to their shared values, and locate them in an arc of change over time.
6. Low-hanging fruit—make short-term gains by prioritizing the technical aspects of the problem situation.

---

platform of the communist party. As the nation's preeminent authority figure, Roosevelt embodied the country's hope for a restoration of order without distorting its core values and institutions. All eyes were on him for direction and protection. His first priority had to be to reduce disequilibrium, to lower the distress so that the nation would be less vulnerable to demagogues and could make progress toward economic recovery.

To do this, Roosevelt had to speak to emotional realities. He had to calm the nation down, both in words and in action. In words, he spoke to people's anxiety ("the only thing we have to fear is fear itself"), to their anger (calling the bankers "money-changers"), and to their disorientation (with intimate and reassuring fireside chats). His actions conveyed the same message, providing hope and calming fears. Roosevelt's decisive and authoritative action—the famous "one hundred days" in which he pushed an extraordinary number of bills through Congress—provided direction and helped reassure the American people that they were in capable hands. Roosevelt knew he was no savior—people would ultimately have to save themselves. But through his words and actions, he lowered the temperature just enough that people could focus constructively on the work ahead.

On the other hand, Roosevelt also knew that accomplishing the adaptive work facing the nation required improvisation, experiments, creativity, and conflict, and he fostered these all around. He orchestrated conflicts over public priorities and programs among the large cast of creative characters he brought into the government. For example, by giving the same assignment to two different people (driving them crazy over the lack of clear role definition), he provoked new and competing ideas, and gave himself more options with which to work. As hard as this improvisation must have been, he got the horns, the drums, and the flutes making music together.

Roosevelt displayed both the acuity to recognize when the tension rose too high and the emotional strength to permit considerable anxiety to exist. He had to resist the strong impulse toward quick fixes. Procrastination and delay were as much a part of his repertoire as decisive action. As Arthur Schlesinger points out, "Situations had to be permitted to develop, to crystallize, to clarify; the competing forces had to vindicate themselves in the actual pull and tug of conflict; public opinion had to face the question, consider it, and pronounce upon it. Only then, at the long, frazzled end, would the President's intuitions consolidate and precipitate a result."[3]

We can see the same principle at work in a very different, and ethically disturbing, example. General Augusto Pinochet of Chile came to power in a 1973 coup d'état amid the political and economic disarray at the end of the Allende administration. Like Roosevelt, he found the level of chaos (rampant unemployment, labor strikes, inflation) intolerably high. Indeed, his rise to power was an explicit effort to restore order in a nation caught between superpowers and riven with conflict. He used his authority—that is, military might and political repression—to restore order. The costs in human lives and individual freedom were enormous.

However, Pinochet understood that too much order would make meaningful change impossible. So while he treated dissenters brutally, he used the stability he created to challenge the traditional power elites on the economic front. He proceeded to turn up the heat on the private sector, eliminating protective tariffs and government subsidies, thus forcing businesses to adapt to international competition or die. Some did die, but others adapted, and many new businesses and industries flourished in the new environment.

Pinochet deserves to go down in history as a controversial figure. For seventeen years, he forcibly guided his society through an adaptive transformation, but Pinochet's repression outlived any usefulness it might have had, and political democracy was restored. His methods for restoring order were savage and criminal. There is no denying that he understood the need to control the temperature in his country in order to accomplish needed economic change. Chile has a strong growth record with a modern economy more productive than before, but it still wrestles with its scars.

The U.S. presidential election in 2000 provides a less extreme illustration. After five weeks of intense and acrimonious partisanship following the inconclusive results on election day, both the winner, George W. Bush, and the loser, Al Gore, used their victory and concession speeches to calm the waters rather than fan already inflamed passions even further. Bush could have used the opportunity to advance his agenda and Gore could have used the moment to air his grievances. Many wanted them to do that. But both understood that the nation was reaching the limit of tolerance for such disequilibrium, and that this was not the time to advance contentious and provocative perspectives or issues.

These are large-scale examples, to be sure, but the principle remains unchanged at any level: You must use the resources at your disposal to regulate the stress of your colleagues so that they can deal creatively with the underlying challenge causing the stress. In our experience, most people and organizations find it more difficult to raise the temperature than to lower it. We often encounter people in our work who resist making their communities uncomfortable, expressing something close to a moral revulsion against doing so. This is quite natural—we often create a moral justification for doing what we want to do, and most people want to maintain the status quo, avoiding the tough issues. In an effort to maintain equilibrium, we keep the tough issues off the table altogether, "so as not to upset anyone."

To exercise leadership, you may have to challenge the assumption that the needed change is not worth the upset it will cause. You'll need to tell people what they do not want to hear. This may mean raising the temperature to a point where addressing the problem becomes imperative in order to move forward, or at least seems as likely a way to restore calm as continued avoidance.

In the brilliant 1957 movie *Twelve Angry Men*, raising and lowering the temperature plays a central role, both literally and metaphorically. All but three minutes of the 132-minute film take place in a sixteen-by-twenty-four-foot jury room, a kind of pressure cooker.

Only a few minutes into the film, we see the twelve white males on the jury file into the cramped, almost claustrophobic space. They have sat though a long first-degree murder trial. An eighteen-year-old boy is accused of stabbing his father to death after an argument. Under state law, a guilty verdict will result in the electric chair for the defendant. It is a late summer afternoon in New York City and the early conversation among the jurors is all about the heat and stifling humidity. They pry open the windows to get some air in the room. The fan doesn't work.

Martin Balsam, in the role of the jury foreman, calls for a preliminary vote. Everyone except for the straitlaced architect played by Henry Fonda votes "guilty." Without any conversation at all, it is 11–1 for a conviction. People are obviously tired. Some are sweating from the heat. They want to be done with it. But the decision must be unanimous, and Fonda has already disturbed the equilibrium in the room by holding out. The small talk about the weather, sports, and the stock market stops. Fonda tells them that he is not sure the boy is innocent, he's just not certain that he is guilty, either. There is grumbling. One juror has tickets to a baseball game that night. Others are worried about getting back to their businesses.

Fonda insists on hearing the jurors out, one by one, going around the room and listening to their arguments, finding out first where people are. He questions them and they push back at him, hard. He is attacked personally: "You think you're a pretty smart fella, don't ya?" the character played by Lee J. Cobb snarls as Fonda gently, patiently probes their arguments. He is threatened. At one point he seems physically in danger when Cobb grabs him to demonstrate how the murderer must have used the knife to stab the victim. When they come at him, Fonda resists escalating the instability. He knows that they are close to the point of throwing in the towel and declaring a hung jury, a tempting prospect as the deliberations linger into the evening.

Early on, as the tension rises and it appears that the majority will run roughshod over him and his doubts, Fonda cools things off temporarily by putting forth a high-risk proposition. He calls for a secret ballot. If he is still the only one for acquittal, he will back off and vote for conviction. But they all agree that if there is another vote for acquittal the group will commit to staying and talking it out. The additional vote, of course, comes through, and the tension level is lowered as everyone realizes they're not going anywhere for a while. No quick conviction. No quick hung jury.

For most of the next hour Fonda carefully manages the level of distress in the room. He raises the temperature with the dramatic production of a knife that looks just like the murder weapon, which is shortly followed by taking a break from their deliberations. He attacks Cobb, baiting him, until Cobb explodes and threatens to "kill" Fonda, thus making Fonda's point that people often use that language without really intending to follow through. Whenever

Fonda senses that the group is too tired or too stressed he backs away a little, allowing for some cooling off time. But he is just as sensitive on the other end, raising the tension in the room enough to prod them to address his concerns, perhaps just to get him to calm down.

Fonda's skill was in absorbing and controlling the heat of conflict. He increased and reduced the disequilibrium so that it was high enough to get his fellow jurors to focus on a reality other than the one they preferred but not so high so as to cause them to break apart, throw in the towel, and declare a deadlock.

Typically, as it was in the movie for Fonda, people push back hard on dissident voices to try to restore calm. Fonda was criticized and attacked, as other members of the group sought to turn the conversation onto him and avoid dealing with the questions he raised. The attacks on him were a diversion. For several members of the group, Fonda's persistent prodding uncovered their own biases that had affected their assumption of guilt. In the end, Cobb understood an awful truth: that his guilty vote was more about his anger, frustration, and mostly sadness about his relationship with his own son than it was about the evidence. Without his combination of relentlessness and careful modulation of the temperature in the room, Fonda would not have been able to survive the overwhelming desire of the group to convict and go home.

Of course, there's a significant chance that when you generate the heat, and take it in return, you may simply end up in hot water with no forward progress to show for your effort. But if you don't put yourself on the line and take the step of generating that constructive friction, you'll deprive yourself and others of the possibility of progress.

Pace the Work

Leadership addresses emotional as well as conceptual work. When you lead people through difficult change, you take them on an emotional roller coaster because you are asking them to relinquish something—a belief, a value, a behavior—that they hold dear. People can stand only so much loss at any one time. You risk revolt, and your own survival, by trying to do too much, too soon.

In the early 1990s, the two senior authority figures in the U.S. government made this mistake within months of each other.

In 1993 and 1994, President Bill Clinton recommended sweeping health care reform that involved radical changes in the financing and delivery of health care services. Health care represented one-seventh of the U.S. economy and touched the lives of every American citizen. To generate change of that magnitude, Clinton may have needed a strategy to educate, explain, and persuade that would have taken years, with small experiments all along the way. People always want better and cheaper health care, but those who were insured were not fundamentally dissatisfied with what they were already receiving. They weren't certain that any new system would improve their lives.

Many health care providers and most insurers—that is, those who would have to implement a new plan—actively opposed Clinton's proposed reforms, and the public did not find this reassuring. Clinton believed his election in 1992 gave him a mandate and, treating health care reform as a technical problem rather than an adaptive challenge, he acted as if members of Congress and the public could be persuaded that his plan was the best policy and the right course of action. They weren't persuaded, and his plan died without coming to a vote. His own popularity crumbled quickly, constraining the success of other initiatives. The media wrote stories about whether he was still "relevant," and his political opponents took advantage of his weakness. His failure to pace the work of changing the health care system contributed significantly to Republican victories in the 1994 congressional elections.

The main architect of that Republican electoral success, and its chief individual beneficiary, was Congressman Newt Gingrich, elected Speaker in January 1995. But soon afterwards Gingrich followed suit, making the same basic mistake by failing to pace the adaptive work that he now identified for the nation. Gingrich had designed the 1994 national Republican congressional campaign around a series of dramatic reforms including term limits, tax and welfare reform, a strong national defense, and a dramatically smaller federal government. These were packaged together under the rubric "Contract with America." Nearly all of the Republican candidates for the U.S. House of Representatives endorsed the Contract. The strategy worked. Gingrich gained what no Republican leader of the House had enjoyed since Dwight Eisenhower's presidency, a Republican majority. Inspired by his enormous electoral success, Gingrich set out to enact the entire Contract with America agenda as quickly as possible in the early days of the 1995 session. He had the votes. And he had what he thought was an electoral mandate for a very specific set of changes.

Despite the votes and the mandate, however, Gingrich ran into great difficulty. Neither the public nor its elected representatives were ready to make so many changes so fast. Voting for candidates who endorsed the Contract with America was quite different from supporting quick enactment of all of its far-reaching elements.

Gingrich failed to appreciate that no matter how much enthusiasm the public felt for the contract as an idea, in reality people needed more time to get their heads around so many deep and significant changes. Gingrich didn't seem to consider how best to pace the work. How much radical change could people absorb at once? Parceling out the change, spreading the agenda over a longer period of time, would have enabled people to assess the value of the new versus the loss of the familiar, through every step of the process. Debated one-by-one over time, the individual items would have seemed more doable and would have been more easily understood in terms of the broad themes of the Contract, which had been so popular in the election. After all, the broad themes—the idea of a smaller, more responsive government—had given the Contract its appeal, rather than its individual parts.

Gingrich's insistence on enacting the whole agenda right away had the effect of frightening people rather than inspiring them. His personal vulnerability increased when he was held largely respon-sible for the government closing down in late 1995. By 1996, little of the Contract had been passed into law and the momentum behind it had been dissipated in the misguided effort to get Congress, and the people, to swallow it whole. Clinton, on the other hand, survived and regrouped successfully, winning reelection handily in 1996 after making some dramatic midcourse corrections. Gingrich was not so fortunate, and his impatience cost him dearly. After the 1998 election, he lost the post of House Speaker and left the Congress.

Pacing the work is not a new or complicated idea. Mental health professionals have said for a long time that individuals cannot adapt well to too many life changes at once. If you suffer a loss in the family, change jobs, and move all within a short time, your own internal stability may break down, or show signs of serious strain. The same is true of organizations and communities. Change some-times involves loss, and people can sustain only so much loss at any one time.

Yet pacing the work is often difficult because your own com-mitment and that of your enthusiasts push you forward. It would have been hard for Clinton and Gingrich to resist the importuning of their most fervid followers and slow the process. Following their most passionate constituencies must have felt like the path to sur-vival as well as success. True believers are not known for their sense of strategic patience.

Pacing the work can be ethically complicated because it can involve withholding information, if not outright deception. Once Clinton's health care program had been designed, sequencing the work wisely may have required him to appear more open to options than perhaps he was. He would have been engaging in a process of persuasion under the guise of education. Pacing typically requires people in authority to let their ideas and programs seep out a little at a time, so they can be absorbed slowly enough to be tested and accepted. This kind of patient withholding of information must be done carefully, with an openness to the testing and revision of one's ideas, lest it be interpreted as deceitful or misleading.

If you have some authority, you can use some of the basic functions of your position as resources for pacing the work. You decide which ingredients to mix and when. For example, in setting agendas, postpone the most threatening or provocative issues, either by ruling them off the agenda or by excluding their advocates from participation in the early stages. This will help modulate the rate of change. Also, in determining decision rules, think strategically about how decisions are made; draw out this process so the group is not faced with too much too soon.

Each of these techniques for pacing might be interpreted as simply putting off the hardest issues, as a kind of work avoidance. But it's not avoidance if you in fact are preparing people for the work that lies ahead. Rather, you are taking control and making change a strategic and deliberate process.

How you pace the work depends on the difficulty of the issue, the tolerance of the community, and the strength of your authority relationships and the holding environment. Assess the situation. Calculate the risks. Then decide how to pace the work, knowing that this is an improvisation. Not only must you be open to the possibility of changing course in midstream, you should expect that after seeing people's reactions, you will have to reassess and take ongoing corrective action.

Show Them the Future

To sustain momentum through a period of difficult change, you have to find ways to remind people of the orienting value—the positive vision—that makes the current angst worthwhile. For Roosevelt, that meant creating a New Deal for Americans, saving the free-market system, and protecting democracy in the era of Stalin and Hitler. His vision, however abstract in his high rhetoric, moved people.

As you catalyze change, you can help ensure that you do not become a lightning rod for the conflict by making the vision more tangible, reminding people of the values they are fighting for, and showing them how the future might look. By answering, in every possible way, the "why" question, you increase people's willingness to endure the hardships that come with the journey to a better place.

That was Martin Luther King, Jr.'s, aim in his famous 1963 "I Have a Dream" speech, in which he pointed to a future where "little black boys and black girls will be able to join hands with little white boys and white girls and walk together as sisters and brothers."[4]

Sometimes it is possible to make the future even more concrete than King was able to do in that speech. In 1983, the Spanish government appointed Ricardo Sanchez to be the Director General of IPIA, the regional industrial promotion agency for the Andalusian region of Spain.[5] The government gave him the job of reversing the pattern of economic stagnation that characterized the region. The local industries struggled along with antiquated production methods, primitive marketing, and an assumption on the part of the citizenry that being an economic backwater was an inevitable and permanent condition. Not only was there no innovation, there seemed to be no interest in it or spirit for it.

Sanchez focused his attention on the marble industry in the Macael region, located in the desert mountains of eastern Andalusia. Although Macael enjoyed one of the world's largest deposits of white marble, production and profit were way below its competitors. The Macael marble industry specialized in primary marble production, a low-profit and fragmented segment of the marble market compared to the more lucrative finishing processes. There were more than 150 small marble firms in the region, averaging seven employees. Firms did little or no marketing, had no brand identity, and were vulnerable to competition from larger firms and to the market power of both suppliers and customers. The owner-managers of these small firms valued their independence above all else, even above profit and growth. Sanchez came to Macael to promote growth, but he had virtually no resources at his command. He found himself with no funds to dispense, no authority with which to organize people, and a formidable adaptive challenge.

Sanchez realized that one powerful way he could help his people face the need to give up a way of life they loved was to show them a better future. He knew that the members of the employers association could not envision any organizational model different from the one in which they had been embedded for generations. So, he took a group of them on a bus trip to the Carrara marble region of Italy. Most of them had never traveled outside of Spain. They toured quarries and fabrication facilities, marveled at the automated equipment, and talked with their counterparts, who were accustomed to the most modern technology and took advantage of economies of scale. The Spaniards began to appreciate the benefits of marketing and branding. The group returned with a different attitude, a greater willingness to entertain the possibility that their lives could be both different and better, that there might be something worth giving up what they loved. They had seen for themselves a future that might be theirs.

It is not always possible to show people the future. It might not exist. You might not even be able to envision it yourself. But if it is possible, revealing the future is an extremely useful way to mobilize adaptive work and yet avoid becoming the target of resistance. If people can glimpse the future, they are much less likely to fixate on what they might have to shed. And if someone else has been there before them and achieved the vision, it increases their confidence not only that the future is possible, but also that you are the person to get them there. You come to embody hope rather than fear. Confidence in the future is crucial in the face of the inevitable counterpressures from those who will doggedly cling to the present, and for whom you become the source of unwanted disturbance.

· · ·

To lead people, we suggest you build structures of relationships to work the tough issues, establishing norms that make passionate disagreement permissible. But keep your hands on the temperature controls. Don't provoke people too much at any one time. Remember, your job is to orchestrate the conflict, not become it. You need to let people do the work that only they can do.

6

Give the Work Back

You gain credibility and authority in your career by demonstrating your capacity to take other people's problems off their shoulders and give them back solutions. The pattern begins early in school as children receive positive reinforcement for finding the answers, and continues throughout life as you become an increasingly responsible adult. All of this is a virtue, until you find yourself facing adaptive pressures for which you cannot deliver solutions. At these times, all of your habits, pride, and sense of competence get thrown out of kilter because the situation calls for mobilizing the work of others rather than knowing the way yourself. By trying to solve adaptive challenges for people, at best you will reconfigure it as a technical problem and create some short-term relief. But the issue will not have gone away. It will surface again.

Moreover, shouldering the adaptive work of others is risky. As we saw in the last chapter, when you take on an issue, you *become* that issue in the eyes of many; it follows, then, that the way to get rid of the issue is to get rid of you. Whatever the outcome, you will be held responsible for the disequilibrium the process has generated, the losses people have had to absorb, and the backlash resulting from those who feel left behind.

Take the Work off Your Shoulders

When Marty worked on personnel issues in the office of Massachusetts governor William Weld, he often found himself in the position of trying to resolve a conflict between two senior state employees before it hit the newspapers or the evening news. Typically he would call the protagonists into his office to hash out their differences. He took some useful survival lessons from that experience.

First, the people involved usually framed the conflict quite inaccurately, attributing the problem to personality or stylistic differences. Marty would interview them and listen to their separate versions of the story. Most of the time, more was going on than met the eye: The differences they described were not superficial or merely technical but, instead, represented underlying value choices, either individual or organizational. "Personality conflicts" turned out frequently to mask a fundamental conflict in the division of responsibilities, the primacy of cultural values, or even in the vision for the agency. Not surprisingly, the protagonists shied away from addressing the deeper, more difficult issues affecting their working relationship. Second, they looked to him to resolve the problem. Sometimes the only thing they could agree on was to hand the issue over to Marty, saying, "Look, we'll do whatever the governor's office wants us to do here. Just tell us which way you want us to go." A tempting proposition. He could truncate an uncomfortable, tense meeting, put the immediate crisis to rest, and avert a publicly embarrassing story. And if he chose the alternative, attempting to deal with a deeper, more intractable problem, it would take more time and energy than any of them preferred to expend. Sometimes he took the easy way.

Marty discovered that taking the easy way usually resulted in two consequences, neither of which served his or the governor's purposes. First, the underlying issue would inevitably rise again, sometimes in a less controllable form, because it had never been put to rest. Instead, it festered, particularly if the protagonists represented significant factions within the organization. Second, by assuming responsibility for resolving the issue, Marty turned it into *his* issue, or the governor's, or both. Whenever a senior authority in an organization resolves a hot issue, that person's position becomes the story. Winners and losers are created simply by virtue of authority, and no learning takes place. And because the person with authority has taken sides, that authority may later be in jeopardy if the "winning" position on the issue no longer receives adequate support in the organization. Marty created trouble for himself and undermined his own credibility on those occasions when he resolved the issue and, later on, the person or position he chose fell out of favor.

Return to 1994, the NBA (National Basketball Association) Eastern Conference finals.[1] The New York Knicks are facing the Chicago Bulls in a best-of-seven series. Chicago is trying desperately to show that they are more than a one-man team, that they can win without Michael Jordan, who had retired at the end of the previous season (his first retirement). The Knicks have won the first two games, played at Madison Square Garden. Now they are back in Chicago. The score is tied at 102, with only 1.8 seconds left in the game. The Bulls cannot afford to go down 0–3 in the series. Chicago has the ball and they call a time-out to plan a final shot. The players huddle around Coach Phil Jackson, already considered one of the best professional basketball coaches of this or any other era. The discussion is animated, perhaps even heated. Jackson's play calls for Scottie Pippen, the Bulls' number one star now that Michael Jordan has retired, to inbound the ball to Toni Kukoc for the final shot. Kukoc is the only person on the team who could challenge Pippen's status as the new, post-Jordan first among equals. Pippen is angry that he was not selected to take the final, critical shot and is heard mumbling "bullshit" under his breath as the huddle breaks. Jackson says something to Pippen and then turns his attention back to the floor. Then he notices Pippen sitting down at the far end of the bench. Jackson asks him whether he's in or out. "I'm out," Pippen responds, thus committing a dramatic and rare act of insubordination in organized sports: refusing the coach's direction to enter the game. With only four players on the floor, Jackson has to quickly call another time-out to prevent a penalty. He inserts a reserve player, an excellent passer named Pete Myers. Myers tosses a perfect pass to Kukoc. Kukoc spins around and sinks a miraculous shot to win the game. The Bulls are alive, but the euphoria of the win dissipates quickly in the wake of Pippen's action.

The Bulls make their way back to their dressing room. Jackson enters the room. The air is thick. What will he do? Punish Pippen? Pretend the whole thing never happened? Make Pippen apologize? All eyes are on him.

As Jackson is trying to decide what to do, he hears the veteran center Bill Cartwright gasping, overcome with the emotion of the moment. Finally, everyone on the team has reassembled there in the dark, dank room (Jackson describes it as smelling like an "old, forgotten gym bag"), and the coach looks around, making eye contact with the players. Then he says, "What happened has hurt us. Now you have to work this out."

Silence and surprise pervade the locker room. Then Cartwright makes an unusually emotional appeal to Pippen. "Look Scottie," Jackson quotes him as saying, "that was bullshit. After all we've been through on this team. This is our chance to do it on our own, without Michael, and you blow it with your selfishness. I've never been so disappointed in my whole life." Cartwright, known for his quiet stoicism and invulnerability, was crying. Jackson left the room and the team talked.

Jackson knew that if he took action and resolved the issue, he would have made Pippen's behavior a question of insubordination, a matter between coach and player. But he understood that a deeper issue lay at the heart of the incident. This moment had reflected something about the relationship among the members of the team. What did they owe to each other? What was their responsibility to each other? Where was the trust? The issue rested with them, not him, and only they could put it behind them.

By not taking the conflict on his own shoulders, by externalizing it and putting it back on the players, Jackson located the issue
in the only place where it could be resolved, in the team itself. It did
not matter what they decided at that moment; what mattered was
that they and not Jackson were doing the deciding. Jackson said
later when complimented about the way he handled the situation,
"All I did was to step back and let the team come up with its own
solution." With all eyes on him, Jackson got to the balcony and saw
that any intervention by him might solve the immediate crisis but
would leave the underlying issues unattended.

We know from our own mistakes how difficult it is to external-
ize the issue, to resist the temptation to take it on ourselves. People
expect you to get right in there and fix things, to take a stand and
resolve the problem. After all, that is what people in authority are
paid to do. When you fulfill their expectations, they will call you
admirable and courageous, and this is flattering. But challenging
their expectations of you requires even more courage.

Place the Work Where It Belongs

To build new adaptive capacity, people must change their hearts as
well as their behaviors. The Phil Jackson story illustrates that solutions are achieved when "the people with the problem" go through
a process together to become "the people with the solution." The
issues have to be internalized, owned, and ultimately resolved by
the relevant parties to achieve enduring progress. Jackson had to
locate the conflict and place the issue where it belonged.

A boundary of authority separates team and coach, and individual boundaries separate each teammate. But the boundaries
between close-knit teammates can be more easily crossed over than
boundaries that delineate authority or divide highly divergent factions, teams, or parties. Someone within the team could address
the impact of Pippen's action on the team more compellingly than
someone from outside. Jackson situated the issue, placing it within

the group and not between the group and some outside arbitrator. He left a crucial boundary intact, knowing that the most effective work could only be done within the Bulls team "family."

So, taking the work off your own shoulders is necessary but not sufficient. You must also put it in the right place, where it can be addressed by the relevant parties. Sometimes this is within one faction; other times this means getting different factions within the organization to work on the problem together. When those senior officials tried to impose their adaptive work on Marty, his response should have been to push it back on them. In taking on their problems, he also accepted all the risk. Better to agree to endorse whatever resolution the contending parties choose. At those times when he did place the work, Marty found that the resolution was often sustainable, and that the problem was more likely to go away without backfiring. Even if this resolution differed from the one he would have fashioned, or even the one he thought was the best available, the outcome was better (and much safer for him) when he let the people involved determine their own resolution.

Placing the conflict in the right location is not a function or an opportunity that is the sole preserve of those in authority. Ricardo Sanchez (whose story appears in chapter 5) understood this. When he first entered the Macael community, and with the local mayor leading the way, Sanchez spent two days visiting marble production firms and listening to the small-business representatives talk about their issues. He then had the mayor call a meeting of the senior people from both the local employers association and the trade unions. He told them that he understood the problems, but that a solution was not self-evident. Faced with the question of how he could get them to think about collaboration rather than autonomy—without being shown the door—he decided to make a dramatic process intervention. He told them that they needed an action plan, one they would have to develop themselves. IPIA would serve as coordinator, not as author of the plan, and would help mobilize the resources needed to implement it. He placed the work within the community. He was not going to become the person embodying that plan if they refused to collaborate.

Then came the radical part of his strategy. He said that he would walk away from Macael then and there if they did not immediately decide to proceed as he suggested by a *unanimous* vote. Furthermore, he would guarantee his and IPIA's help only if every element of the plan were also approved unanimously. By creating that threshold for his ongoing involvement, he forced the stakeholders to focus on the underlying difficult question: Would they be willing to work collaboratively at the expense of their treasured autonomy? Once they passed that difficult first vote, they would have already begun the process of figuring out how to work together.

Kelly worked as an academic administrator in Colorado and participated actively in the Denver civic and political community. After an eight-year tenure, she left her job as a staff member for the Denver City Council. Friends on the council asked her to be a candidate for appointment by the Council to the Denver Civil Service Commission. She agreed, enthusiastically. But when the retiring incumbent decided to seek one more two-year term, she withdrew her candidacy. The incumbent suggested that she would be an ideal successor two years hence. Two years later she was again approached about her interest in the appointment and agreed to have her name submitted. Once again the incumbent decided to seek reappointment. This time Kelly decided to stay in the game and let the council decide what to do.

With the appointment pending, a newspaper story detailed how the Civil Service Commission had approved the hiring of a police recruit with an extensive history of drug use, domestic violence, and theft from an employer. The ensuing crisis put the commission on the defensive. The media and some self-styled reformers called for change. The brouhaha transformed Kelly's pending appointment into a symbol of reform on the commission, even though it was uncertain which way the incumbent had voted on the approval of the recruit.

For an entire week, the newspapers and radio talk shows focused on some aspect of the story. Kelly figured prominently in all the stories, but only through comments from others about her. Reporters called her. They pressed her to comment on her vision for the commission and her views on the approved appointment of the recruit. She wanted to define herself and felt flattered to be thought of as a force for reform. Moreover, she had a hard time restraining herself from responding to the personal criticisms she received from those who defended the recruit or who favored the reappointment of the incumbent to the commission. But Kelly stayed quiet. She declined to be interviewed and refused to take part in discussions on talk radio.

Eventually, the Council appointed Kelly by a 7–4 vote. She survived because she resisted the temptation to collude with those who wanted to make her a symbol of reform. Otherwise, she would have cast the incumbent negatively and would have created sympathy for him among the council members who had served with him and considered him a friend and colleague. Kelly even held back from responding to public criticism, because that would have made her, personally, a larger part of the story. She tried hard to separate herself from the issue by refusing to take a public position on the hiring of the recruit, even though she had a clear viewpoint on the matter. By staying outside the fray, she kept the dispute as external to her as she could, and kept it located within the commission itself, where it belonged. This increased her chances of winning the appointment and allowed her greater flexibility once she came aboard.

It's a common ploy to personalize the debate over issues as a strategy for taking you out of action. You want to respond when you are attacked or, in Kelly's case, set up to be the attacker. You want to leap into the fray when you are mischaracterized or pigeonholed as embodying someone else's issues. But by resisting attempts to personalize the issues, perhaps by fighting the urge to explain yourself, you can improve the odds of your survival. You prevent people from turning you into the issue, and you help keep the responsibility for the work where it ought to be.

Marty received the first, most powerful, and most painful lesson on placing the issue in the right location early in his professional life. He was fresh out of law school. His friend and mentor Elliot Richardson had been elected lieutenant governor and hired him to be the research and legislative assistant on his small, five-person staff. One day, about three months into the job, Richardson asked Marty to do some research on an issue now long forgotten. Marty did the work and later that week turned in a memo. A couple of hours later it came back to him. Richardson had not written a word on it, not even a pencil mark, nothing to show that he had even looked at it. Marty assumed it had come back by mistake and returned it to Richardson's secretary, asking her to send it to him again. Before he had returned to his desk a short distance away, Marty's intercom was buzzing. "Come in here," Richardson said. The boss didn't sound happy.

Marty found Richardson formidable even when he was in a good mood; an angry Richardson completely intimidated him. When Marty entered the inner sanctum, he saw Richardson's jaw set firmly. He knew he was in for a lecture.

"Is this your best work?" Richardson asked.

"I dunno," Marty mumbled.

"Well, I don't think it is. I can only add about 5 percent on your best work. It's a waste of my time to have to add more than that. So don't send it back in until it's the best you can produce."

Richardson located the issue right where it ought to have been, squarely on Marty's shoulders. He did not take it up himself, even though it would not have taken much time or effort to fix the memo. That would have been a technical solution to an adaptive problem: how to get his new, young staff person to work at a higher level. Both the critical factions existed within Marty himself: the faction that wanted to do the very best work and the faction (which too often won out) that was happy to settle for something perfectly OK, but less than the best he could do.

The worst-case scenario in assuming the conflicts and adaptive work of other people occurs when you place yourself directly in the line of fire. That's what happened to Mark Willes at the Times Mirror Company.

After a successful tenure as vice chairman of General Mills, the giant food and cereal conglomerate, Mark Willes became CEO of Times Mirror on June 1, 1995. His goals were to cut losses, increase profitability, and raise the price of the company's stock. In fairly short order, he presided over the closing of the *Baltimore Evening Sun*, closed *New York Newsday*, sold off the company's legal and medical publishing operations, got rid of some cable operations, and in the process fired over 2,000 Times Mirror employees, all of which earned him the nickname "Cereal Killer." With the newly found cash, however, he was able to buy back stock, boosting share price, and then buy some time from his board and from Wall Street.

Willes's longer-term strategy focused primarily on the *Los Angeles Times* newspaper, the flagship property of the corporation. He named himself publisher of the paper in October 1997. He had ambitious, unconventional, and provocative plans, which he proclaimed at every opportunity, both within the newspaper and to national media. He intended to significantly boost readership at a time when dominant metropolitan newspapers around the country were cutting back on circulation because new readers were more expensive (in terms of print and distribution costs) than they were attractive to advertisers. He would attract these new readers by creating a separate Latino desk and by collaborating with small Los Angeles–based Latino and Asian newspapers. Willes ordered coverage that would have as its objective improving literacy among elementary school children so that they were more likely to become newspaper readers as adults. He even talked about, but never implemented, tying editors' compensation to the number of times women and minorities were quoted in articles under their jurisdiction.

All of these steps challenged conventional journalistic values about the sanctity of the editorial product and its separation from commercial considerations. But the most radical idea, which he trumpeted loudly, was to blow apart the traditional thick wall that separated the news and business sides of the organization. In his initial and dramatic effort to cross this divide, he assigned a business-side person to each of the senior editors, with the goal of working together to increase profitability. He was trying to create a partnership between factions that had traditionally remained at arm's length from each other in mutual suspicion, if not outright hostility.

Willes had gained some support for this objective from his board, from sales and marketing, and even from a few folks on the editorial side. But Willes was not a journalist, and he had never worked in a news organization. Everyone knew Willes was boss, but most people on the news side of the organization saw him as an outsider, trying to change a deeply held value within the newsroom. From their perspective, collaborating with the business side threatened their independence and integrity, and because it was Willes's cause, they aimed their firepower at him, not at their colleagues in circulation and advertising.

The board had invested heavily in his strategy and its success. They backed him initially and Willes survived the first couple of skirmishes. He met with enormous criticism from both inside the *Times* newsroom and from national media watchers. Some industry people acknowledged that he was raising important issues and appropriately challenging previously unquestioned assumptions. However, Willes had clearly moved out on the limb alone, and people were watching him closely both inside and outside his own organization.

Having survived the initial attacks, in mid-1999 Willes turned the publisher's job over to a protégé from outside the newspaper. The stock price had moved steadily upward and the board had rewarded him handsomely. Then, in the fall of that year, the *Times* made a deal to split the advertising revenue from a special edition of its Sunday magazine with the Staples Center, the new sports and convention facility that was the subject of the special issue. Such an arrangement was way outside conventional practices, and a firestorm of protest erupted inside the newsroom and from national newspaper-watchers. The editor assigned a respected reporter to do a lengthy investigation of how the deal came about, and the publisher had to make a very public apology to calm the waters. The criticism focused on whether the Staples Center deal was the inevitable result of Willes's aggressive drive to smash the separation of news and advertising domains. The public critics included Otis Chandler, scion of the family that started the paper and Willes's predecessor as CEO.

Less than six months later, Willes was out of a job. The Chandler family, which controlled the board, sold the company out from under him without even letting him know that negotiations were underway. Even though they had rewarded him when the stock rose, he didn't realize how his strategy—or, more precisely, how he implemented his strategy—might make him expendable when the heat rose. Willes had allowed himself to become the issue. He never placed the issue of the relationship between the business and editorial sides of the organization in the newsroom. He never made collaboration with business employees a subject of debate among the news employees, forcing editors and reporters to come to grips with current realities, to question each other and explore their own conflicting assumptions. He did not even try to orchestrate the conflict between the news and business factions, in order to generate greater mutual understanding. As long as he was willing to take it all on himself, most people on both sides were happy to sit back and watch the war between him and the traditional journalists and see who would survive.

Make Your Interventions Short and Simple

Exercising leadership involves interventions. These need to be both strategic and tailored to the particular situation. Generally, short and straightforward interventions are more likely to be heard and to be accepted without causing dangerous resistance.

Four types of interventions constitute the tactics of leadership: making observations, asking questions, offering interpretations, and taking actions. In practice, they are often combined with one another. Which you choose will depend on your own skills, your particular purpose, and your assessment of which intervention is most likely to move the organization's work forward and leave you unscarred. The interventions you make will of course be calculated to have different effects. Some are meant to calm and others to disrupt; some will attract attention and others deflect it. And there will always be unintended effects.

When Franklin Roosevelt said during the depth of the Depression, in his first inaugural address, "the only thing we have to fear is fear itself," he was making an interpretation of the emotional state of the nation and its paralyzed economy. He intended to calm the nation and, followed by an action-filled 100 days, he succeeded. On the other hand, in his famous "malaise" speech at the height of the 1979 oil crisis, Jimmy Carter said the nation was also suffering from a crisis of confidence. Carter was making an interpretation that the problems of the country lay in the attitudes of the people themselves. At first, he was very well received and his poll numbers jumped 11 percent. But two days later, he fired his entire cabinet. In facing both of these crises, the country needed their president to provide a strong holding environment, to be a rock of stability. If the people were going to take up his challenge, they needed to trust him. By firing his cabinet, Carter suggested he had no trust in his own administration. If he had no confidence, why should they? Carter then became the crisis.[2]

Observations

Observations are simply statements that reflect back to people their behavior or attempt to describe current conditions. They shift the group momentarily onto the balcony so that they can get a little distance from and perspective on what they are doing. For example, when a heated argument breaks out in a meeting, someone might say: "Wait a second. It seems to me the tensions are getting really high here. Everything was going fine until Bob's comment."

In and of themselves, observations are no more than snapshots from the balcony. For that reason, observations tend to be less threatening and less catalytic than other interventions, although simply calling "time-out" and reporting what you see may be stimulating and productive.

Questions

When making an observation, you can either let it rest, letting the group fill the void, or go a step further with a question or an interpretation.

A question such as: "What's going on here?" or "Was there something in what Bob said that was disturbing?" may have the effect of giving the work back to the group. You might use a question because you really do not know the answer and therefore cannot render an interpretation. You might simply think it is important for people to address the issue on their own, or you might use a question because you want to stay as much out of the line of fire as possible, while still getting the issue addressed.

Of course, when you inject your understanding of events into the way you frame the question, it becomes a loaded question. Frequently, this ploy annoys people unnecessarily. Rather than simply making your interpretation of events available for discussion, people sense that you are trying to manipulate them into assuming your interpretation is true and then starting the discussion where your assumptions leave off.

Interpretations

A bolder and generally more useful alternative to a loaded question is to follow an observation with an interpretation. For example, instead of merely observing and asking about the fight, you might say, "I don't think this conflict is really about X. I think it's really about Y, a separate issue that's been simmering in our meetings for the last four months. Until we resolve that issue, I don't see how we can make progress on this one."

This technique might be useful if you had been worried for some time about a hidden issue, but wanted to wait until either more data or a relevant situation surfaced.

In offering an interpretation, you may not be fully certain of its accuracy. Clues on that score will be forthcoming from the response. Offer the interpretation, then hold steady and listen for the way the group treats your perspective.

Interpretations are inherently provocative and raise the heat. People by and large do not like to have their statements or actions interpreted (unless they like your assessment). When you make an interpretation, you reveal that you have spent some time on the balcony, and that makes people suspicious that you are not "on the team." They may think you are somehow "above" them.

Actions

Every action has an immediate effect but sends a message as well. Actions communicate. For example, when someone walks out of the room during a meeting, you lose that person's contribution. But the departure also communicates messages, such as: "You're not addressing the key issues I see," or "This conversation is too tense for me."

Actions as interventions can complicate situations because they frequently are susceptible to more than one interpretation. For example, when the United Nations coalition invaded Iraqi-controlled Kuwait in January 1991, the message to Saddam Hussein was pretty clear. But what message was being sent to the rest of the nations in the Middle East? Could they too rely on UN intervention to protect their borders? Was the United States declaring a more active commitment to peace in the region? Did the alliance with Syria represent a temporary marriage of convenience or a shift in relations with ongoing relevance to regional politics?

The protests of 1968 illustrate the complexity of communicating through action. The beating of men and women by Chicago policemen during the 1968 Democratic National Convention did not help the cause of the anti-Vietnam War protesters. Inadvertently, it probably helped the more hawkish presidential candidate, Richard Nixon, win the election. It made the Democratic Party look chaotic and unable to manage its members, a party of rioters and overzealous police, especially since Democratic stalwart, Mayor Richard Daley, was responsible for law enforcement in the city.

As attempted leadership interventions, the protests failed to highlight the issues clearly and place the work where it belonged. The protests took place in a political context in which the president who was held responsible for the war, Lyndon Johnson, had already withdrawn from the presidency. The Chicago police used violence unnecessarily and outrageously, but both sides acted provocatively, and neither side was directly connected to the issue: Chicago cops versus a group of kids led by adults, most of whom were beyond military draft age. Rather than draw attention to the tough issues facing the society, the protesters created a side issue, law and order. The actions were easily misinterpreted and the work easily displaced, as the television audience watched the proxies battle it out on a side issue. In other words, the protests failed to instill in the American public a sense of responsibility for the war.

Not all actions send ambiguous messages. When Martin Luther King, Jr., and his strategists marched from Selma, they sent a clear message illustrating the brutality of racism in America. Black people would have to choose between passive compliance and protest. White people would have to face the contradiction between the values the country stood for and the values it actually lived. In this case, action as intervention spoke far more powerfully than other modes of communication. Televised scenes of white police beating peaceful black men, women, and children forced images into the national consciousness. Millions of citizens in their living rooms across the country got the message.

Actions draw attention, but the message and the context must be crystal clear. If not, they are likely to distract people, who may then displace responsibility.

. . .

You stay alive in the practice of leadership by reducing the extent to which you become the target of people's frustrations. The best way to stay out of range is to think constantly about giving the work back to the people who need to take responsibility. Place the work within and between the factions who are faced with the challenge, and tailor your interventions so they are unambiguous and have a context. In the ongoing improvisation of leadership—in which you act, assess, take corrective action, reassess, and intervene again— you can never know with certainty how an intervention is received unless you listen over time. Therefore, just as critical as the quality of your actions will be your ability to hold steady in the aftermath in order to evaluate how to move next.

7

Hold Steady

We've explored why adaptive work generates heat and resistance, the forms of danger this resistance takes, and how to respond. But taking action to manage political relationships, orchestrate the conflict, or give back the work assumes that you are able to meet a more basic challenge—maintaining your poise so that you can plan the best next step. Holding steady in the heat of action is an essential skill for staying alive and keeping people focused on the work. The pressure on you may be almost unbearable, causing you to doubt both your own capacities and your direction. If you waver or act prematurely, your initiative can be lost in an instant.

Take the Heat

Learning to take the heat and receive people's anger in a way that does not undermine your initiative is one of the toughest tasks of leadership. When you ask people to make changes and even sacrifices, it's almost inevitable that you will frustrate some of your closest colleagues and supporters, not to mention those outside your faction. Your allies want you to calm things down, at least *for them,* rather than stir things up. As they put pressure on you to back away, drop the issue, or change the behavior that upsets them, you will feel the heat, uncomfortably. In this sense, exercising leadership might be understood as disappointing people at a rate they can absorb.

No two people are wired exactly alike, and so we all respond differently to our environment. Some of us have a higher tolerance for heat and stress than others; indeed, there are those who thrive under peak pressure. But for most of us, who prefer to minimize opposition or avoid it altogether, the truth is that rarely, if ever, can we escape people's anger when leading any kind of significant change. Thus, the more heat you can take, the better off you will be in keeping your issue alive and keeping yourself in the game. As we saw in chapter 5, Henry Fonda's character took intense heat from his fellow jurors in *Twelve Angry Men*. They attacked him verbally and threatened him physically, hoping to get him to back down. His willingness to be the "skunk at the lawn party" and then to take the heat gracefully was essential to keeping himself, and the legitimacy of his position, alive in that jury room. Increasing your capacity for taking the heat takes practice. Again and again, you must train yourself to be deliberate and keep your cool when the world around you is boiling. Silence is a form of action.

For over a decade, Mary Selecky administered public health programs for a three-county health district in rural northeast Washington State.[1] She also played an active role statewide at the forefront of several successful legislative initiatives, including the AIDS Omnibus Act, which required local health agencies to provide AIDS-related services, as well as the law establishing the state Department of Health. Her success led to her appointment as acting secretary of health for the state of Washington on October 1, 1998, when Governor Gary Locke made her the head of the agency she helped to create.

From the moment of her appointment, she found herself in the midst of a ferocious ongoing controversy over whether people who tested HIV-positive should be reported to the department by name or by a unique numerical code. AIDS activists argued adamantly that the reporting should be by numbers to protect the identity of the patients and to encourage people to be tested for HIV. Public health officials insisted that the interests of public health required that names be used. They argued that this was the simplest and most accurate system to administer and that it could more quickly and easily track the spread of the disease, better facilitate counseling and notification, and more effectively protect against further infections. Reporting by name was the standard procedure for the other fifty-four illnesses on the state's list of reportable diseases.

The previous February, the Governor's Council on HIV and AIDS, dominated by AIDS workers and activists, voted overwhelmingly (14–4) in favor of using numerical identifiers. Supporters of numbers expected the governor to accept the recommendation and pass it on with his approval to the state Board of Health, which had the statutory responsibility for adopting regulations governing the reporting of diseases. The governor enjoyed widespread support in the gay community, which made up the core of the pro-numbers constituency, and he had been a strong privacy advocate throughout his political career. Instead, the governor stuck with his neutral position. He tried to form an ad hoc committee to resolve the issue, but was not able to put together a group that would be acceptable to both sides.

Finally, he asked the state Board of Health to settle the matter, which then placed it on the agenda for a preliminary vote at the board's October meeting. The board consisted of ten gubernatorial appointees, all members of the health professions. Selecky served as an ex officio member of the board, and therefore would have to cast her vote on this highly divisive issue just two weeks after coming into the job. Although she did not chair the board, as state health secretary her words and actions would have a strong impact on the proceedings.

In her previous job at the county level, Selecky sided with her public health colleagues in favor of using names. But now she found herself in a different environment. She had a new role with different responsibilities, a new mix of constituencies, and little guidance from her appointing authority. She assumed that Locke knew she had earlier taken a public position on the question at hand.

There would be a discussion and a vote at the board meeting, and Selecky would have to declare herself. The board's vote would not be final, but it would serve as the basis of a draft rule, subject to further discussion and public hearings. There would be considerable political momentum behind whatever position it took.

As the meeting date approached, Selecky gave no indication of her plans, though her staff was heavily weighted toward reporting by name. At the meeting, the extensive prevote discussion made it clear that the public health professionals, supporting names-based reporting, had done their homework. Selecky said nothing throughout the conversation. She waited until some but not all of the council members had voted. All eyes were on her. She abstained. The vote was 7–0 for names-based reporting and Selecky's department was now charged with drafting a preliminary rule reflecting that vote.

Her action, or inaction, upset almost everyone. Both sides expressed disappointment that she did not vote with them, but they agreed on one thing: She had abdicated her responsibility. The governor's office also expressed concern.

Selecky endured a trying period in the aftermath of that meeting. Criticism came at her from many quarters. Outraged AIDS activists protested with public demonstrations. But Selecky took the heat and held steady, refusing to cave in or even to respond to the pressure to take a stand.

Then, slowly and hesitatingly at first, she began to meet with the two sides, first separately and then together. Neither felt happy with what she had done, but both would have been much more upset if she had sided with the other. Eventually they came to a compromise. The names of people infected with HIV would be destroyed after ninety days. Local health authorities would record the names but would provide the state only with numerical identifiers.

Selecky found herself tested here, not for the technical aspects of the issue, the right or wrong of policy options, but rather for her tolerance for taking heat. She had to willingly incur everyone's anger and disappointment, and then absorb it. Her old public health colleagues had every reason to think her views on the issue would remain consistent with those she had taken previously. And the AIDS activists had known her and the governor to be sympathetic to their cause.

She found it difficult to get through that period. She had to absorb intense criticism from people whose friendship, collegiality, and support she had valued and enjoyed in the past. By holding steady, however, she retained access to everyone and eventually found a way to get the two sides to face each other and to accept the legitimacy of each other's concerns.

Taking heat from your friends and allies is very tough. In a way, it's easier to tolerate abuse from the opposition. After all, you know you must be doing something good if the forces of evil are after you, calling you names. The people who speak in front of an angry crowd or submit to interviews on a hostile talk radio show may appear especially courageous, but those who have been in that role know the ameliorating secret: When the enemy throws tomatoes in your face, a part of you feels ennobled and reaffirmed.

As Henry Fonda's character and Mary Selecky illustrate, the challenge of exercising leadership often involves taking intense heat from people whose support you value and need. Neither of them could have accomplished their aims without the help of those they were frustrating and disappointing. To withstand such pressure demands a broad perspective and extra measures of patience, maturity, courage, strength, and grace.

The people you challenge will test your steadiness and judge your worthiness by your response to their anger, not unlike teenagers, who want to know that they can blow hot without blowing their parents away. Receiving people's anger without becoming personally defensive generates trust. If you can hold steady long enough, remaining respectful of their pains and defending your perspective without feeling you must defend yourself, you may find that in the ensuing calm, relationships become stronger.

History delights in people who demonstrate this capacity. Nelson Mandela, Martin Luther King, Jr., Gandhi, Margaret Sanger, Elizabeth Cady Stanton, Joan of Arc, Mohammed, Jesus, Moses— all gained extraordinary credibility and moral authority by receiving anger with grace. Receiving anger, then, is a sacred task because it tests us in our most sensitive places. It demands that we remain true to a purpose beyond ourselves and stand by people compassionately, even when they unleash demons. Taking the heat with grace communicates respect for the pains of change.

Let the Issues Ripen

In your efforts to lead a community, you will often be thinking and acting ahead of them. But if you get too far ahead, raising issues before they are ready to be addressed, you create an opportunity for those you lead to sideline both you and the issue. You need to wait until the issue is ripe, or ripen it yourself. True, patience is not a virtue typically associated with people passionate about what they are doing. But holding off until the issue is ready may be critical in mobilizing people's energy and getting yourself heard.

Of course, most organizations and communities have a whole spectrum of challenges confronting them at any given time. Common sense tells us we can't tackle them all at once. The availability of resources often dictates the agenda—we attack a problem when we have the wherewithal to do so. But resources are just one factor in determining the willingness of people to tackle an issue. The primary factor consists of the psychological readiness to weigh priorities and take losses. The political question becomes: Has the psychological readiness spread across enough factions in the organization or community to provide a critical mass?

An issue becomes ripe when there is widespread urgency to deal with it. Something that may seem to you to be incredibly important, requiring immediate attention, may not seem so to others in your organization, at least not at the moment. But it may become important to them in time. The activism of individuals, like Maggie Brooke, who took on alcoholism in her community, can ripen an issue over time by drawing people's attention to the contradictions in their lives. Or dramatic events, like the attacks on September 11, 2001, can immediately accelerate work on a whole set of issues.

Once again, this is a matter of perspective. Think back to the story in chapter 3 about Amanda and Brian, in which Amanda's intervention went nowhere and Brian's almost identical comment, made a little while later, engaged the attention of the people at the meeting. You probably have had a similar experience, raising an issue in a meeting and having it fall on deaf ears, only to see the same issue come up again later and dominate the conversation. Though the process may confuse you and generate dismay, notice the outcome: The issue became ripe.

The history of the civil rights movement in America provides a powerful illustration at the national level. By 1965, after ten years of demonstrations, the civil rights movement had succeeded in creating national demand for civil rights legislation. They had ripened the issue by using demonstrations to draw attention to the unlived values in America. Yet in many parts of the South, black people still could not vote. In spite of the historic 1964 Civil Rights Act, the issue of voting rights had not yet ripened. The 1964 legislation had avoided the issue intentionally—it was one thing to let black people onto white buses and into white restaurants and bathrooms, but quite another to give black people access to power.

The men and women who allowed themselves to be beaten by Alabama policemen in the 1965 voting rights marches in Selma ripened the issue, not only because they built upon previous progress, but also because they illustrated the problem of racial injustice clearly and dramatically. By keeping the demonstrations peaceful, no one could turn this into a law-and-order issue. The organizers made sure the television cameras were capturing scenes for the American audience, and the demonstrations themselves showed the problem's central stakeholders playing their roles: black adults who were of voting age and white officials standing in their way.

Having galvanized widespread political will, the demonstrations cleared the way for President Lyndon Johnson, who quickly seized the opportunity to send before Congress what soon became the 1965 Voting Rights Act.

In the United States, drug abuse surfaced as a ripe issue during the late 1980s and early 1990s. Global warming, poverty, and health care did not. Health care surfaced briefly in 1993–1994, but the new Clinton administration formulated a solution that was so far beyond any prevailing conception of the problem that it never stood a chance. Yet Clinton's massive initiative did sow the seeds for future steps. Several years later, pieces of the issue—the plight of uninsured children, the high cost of prescription drugs for seniors, and accessibility for all—began to gain momentum.

What determines when, or whether, an issue becomes ripe? How does it take on a generalized urgency shared by not just one but many factions within the community? Although there are many factors, we have identified four key questions: What other concerns occupy the people who need to be engaged? How deeply are people affected by the problem? How much do people need to learn? And what are the senior authority figures saying about the issue?

First, what else is on people's minds? If most of the people in your organization are handling a crisis, you may have greater difficulty getting them to shift their attention to the issue you think is most important. Sometimes you can get a better hearing by postponing your issue to a later time. During the Persian Gulf War in early 1991, the attention of many nations in the world focused on the Middle East. In these nations, issues other than the Middle East could not compete for popular attention. No other problems were going to be seriously addressed. In contrast, at the same time, within the former Soviet Union, the stirrings of a capitalist economy began to raise expectations. A growing discontent would threaten the fledgling capitalist economy if the Soviets could not meet the expectations of citizens to provide basic commodities at reasonable prices. Yet because of the Gulf Crisis, you would have found it extraordinarily difficult to get a serious hearing in the

NATO countries for the predicament of the Soviets. And conversely, because of the economic crisis in the former Soviet Union, you would have found it extraordinarily difficult to get the Soviet people to concern themselves with peace in the Middle East.

Sometimes, you have to hold steady and watch for the opportunity. However, if you notice that there is never a time for your issue, you may have to create the opportunity by developing a strategy for generating urgency. When Lyndon Johnson told Martin Luther King, Jr., after passage of the 1964 Civil Rights Act that he would have to wait years before anyone would be ready to act on voting rights, King replied that black people had waited too long already, and that he would begin marching in Selma the following January. Johnson advised against it, but told King that if he and the organizers could raise public urgency, Johnson would use the presidency to seize the moment, which he did.[2]

Second, how deeply are people affected by the problem? If people do not feel the pinch of reality, they are unlikely to feel the need to change. Why should they? Sometimes, fortuitous events ripen an issue by heightening the severity of a problem. Used properly, a crisis can provide a teaching moment.

For example, when President Richard Nixon and Postmaster General Winton Blount tried in 1969 to reverse two hundred years of political patronage at the U.S. Post Office by turning it into a government corporation, few people cared enough about the issue to support such massive reform. Post office patronage was close to the hearts of the members of Congress who, after all, were going to have to vote on the proposal. But members of Congress were hearing from every postal employee in their district about the need for a pay raise, and very little from anyone at home about the need for reorganization.

A wildcat walkout of postal workers in New York City, followed by a nationwide strike to demand a pay raise, changed all that. Most people, particularly businesspeople, felt an immediate and devastating impact. Millions of dollars were lost, important documents fell into limbo, and social security checks were delayed. There were threats of a court order and on March 23, 1970, Nixon threatened to send in the National Guard to deliver the mail. Bringing in the military had the effect of breaking the strike, and most postal workers were back on the job by March 25.

The postal strike became the number one news story throughout the country. It affected almost everyone. Because the public largely supported postal pay raises, the administration feared that the strike would actually set back reform efforts. What they had not anticipated was that the strike brought home to people just how dependent they were on a smoothly functioning postal service. Because the public had felt the effects of the mail's disruption, the administration was able to pressure the unions to link the pay bill with union support for reform, and on August 6, 1970, the Congress sent a pay raise/reorganization package to the White House. Although the strike was not about the reorganization of the post office, the disruption in people's lives made the issue of post office operation salient. People felt they had experienced the problem and, for the first time, wanted something done to ensure that delivery of the mail would be in the hands of capable professionals.[3]

Events ripened the issue of nuclear safety in 1978 when the reactors at Three Mile Island began to melt down. For many years, warnings about the danger of a nuclear energy plant meltdown had come only from marginalized interest groups long identified as antinuclear. Their claims were not taken seriously, and an energy-guzzling public eagerly accepted the assurances from government and industry that all was safe and well. After that frightening incident, the claims of the nuclear power industry regarding the safety of nuclear energy plants sounded very different than they had before (even though no deaths and apparently very little significant, long-term damage resulted from it). Coincidentally, the film *The China Syndrome*, a fictitious account of a nuclear power plant disaster, was released at the same time as the incident, ripening the issue further. Building nuclear power plants suddenly became highly problematic. The issue of safety versus the need for more energy had ripened. People began to face the trade-offs.

Third, how much must people learn in order to make judgments? The lack of knowledge on an issue is almost always in direct proportion to its lack of ripeness. A crisis can change this quickly. The risks of nuclear power were not well understood until the accidents at Three Mile Island and Chernobyl. Those incidents generated public learning in short order. On an even larger scale, the events of September 11, 2001, and their aftermath schooled the nation, and to a significant extent the world community, on the grave risks and potential consequences of terrorism, and the need for new international norms and cooperation. By contrast, global warming is an issue that is slowly, gradually impressing itself on the public consciousness. As weather patterns change and new trends emerge, affecting people's lives, education increases and the issue develops. No doubt a teaching moment will develop in this area when we experience a string of catastrophic and weird weather events with losses of life and property.

Because crises and tragedies generate the urgency to tackle issues, sometimes the only way to bring focus to an issue and move it forward is to create a crisis. These can be small, like budget crises, which are often available to draw attention to the need to reevaluate priorities and direction. Or they can be large. Martin Luther King, Jr., lived in constant fear for his life, but in Selma he deliberately created a situation that was almost certain to result in violence. He knew he was putting not only his own life at risk, but many other lives as well. The marchers understood the dangers, to be sure, but that did not make King's decision any easier, particularly when three people were killed.

If you do not take into consideration how difficult the learning will be, the organization or community will box you off as an outcast, impractical visionary, or worse. You may have to take baby steps. It may take years to ripen the issue in an organization to the point that people understand what is at stake and can decide their fate. As we saw in chapter 1, the IBM corporate culture of 1994 did not recognize the new challenge of business on the internet. At that time, IBM operated from a full agenda that had no place for dealing with it. People were busy with other things. So it was up to engineer Grossman, middle manager Patrick, and other volunteers with little authority to ripen the issues in baby steps over a five-year period.

Fourth, what are the people in authority saying and doing? Although the rhetoric and even the commitment of authorities often are not enough by themselves to ripen an issue, they always figure significantly. Formal authority confers license and leverage to direct people's attention.

Notice an important distinction between the U.S. Post Office reorganization and Selma. With the post office, the Nixon administration took advantage of a tangential event to focus attention on an issue and thus make it ripe for political action. But in Selma, King took the initiative himself to ripen the issue. Worse than lacking authority, King had to challenge authorities across the nation— first the Alabama police, then the federal court, and finally the Congress. The less ready a group is to resolve an issue, the more you may need to challenge authority.

Of course, King also had a major ally among the nation's authorities, namely Lyndon Johnson, the president. So you might ask, "Shouldn't the president have just taken the lead and persuaded Congress it was wrong to keep black people from voting?" After all, people expect their authorities to persuade people to do what they should do. Furthermore, society has formal rules and procedures for authorities to take charge. The person running the meeting prepares an agenda. The president gives a State of the Union message. The head of the labor union proposes a set of target goals for the upcoming negotiation.

If you are the person in authority, you are not only expected to set the agenda, but also to select the issues that warrant attention. You cannot keep your authority in your organization if you insist on projects that your organization opposes. In other words, those who have authority put it at risk by seeking to raise unripe issues. For example, while jogging before dawn during his first week in the White House in 1993, Bill Clinton felt cornered by reporters to comment on "gays in the military." By taking a stand long before the public, Congress, or the military had had the chance to work through this issue, Clinton inadvertently became a lightning rod and created a spectacle. Forced to expend an enormous amount of energy on developing and defending his position, he sacrificed a significant measure of the credibility and goodwill he needed to establish other priorities and launch his presidency.

In contrast, Lyndon Johnson approached civil rights strategically. He did not move out front to take a stand. Instead, he helped other people ripen the issue so that his hands were free to orchestrate the ensuing conflict. For example, to gain enough Republican votes to end a filibuster by Southern Democrats on the 1964 Civil Rights Bill, Johnson personally prodded Roy Wilkins and other civil rights leaders to woo Senator Everett Dirksen, the Republican leader, with the possibility of black electoral support in the coming presidential election and beyond. Johnson was in no way authorized to be a behind-the-scenes civil rights strategist, advising activists on techniques for winning Republican support. If he had been exposed, he would have lost credibility. He went outside his authority, but he did so in a way that minimized the risk of undermining his position. He did not, for example, hold a press conference in which he declared the priority of civil rights. He helped others ripen the issue.

For people exercising leadership without or beyond their authority, ripening an issue becomes more difficult, requiring more dramatic and therefore riskier steps. For example, in a meeting for which the chairperson has set the agenda, you decide that your best chance for drawing attention to an important issue is to put yourself forward and change the course of the meeting. When the time for new business comes, you stand up and start to speak. At that moment, you become the center of attention, a likely lightning rod for, and personal embodiment of, the issue. Parties on different sides of the issue will perceive you as a threat, upsetting the status quo. Some will likely move to restore equilibrium by finding a way to silence your voice, perhaps by criticizing your style or noting that the meeting is running late. Perhaps they will look to authority to fend off the challenge. But if you hold steady, taking the immediate heat and keeping your intervention short and clear, your odds of success increase. Your position may be heard and people may respect you for putting yourself on the line. If you back down quickly, you merely reinforce your lack of credibility.

Focus Attention on the Issue

Getting people to focus their attention on tough problems can be a complicated and difficult task, particularly in large organizations or communities where, typically, ways of avoiding painful issues—work avoidance mechanisms—have developed over many years. The most obvious example of work avoidance is denial. Even our language is full of shorthand reminders of this mechanism: "out of sight, out of mind;" "swept under the carpet;" "if it ain't broke, don't fix it." Other typical work avoidance mechanisms are seeking a Big Man to fix things, scapegoating, reorganizing (yet again), passing the buck (setting up another committee), finding an external enemy, blaming authority, character assassination, and physical assassination. Actual physical assassination usually represents an extreme act of work avoidance.

These mechanisms reduce the level of distress in an organization or community by deflecting attention from the tough issues and shifting responsibility away from the people who need to change. In leading, you need to hold steady in the face of these distractions, counteract them, and then redirect attention and responsibility to the issue at hand. In an important sense, this book is about sensing and counteracting work avoidance mechanisms that will endanger you and your organization.

Again, a person in authority can more easily redirect attention than someone lower on the ladder. Typically, authority figures have established mechanisms for focusing attention: calling a meeting, sending a memo, holding a press conference. However, these methods do not always succeed. If you employ a routine mechanism for getting attention, people may well see the problem as routine and ignore it. So even with authority, you need to find creative ways to signal that the new situation is different.

When John Lehman became secretary of the Navy in 1981, he faced the very big challenge of reasserting the Navy's control over its major contractors, including General Dynamics and its subsidiary Electric Boat, which built Navy submarines.[4] Electric Boat had not delivered any of the ships promised in 1980, and the company was incurring huge cost overruns, which it wanted the Navy to absorb. This was both a money issue and a production issue for Lehman, who had made creating a 600-ship Navy the key goal of his tenure. He needed General Dynamics to back off on its financial claims and to dramatically speed up its work, and he knew that neither would happen without putting some pressure on the company.

Initially, Lehman used conventional strategies to try to focus the attention of key parties on the issue. He sent a vice admiral to testify at a congressional hearing. He called David Lewis, the CEO of General Dynamics, to the Pentagon and told him he was canceling a request for bids on new attack submarines and negotiating sole source contracts with Lewis's only competitor. Intent on avoiding responsibility for its delays and cost overruns, General Dynamics counterattacked in predictable fashion, revving up support from its favorite senators and representatives. These included the late John Chafee (R-RI), himself a former Navy secretary, whose state of Rhode Island reaped significant economic benefits from the presence of Electric Boat in Groton, Connecticut, close to the Rhode Island border. Chafee dragged Lehman out to Groton and forced Lehman to speak in a more conciliatory tone lest he alienate a key senatorial ally.

Back and forth it went throughout most of the spring and summer. There were meetings, reports, threats, and counterthreats, most of them reported in the press. Lehman seemed to vacillate, sounding critical, offering an olive branch, and then taking it away. Lewis and Lehman were engaged in an elaborate chess game, in which they both followed the rulebook fairly closely. But then, in early August, Lewis went over Lehman's head to see presidential counselor Edwin Meese III in the White House in an effort to get Lehman to back off. Lehman realized that unless he did something dramatic, he was in danger of losing the issue. Rather than continue the back and forth pattern of press conferences, meetings, and leaked memos and reports that had characterized the past six months, Lehman decided to make a speech at the National Press Club in Washington. The Press Club was a venue that would ensure broad coverage, forcing all the relevant players—General Dynamics, the White House, Congress—to take definitive steps. For the same reason, the move was extremely risky, putting his credibility squarely on the line. If he did not have enough support within the White House, the Congress, and interest groups, his strategy could backfire, resulting in a solution that would set back his objectives and undermine his tenure.

The Press Club speech was a major departure from routine. Ordinarily, someone in Lehman's position might never give an address there. The coverage of the speech, which Lehman followed up with an op-ed synopsis in the *Washington Post*, forced all those involved to put the issue at the top of their agendas. For the first time since he had begun to engage the company, everyone's attention began to sharpen. A week after the speech, Lehman and Lewis had an intense and difficult meeting that led, a month later, to an agreement between the Navy and General Dynamics, capping the government's financial exposure and tying Electric Boat to clear performance measures in return for more work.

In a more routine way of signaling the nonroutine, the senior management at Xerox Corporation drew attention in the early 1990s to the enormous challenge of becoming a customer-responsive organization by holding a series of three-day retreats with their top managers. Moreover, in a period of cost containment, they hired an expensive consultant who could make the case for the need to change cultural norms. At that time, the Xerox frontline sales and service personnel had no latitude whatsoever to respond creatively and quickly to the needs of customers. Instead, they were expected to follow the rulebook, even if it meant angering clients needlessly. People down the line were controlled rather than entrusted.

It would have been easy for senior management to pull people together at corporate headquarters, where they interacted regularly anyway. But doing so would have signaled that the message was nothing out of the ordinary. By meeting off-site, with presentations and discussions orchestrated by outsiders who had spent months interviewing and assessing the company, they generated serious-ness and new focus for the company's adaptive work.

If you are not in a position of authority, drawing attention entails risks as well as greater challenges. You might form alliances with people who have more authority and can direct attention to the issues you see. For example, at IBM, Grossman luckily found Patrick, who had far greater authority and credibility with which to draw companywide attention to the internet challenge, and in ways less provocative than barging alone into Armonk Headquarters.

To get the attention of higher-ups, chances are you will need to escalate your behavior or rhetoric to a level that creates some personal risk. For example, you might generate a story in the press. Leaking a story to a reporter might be effective in focusing people on your issue, but will likely be considered an act of institutional disloyalty if you are discovered. Rising to ask a CEO a provocative question at a companywide picnic will surely get attention, but it may well be focused exclusively on you and not the issue. Your impertinence could even cost you your job, or at least cause some of your colleagues to put themselves at a safe distance from you.

A friend told us of a situation in which her lack of author-ity seemed to her an insurmountable barrier in mobilizing people to focus on an important issue. She had been at a meeting of the senior management team of a small company when a new depart-ment head asked what seemed like a perfectly reasonable question. The CEO responded with an outburst, attacking the idea as "the most stupid thing I have ever heard." This stunned everyone, and the question was dropped. The meeting deteriorated, as everyone else felt silenced. She realized that a nerve had been touched and some unspoken issue had surfaced, but she felt unable to pursue it in her role as just another member of the group. She also realized that the department head's appropriate and important question would not be addressed. She discovered later that the issue underlying the CEO's outburst was his hope that the new department head would relieve him of some of his responsibilities. He felt stretched too thin. He took the question as a deeply frustrating signal that the new colleague was not experienced or knowledgeable enough to help him out.

Could our friend have intervened in that situation without putting herself at risk? Could she have put the department head's question back on the table? More critically, could she have helped the CEO and the group address the issue of the overburdened CEO and the need for more talent? How could she have refocused the attention of the group?

A few possibilities: She might have waited a short while and then asked the question again, in a different way. She might have offered the observation that the CEO's strong response seemed disproportionate to the question, or she could even have asked him why he felt that way. Perhaps after the tenor of the meeting changed, she could simply have stated what everyone knew to be true, that something was getting in the way of being productive.

Getting a group to focus on a tough issue from a position without authority is always risky business. But you can lower the danger by speaking in as neutral a way as possible, simply reporting observable and shared data rather than making more provocative interpretations. It may be more than enough simply to ask a straightforward question in order to bring the underlying issue to the surface.

When you are operating beyond your authority, you tread a thin line between acting out of role such that people will notice, and being so extreme that your issue (and perhaps you) will be dismissed. The late Silvio Conte, a U.S. congressman from Massachusetts, once took the microphone in the House of Representatives wearing a pig mask to debate a budget bill that he thought contained a lot of "pork." As a member of the minority party, Conte had little hope of mustering the votes to eliminate the items he questioned. Most members wanted to avoid focusing on the merits of his issue. He risked drawing attack and ridicule, professionally and publicly. But he also struck a responsive chord and got the attention of reporters and key colleagues—which led to some changes in the budget.

Once again, Martin Luther King, Jr., provides an example of the gambles of provocation. In the early days of the civil rights movement, without the authority to require the nation to address racial injustice, he engaged extensively in demonstrations and nonviolent civil disobedience. Although he did not know for certain that there would be violence along the way, he knew that if he kept it up long enough there would likely be trouble. All King could do was make sure that if violence did occur, the media would be there. When Sheriff Bull Conner brought out the attack dogs, King had a national audience. Once he had people's attention, King did not have to be so provocative. He began to have moral authority, and as his authority grew, he had a wider spectrum of attention-getting devices at his disposal. In 1963 it was numbers, not violence, that focused the nation on civil rights, when 240,000 marched with him in Washington, DC, and heard him say, "I have a dream."

. . .

Undoubtedly, you have experienced and observed the pressure on you to back off when you point to difficult, conflictive, value-laden issues in an organization or community. Although hard to do, holding steady allows you to accomplish several things at once. By taking the heat, you can maintain a productive level of disequilibrium, or creative tension, as people bear the weight of responsibility for working their conflicts. By holding steady, you also give yourself time to let issues ripen, or conversely to construct a strategy to ripen an issue for which there is not yet any generalized urgency. Moreover, you give yourself time to find out where people are so that you can refocus attention on the key issues.

Holding steady under a barrage of criticism is not just a matter of courage; it also involves skill. In part two of this book, we
have suggested a series of approaches to keep your bearings when
you are under fire. For example, getting to the balcony, finding
partners, adjusting the thermostat, pacing the work, making your
interventions unambiguous and timely, bringing attention back to
the issue, and showing the relevant communities a different future
than the ones they imagine are all methods of dealing with the disequilibrium that you generate. In addition to these ways of assessing and taking action, however, we suggest a series of perspectives
and practices that address the personal challenges of sustaining the
stresses of leadership. We explore these in part three.

PART THREE

Body and Soul

8

Manage Your Hungers

From our own observation and painful personal experience, we know that the cleanest way for an organization to bring you down is to let you bring yourself down. Then no one else feels responsible. All too often we self-destruct or give others the ammunition they need to shoot us down.

Frequently people are defeated because, though they are doing their best, they make mistakes in how they assess and engage their environment, as we have explored so far in parts one and two of this book. But sometimes we bring ourselves down by forgetting to pay attention to ourselves. We get caught up in the cause and forget that exercising leadership is, at heart, a personal activity. It challenges us intellectually, emotionally, spiritually, and physically. But with the adrenaline pumping, we can work ourselves into believing we are somehow different, and therefore not subject to the normal human frailties that can defeat more ordinary mortals on ordinary missions. We begin to act as if we were physically and emotionally indestructible.

Marty remembers a particularly stressful time many years ago when he managed a large piece of a statewide political campaign. He kept coming into the office earlier and staying later. He was putting in seventy hours a week or more when, slowly but surely, the quality of his work began to fall off, reflecting his utter exhaustion. But he was the last to notice. Finally, a key adviser to the campaign took him aside, ordered him to take a week's vacation, and told him that if he could not get the job done in a sixty-hour workweek, they would find someone else to do it.

Bill Clinton came to the White House in January 1993 sleep-deprived and physically drained. According to David Gergen, the presidential adviser and observer, rather than "prepare himself physically for the ordeal ahead," Clinton spent the period between the election and the inauguration working, playing, and celebrating in endless twenty-hour days.[1] By the time Clinton got to Washington, he "seemed worn out, puffy and hyper. His attention span was so brief that it was difficult to have a serious conversation of more than a few minutes." Gergen is convinced that the stumbling start to the Clinton administration was a product in part of the new president's physical condition. He refused to rest. It may be that Clinton had a real drive to keep that pace. We are, all of us, vulnerable to falling prey to our own hungers. Self-knowledge and self-discipline form the foundation for staying alive.

We all have hungers, which are expressions of our normal human needs. But sometimes those hungers disrupt our capacity to act wisely or purposefully. Perhaps one of our needs is too great and renders us vulnerable. Perhaps the setting in which we operate exaggerates our normal level of need, amplifying our desires and overwhelming our usual self-controls. Or, our hungers might be unchecked simply because our human needs are not being met in our personal lives.

Every human being needs some degree of power and control, affirmation and importance, as well as intimacy and sexual pleasure. We know of no one who prefers to feel entirely powerless, unimportant, or untouched in life. Yet each of these normal human needs gets us into trouble when we lose the personal wisdom and discipline to manage them productively and fulfill them appropriately.

Recognizing and managing these hungers is an individual effort, because each of us is unique. To employ a musical metaphor, you can think of yourself as a harp whose strings are tuned in a unique way by both your upbringing and your genetic heritage. Since each of us has our own distinctive harp strings, it follows that each person resonates a bit differently to the same stimulation. There's no such thing as a perfectly tuned harp. Each of us is highly sensitive to particular social dynamics and issues, and each of these sensitivities becomes a source of strength and weakness. You may notice an issue before anyone else does and be primed for action, but you may also see it when it's not there, or react in the wrong way or at the wrong time. Moreover, you probably miss hearing other parts of the music for which you have a tin ear.

In leading people, you will tune into their needs as well as your own. In connecting with their hopes and frustrations, it is easy to become the storehouse of their yearnings. However, the desire to fulfill the needs of others can become a vulnerability if it feeds into your own normal hungers for power, importance, and intimacy. This is especially true if you have strong hungers to begin with, or if your own needs are not being adequately met. Thus, all too frequently, people end up bringing themselves down. They get so caught up in the action and energy that they lose their wisdom and self-discipline, and slip out of control.

We're not suggesting that leadership requires repressing your normal human passions. (Quite to the contrary, as you'll read later.) But to return to our original metaphor, it is crucial to get to the balcony repeatedly to regain perspective, to see how and why your passions are being stoked. When you take on the tasks of leading, invariably you resonate with many feelings expressed by people around you. No doubt some of the feelings you bring to your professional role are "inherited"; we all carry both virtues and baggage from our parents and previous generations. Many other feelings in your job are produced by the way you resonate with the job environment itself. In each professional role you take on, you must be careful about your emotional inclination to carry the issues and sentiments of others in the organization, and be aware of how others in the environment affect you.

When you lead, you participate in collective emotions, which then generate a host of temptations: invitations to accrue power over others, appeals to your own sense of importance, opportunities for emotional intimacy and sexual satisfaction. But connecting to those emotions is different from giving in to them. Yielding to them destroys your capacity to lead. Power can become an end in itself, displacing your attention to organizational purposes. An inflated sense of self-importance can breed self-deception and dysfunctional dependencies. Inappropriate sexual relationships can damage trust, create confusion, and provide a diversionary justification to get rid of you and your perspective on the issues. We turn now to exploring these temptations and the ways our normal hungers can become distorted.

Power and Control

The hunger for power is human. Everyone wants to have some measure of control over his or her life; everyone wants to experience a sense of agency. Yet some people, perhaps as a product of their upbringing, have a disproportionate need for control. They might have grown up in a household that was tightly structured, or unusually chaotic; thus they might react strongly in the midst of any social disturbance, having spent many years satisfying their hunger to take control. Their mastery at taming chaos reflects a deeper need for order.

That need, and that mastery, can turn into a source of vulnerability. Consider what can happen when someone with that profile plugs herself into a stressed organizational circuit. Imagine the scene: People are experiencing high levels of disequilibrium as they struggle with difficult issues; there is great chaos and conflict. Rhonda rides in on her white horse, ready and willing (and desperate inside) to take charge of the situation. Indeed, she appears to be a godsend to folks in the organization. And sure enough, she restores order.

This is indeed a blessing initially, because when people in a social system are overwhelmed, they cannot learn properly. Social learning requires some challenge to the social order, but within a productive range of disequilibrium. So someone who can bring a semblance of order to the chaos, lowering the stress to a tolerable level, provides a vital service. Rhonda keeps the pressure cooker from blowing up.

But the hunger for control can lead Rhonda to mistake the means for the end. The person who has a disproportionate need for control, who is too hungry for power, is susceptible to losing sight of the work. Rather than keeping an eye on the ongoing effort required to mobilize progress on the issues, Rhonda is likely to focus on maintaining order as an end unto itself. Returning to the political work of clarifying commitments and facing tough trade-offs would lead back to the chaos she cannot abide. She says to herself, "Everything must be just fine because the situation is under control." The people in the organization are happy because they prefer calm to distress. All seems well. Unfortunately, Rhonda has now become vulnerable to, and an agent of, the organization's desire to avoid working its contentious issues.

James Kerasiotes was one of the most successful public managers we have known. He got things done. In the mid-1990s, Kerasiotes's biggest challenge was managing the Big Dig, the $14.5 billion-plus public works project in Boston designed to move the Central Artery—the highway that splices the city—underground and build a third harbor tunnel to Logan Airport. By all accounts he did an extraordinary job, and for a long time. Then his need to feel in control caught up with him. The project went seriously over budget, but Kerasiotes told no one. He did not even inform the governor, who was running for reelection. He thought he was being noble and doing everyone a favor by controlling the situation and keeping the problem a secret until he could fix it himself.

If he had made the problem known when he first discovered it, the energies of federal, state, and local officials and citizens might have been marshaled to figure out a solution. Instead, the problem came to light as a result of outside scrutiny. Kerasiotes's management then became the issue, and he was fired. His hunger for control had become the driving purpose, blinding him and preventing him from finding a strategy of sharing the work that would have enabled him to survive with his reputation intact.

Perhaps more than any other institution, the military prepares people to operate in the midst of chaos and to exercise raw power to restore order. It tends to attract people who have a need for control and in fact prepares them to take control. If you are in a newly formed group struggling to organize itself and a military person is present, you may find that the military person steps forward with the skill, and the need, to get things moving. Heroically, when the passengers of United Airlines Flight 93 discovered from cell phone conversations over Pennsylvania that hijackers were probably going to crash their plane with the intent of killing many people on the ground, the men who acted to take back control of the plane had backgrounds in the martial arts and the military.[2]

On a much larger scale, when a government in the midst of political chaos no longer seems able to contain the conflicts and distress within the nation, the military frequently operates as a stabilizing force—the holding environment of last resort. This may prove a most important function that, in a dangerous and emergent situation, might save many lives. But because they are trained to suppress chaos and maintain order, the military may also go too far, suppressing the diversity of views needed to make progress on vital political, economic, and social issues. Containing conflict and imposing order may create some of the conditions for progress, but they are not progress itself.

If you find yourself heroically stepping into the breach to restore order, it is important to remember that the authority you gain is a product of social expectations. To believe it comes from you is an illusion. Don't let it get to your head. People grant you power because they expect you to provide them with a service. If you lose yourself in relishing the acclaim and power people give you, rather than on providing the services people will need to restore their adaptability, ultimately you jeopardize your own source of authority.

Affirmation and Importance

When you take the lead, some will oppose your views and others will affirm them. As we discussed in chapter 4, there are many good reasons to keep the opposition close. You need to comprehend them, learn from them, challenge them productively, and certainly, be alert to attack. But it is just as important to keep a critical check on the positive feedback you receive. We all need affirmation, but accepting accolades in an undisciplined way can lead to grandiosity, an inflated view of yourself and your cause. People may invest you with magic, and you can begin to think you have it. The higher the level of distress, the greater are people's hopes and expectations that you can provide deliverance. They may put too much faith in you.

Sometimes there are good strategic reasons to sustain people's illusions, at least for a while. In times of severe distress, people need to hope against hope. You may have to show more confidence than you personally feel. Following the September 2001 terrorist attacks, President George W. Bush maintained his poise and provided much-needed reassurance to the nation. He proclaimed that the people behind the raids would be caught and brought to justice, and that while the struggle against terrorism would be long and difficult, we could and should go on with the normal course of our lives. His approval rating nearly doubled. In the meantime, of course, the tough trade-offs lay ahead.

As a senior authority during an organizational crisis, you may decide to withhold some bad news and allow your people to revere you temporarily; this strategy gains a little time if you are uncertain how much conflict they can tolerate and how fast they can take on the challenges ahead. But be careful to keep your thinking clear and strategic, and don't be lulled into complacency and overconfidence by their affirmation. As quickly as possible, people need to know the truth so that they can wrestle with the issues and the changes they may need to make. Over time, if you pretend to have more answers than you do, reality will catch up with you; ultimately, you risk your credibility by feigning wisdom.

In a similar vein, there may be zealots among your followers, passionate for your causes and eager to use their influence on you. In their exuberance, they may argue that your pacing strategy is an avoidance of the issues. Zealots are terrific at pushing the envelope, but they frequently set the wrong pace by failing to respect the views, stakes, and potential losses of their adversaries. Indeed, one of the great seductions of leadership comes from zealots who play to your need for affirmation and pressure you to move dramatically—and sometimes unwittingly over a cliff. Something like that may have happened to President Bill Clinton when he brought out too much of his health care plan too fast.[3]

In ancient Rome, the emperors had a man stand close to them at all times whose job was to remind them of their mortality. For an authority figure in an environment of unbridled political cunning and savagery, having someone perform this task was no doubt necessary for day-to-day survival, not to mention success. It is not so different for you as you strive to enact deep, perhaps unwanted, change. We suggest that you find someone to do this job for you—someone not subject to your authority.

The skill of managing any tendency you might have toward grandiosity goes hand in hand with remaining mindful that people see you in your role more than they see you as a person. Indeed, what those in your professional surroundings see is the fulfillment of their goals or, conversely, the disturbing questions you represent. They see not your face but the reflection of their own needs or worries. These dominate their perceptions of you. To believe you have inherent power is a trap, both for you and for them. In the long run, dependency entraps people, and you must control your desire to foster it. Dependence can readily turn into contempt as the group discovers your mortal failings. Indeed, a hunger for importance can make you discount obvious warnings that you are in danger. In Shakespeare's *Julius Caesar*, when someone warns him from the crowd, "Beware the ides of March," he discounts the warning, saying, "He is a dreamer; let us leave him: pass." Caesar was cocksure of himself because he believed that he, rather than his office, was the center of everybody's world.[4]

Managing one's grandiosity means giving up the idea of being the heroic lone warrior who saves the day. People may beg you to play that role; don't let them seduce you. It robs them of the opportunity to develop their own strengths and settle their own issues. Don't begin to believe that the problem is yours to carry and solve. If you carry it at all, make certain you do so only for a limited period of time, while people accustom themselves to their need and ability to take responsibility for the challenge.

Pete, the fellow in chapter 4 who was trying to site a facility for the mentally disabled, was defeated in part because his self-importance made him vulnerable. He suffered from a kind of hubris. We asked him why he didn't see the opposition coming. Here's what he said: "I thought I had all of the law on our side. I could have won in court. I figured I had the big stick. It was based on my experience in 1992 when neighbors tried to block us from taking over an abandoned army base. We met with them for about a year and had found them implacable. So I tried that route and it hadn't worked. This time I had all of the political power on my side. It gave me a false sense of invulnerability. The voices I was listening to were saying that this was the right thing to do and the right place to do it. Several people on my board were cautionary, but I never paid attention to their concerns." Blinded by his impatience and certainty, he listened only to affirming voices and stopped listening to critical ones—and the latter brought him down.

Of course, every human being hungers for importance and affirmation. Every person wants to matter in life, at least to somebody; but some of us are more vulnerable than others in this regard. We include ourselves in this group. We love feeling needed and important. Like many people with this need, we spent many years of our lives learning how to solve problems for people, investing enormous personal energy and discipline in formal and on-the-job education. If we can solve people's problems, then we become important to them, or so the logic goes.

People with an exaggerated need to be needed scan the horizon for situations offering problems they can solve. They're not happy unless they are helping someone solve a tough issue, and the harder it is, the more important they feel. Their motto is "You've got a tough problem . . . I've got a solution." In a sense, they are professional scab-pickers (think "consultant"), examining people's fresh wounds, getting them to bleed a bit more, and then telling them: "We've got the remedy!" Make no mistake, these people are often wonderful and make extraordinary contributions. Just be aware that part of what impels them to serve people is their need to matter. Kept in balance, the feeling that you're on this earth for a reason generates meaning and caring, but this need can easily become a source of vulnerability. Imagine you are someone who needs too badly to be needed, and after coming into an ailing company you make one or two significant fixes. Your people say, "Wow, you're terrific!" and proceed to latch onto you in a state of uncritical dependency— just what you want! The problem is, you may start to buy into their misperception, believing you've got all the answers and can fulfill all sorts of needs. If the people around you aren't questioning you, and you've lost your capacity for self-criticism, an unconscious collusion begins to take place in which the blind lead the blind.

This collusion can potentially take a much more menacing turn. History is replete with charismatic authorities who, with their self-importance and air of certainty, galvanized people looking for answers. Cult figures Jim Jones, David Koresh, along with Osama bin Laden and his band of religious extremists, are but recent and tragic examples. Hitler is the archetype, representing on an almost unimaginable scale the dangerous dynamic in which a suffering and disoriented people, desperate for someone to "know the way," collude with the grandiosity of a demagogue.

Most people who preach or teach know something of this appeal. There is a strong temptation to believe it when people say,

"You're the One." Of course, you may indeed have valuable wisdom, but the need to be of special importance creates a dangerous condition, where leading can become misleading.

Some people are very lucky to have a bruising experience that serves to awaken them early in their career, before anyone else gets hurt. Tony Robinson, the senior minister at Plymouth Congregational Church in Seattle, describes the experience of how he fell from his pedestal. "When I first started out, I moved to Honolulu to take over the ministry of a church where my predecessor had committed suicide. When I arrived, I asked myself, 'What do I want to do with this?' Like many folks who've gone to the ministry, however, we have ourselves confused with God. I thought I'd just fix it; instead it fixed me. My experience of this leadership failure led me to deeper clarity of who I was, what I was called to do and what I couldn't do." In the same vein, Pete Powell, another minister, quotes standard advice given to many young ministers during their training: "If you act like Christ, you're going to end up like him."[5]

Some people may never learn. When Ferdinand Marcos became president of the Philippines in 1965, the people hailed him as a savior. He promised to vanquish poverty and set his country right. But after two decades of political domination in which he continued to see himself as the indispensable source of wisdom and order, the people were still poor (and Mrs. Marcos had all the shoes). Their hungers were fully out of control, and the people finally threw them out of the country in 1986.

Grandiosity sets you up for failure because it isolates you from reality. In particular, you forget the creative role that doubt plays in getting your organization or community to improve. Doubt reveals the parts of reality that you missed. Once you lose your ability to doubt, you see only that which confirms your own competence.

Of course, the experience of going beyond your competence is also a necessary part of leadership. How can you possibly imagine yourself to have sufficient knowledge and skill to tackle the innumerable and ongoing adaptive challenges that will confront your business or community? Indeed, it's in the nature of adaptive work to be on the frontier of new and complex realities. If all were within your competence, life would be a string of mere technical challenges. But boldness is not the same as bravado. You can move courageously into new terrain even if you're not convinced that you know what you're doing. Acknowledging the limits of your competence is a way to stay open to learning as you blaze a trail.

At its peak, Digital Equipment Corporation (DEC) rivaled IBM in the computer business, employing 120,000 people. Ken Olsen founded the company, but unlike many entrepreneurs, he also succeeded in building the company and leading it to a top position in the marketplace. A deeply generous man in his community, he treated his employees extraordinarily well and experimented with all sorts of personnel policies to increase the creativity, teamwork, and satisfaction of his workforce. Due to his outstanding success, top management looked to Ken to make the key business decisions. He seemed always to know the way and to "do the right thing." He had gotten it right so many times before.

But his success also led to his downfall. In the early 1980s he predicted, quite reasonably, that nobody would ever want to own a personal computer. There was simply no reason to have one. It would always be more cost effective, he argued, for people to use mainframe computers connected to terminals on their desks. Consequently, he kept DEC out of the personal computer market until it was too late.

Of course, everyone in business makes good and bad predictions and decisions. The vulnerability here was not in Olsen's decision itself, but in the dependency that he had fostered around him, which meant his decisions remained unchallenged by his colleagues for too long. In contrast, a decade later, Bill Gates made the faulty decision to keep Microsoft out of the internet business, only to make a 180-degree turn shortly thereafter. Watching the rapidly changing computer industry and listening carefully to colleagues, he reversed himself with no permanent damage to his sense of pride, and probably an enhanced reputation due to his nimble change of course.

Finally, when we hunger for recognition and reward in our professional lives, we may put on blinders that can cause us to run roughshod over our personal commitments and values. A close colleague experienced this himself after writing his first book. Having invested ten years in it, he then promoted it around the country, telling people in a variety of ways how much they needed what he had to say. For six months, he taught classes two days a week, went on the road the other days, and gave interviews to newspapers, radio, and television, talking to whoever would listen.

One night he came home from a book promotion trip and his wife suggested that they take a bath together after the kids were in bed. "Oh, wow," he thought, "a little pleasure after all my hard work running around pushing the book. Do I deserve that or what?"

The kids were washed, brushed, and read to. Husband and wife proceeded to the bathroom. They ran the water, added some wonderful smelling stuff, disrobed, and got in the tub. But his fantasies were dashed before his fanny hit bottom. It turned out, he now understood, that this was not some sensual celebration. This was a meeting.

They spent two hours in that tub, cooling his jets, so to speak. She pointed out to him what had been happening at home and in his office while he was so preoccupied and pleased with what he had done. The world is still spinning along, she said, and if he didn't pay attention to it, it would be very changed when he decided to step back in.

He resisted her message in every way he knew how. He "listened." He interpreted her "hypersensitivity to his absence." He got angry. He acted sweet and seductive. He tried to reason and compromise. He even acted pathetic. His wife refused to get defensive or drawn in, and held steady. During the second hour of the meeting, while the water was getting cold, he began to learn. He began to comprehend what she meant when she said, "You're really losing yourself. You're flying around all the time; you're on this radio program and complaining about not being on that one. You're in the *New York Times,* but you complain about not yet getting into the *Washington Post*. Furthermore, you're away so much, and so preoccupied with yourself, that you don't seem really to be present to our young children; and *I'm never going to finish my PhD!*"

So he began to discover in that bathtub what he calls his "Zone of Insatiability," that place in him where no matter how much he does and how good it is, it's never enough. To someone with an exaggerated need to be needed, it was just awful for him to answer the question, "What's precious and what's expendable?" Of course, there were many conversations over many months. Our colleague had to choose between his espoused values as a father and a supportive husband, and aspects of his behavior that put his career ahead of those values. He wanted it all. Just as his business started to take off, as the phone began ringing with people saying they needed him, sometimes offering big fees, he was being asked to evaluate what truly mattered. Just as his plane got off the runway, his wife told him, in no uncertain terms, to cool his jets.

He pleaded, "How can you do this to my dream?" And then he realized that she was throwing him a life raft. Lost in his zone of insatiability, his never-ending need for importance and affirmation, he might gain the world and lose himself.

Intimacy and Sexual Pleasure

Human beings need intimacy. We need to be touched and held, emotionally and physically. But some of us are vulnerable in the way we experience this need. We may, for example, have a special sensitivity to loneliness from having lost a parent at an early age, scurrying for solace the moment we get anywhere near that feeling. Or we may be particularly susceptible to rejection, so that whenever we begin to feel forsaken, we suspend good judgment and run to anyone willing to provide acceptance, sometimes conflating sexual with other forms of intimacy.

Through your own experience, you may indeed have become extraordinarily good at providing a holding environment for people, containing the tensions during a process of organizational, political, or social change. You may have developed the great emotional and mental energy required to unite people in the midst of conflicting views and values. Indeed, like the walls of a pressure cooker, the holding environment requires strength and resilience.

But who's holding you; who's holding the holder? When you are completely exhausted from being the containing vessel, who will provide you with a place to meet your need for intimacy and release?

In response to our various ways of feeling emotionally strung out, exhausted, "wired," or simply weary, we sometimes do self-destructive things. Take sex, for example. There's no question that being the repository of people's hopes can be arousing, and that this sometimes brings people to behave self-destructively in their sexual lives. Obviously, this may be different for men than for women. When people look to a man as someone special, it sometimes inflates appetite as well as ego. So some men, in this needy state, end up engaging in sexual activity that crosses boundaries inappropriately, doing damage to women (or men), and to themselves, their issues, and the workplace.

Bill Clinton is perhaps the most public example of this in American history. But he's not in any way unique. We know many similar cases. For just a minute, forget Clinton the president, his policies and positions. Look at him as just another middle-aged guy with a lot of power in a large and important organization. Let's try to understand him, and his situation at the time, in the terms we have been discussing: a man who hurt a woman, his family, and himself, and almost took down his presidency because he was unable to manage his own hungers.

Bill Clinton spent a good thirty years, through all of his adult life, dreaming about the presidency. And so here he is, in January 1993, entering the White House as president, with a level of personal excitement that would be difficult for most of us to fathom.

Not only is he excited, Clinton has an ambitious agenda: economic recovery, overhauling the health care system, reducing crime, controlling the deficit, reforming the federal government, passing NAFTA, protecting the environment, and more. He is a man of big appetites, and like some other presidents, he makes the mistake of trying to do too much too fast. He treats adaptive challenges as if they were technical problems, overestimates his authority, and miscalculates the strategy and the pacing of change.

After eighteen months, he hits bottom. In the 1994 elections, voters throw enough Democrats out of office to give Newt Gingrich and his Contract with America an extraordinary mandate as well as control of the U.S. House of Representatives.

In 1995, Gingrich seizes the public imagination, and Clinton tries to recover. He insists that as president, he still has "relevance" to public policy. But he can barely get his message out because all eyes are fixed on Gingrich and the Republicans. Clinton's hopes and dreams are nearly dashed. He just tries to keep from disappearing altogether.

After twelve months of being shunned and ignored by the press and public, Clinton, toward the end of 1995, tries a last-ditch, desperate, all-cards-on-the-table political gamble. He engages with the Republicans in a game of chicken that ends up closing down the government. This is a high-wire act. Clinton cannot know when he places his bet that he can maneuver the Republicans into looking like the bad guys and taking the blame for the shutdown. This is either the end of the line for him, or the beginning of a comeback.

The government shuts down in November 1995, with an unintended side effect. Many of Clinton's staff, allies, and confidants who serve to keep him disciplined cannot come to work. So, after twelve months at an extreme low in his presidency, staking whatever political capital he has left, Clinton finds himself without the daily anchoring provided by his full complement of colleagues in the West Wing of the White House. Moreover, his primary confidant, his anchor of discipline, Hillary Clinton, happens to be out of town. To keep functioning, the White House, operating with a skeleton crew, brings interns (whose stipends are unaffected by the shutdown) to work in the Oval Office.

Now, try to put yourself in Clinton's shoes. You're near the end of your rope, taking the ultimate gamble of your career, with the welfare of many thousands, perhaps even millions, of people at stake. On top of that, there's nobody around; your guardians are missing. It's just you, holding this enterprise together in a time of great risk. And your wife, your most important confidant, is out of town.

You likely feel a kind of light-headed unreal excitement, and perhaps below the surface, some nervous desperation. At least you are back in the game, having demonstrated enormous power in holding the Congress of the United States to a standoff. In such a moment, anyone might need the protection Odysseus gave himself. Odysseus knew that his strength would fail him if he heard the alluring call of the Sirens, and that like so many sailors before him, he would plunge into the water to his destruction. He knew that left alone, he would give way to his hungers. So he prepared himself by having his crew strap him tightly to the mast, and then he put wax in their ears so they would not be tempted either. He ordered them to ignore him when he screamed for them to cut him loose. And then he sailed through those waters, heard the sirens singing their amazing song, went berserk as he anticipated he would, ordered his own release, and was saved by his preparation because his crew ignored his gestures and could not hear him yelling. Perhaps Clinton, too, needed to know himself well enough to ask someone to lash him to the mast.

In the next chapter we explore a variety of anchors to keep you from being swept away in uncharted and risky waters. For now, the point is simply to understand more compassionately our hungers and vulnerabilities. In the midst of an intensely exciting and desperate political gamble, with neither his wife nor his closest colleagues around to keep him tied to the mast, Monica Lewinsky walks in and is smitten with the president. He loses whatever discipline he had, gives in to his appetite, and for a moment's intimacy and delight does incredible damage.

Lewinsky's behavior, too, is an unmanaged hunger. There are few human dynamics more predictable than the attraction of men and women to someone with power, fame, or status. Nearly all of us feel excitement when we get near someone extraordinary. You don't need to work near the Oval Office to know how aggressively people vie to be close to someone in a high position.

We know this hunger firsthand, too. We've both made fools of ourselves by following the urge to get close to men and women in high places, thus sacrificing some measure of integrity, or at least dignity. Indeed, our guess is that many people know the vulnerability that Monica Lewinsky may have felt: the illusion that our self-worth would be enhanced or confirmed by being close to someone "special." In its most blatant form, some men bolster their self-esteem by treating women as trophies, and some women do the same. And we all keep souvenirs of those moments with the Big One, whether photos, autographs, or stained dresses. The shelf above Marty's desk is full of pictures showing him alongside famous people, taken when he was in politics and government. In fact, he remained an autograph hound well into his 60s.

Of course, it's a mirage. No one's worth can be defined by the people they know. Yet many people live so deeply embedded in this illusion that they become lost, without a real sense of their own identity. Talk to anyone in their later years who has been there, done that, and they will tell you it was fun and interesting to get close to "special" people, but it cannot fill any emptiness inside.

These dynamics will not change anytime soon. Temptations will continue to challenge our inner discipline and put our anchors to the test. We need to know better the sexually provocative nature of leadership and authority. Clinton is no rarity. Many men in positions of authority, formal and informal, have trouble containing their heightened sexual impluses. It is no accident that Franklin Roosevelt, John Kennedy, Martin Luther King, Jr., and numerous senators and congressmen in the United States have risked their entire careers on sexual escapades of one sort or another. Mohandas Gandhi was quite open and explicit about his prodigious efforts to control his sexual appetites. The same is likely to be true among many businessmen. The struggle for that inner discipline is a responsibility of leadership and authority. Although it may be that men and women with strong sexual drives seek positions of power, it is probably also true that, as Henry Kissinger put it, power is also a great aphrodisiac. But giving in to the hunger is as sure an indication as any that you are out of control, taking advantage of people, and abusing your position.

Not all men and women have this vulnerability, but we have seen some basic patterns in the stories people have told us. Uncontrolled, the arousal has two basic expressions. People respond to your authority by making advances toward you, or you abuse your power and demand sexual "favors" from them. The advances people make toward you are deceptive, for they are not as sexually attracted to you as they are drawn to your role and power. If you don't believe us, step out of that role and see if they still find you irresistible. In making sexual demands, you not only violate a trust and destroy a productive working environment, but you also often sideline yourself and your issues. Even if you manage to keep your affairs secret, the workplace will never be the same.

Women have described to us different sexual dynamics. Some women lose themselves in the illusion that being with a man in power confirms their worth. And sometimes, to be near him, they will use their seductive strengths. Yet giving in to these seductions leaves emptiness, damage, and disappointment in their wake.

Power can be a potent aphrodisiac and source of attraction for women just as it is for men. But due to gender norms in our culture, women often feel more threatened than men as they rise to positions of authority. In our still-male-dominated world, promiscuity is viewed differently for each sex: For men, it is frequently seen as a mark of prowess and power; for women, a mark of shame and weakness. Would Clinton have survived if he were a woman? We doubt it. Women in power know that engaging in sexual affairs carries the high risk of undermining their credibility and authority, even if the activity remains a private matter. If a woman lets a man cross that boundary, the authority boundary, she knows she may have lost her authority with that man even if no one else knows about it. And if it becomes common knowledge, she risks losing her authority over others as well. In a primitive sense, if she lets herself "be taken," her authority among women and men will be discounted.

Consequently, women work hard to maintain the boundary. Every day many professional women devote some of their attention, consciously and unconsciously, to staying mindful and a bit wary of who is coming at them and why. After a while, it becomes part of a woman's intuition, and she may not even know that she is on guard.

To keep that boundary intact, women have to manage not only how they behave around men, but also how they feel. Men's and women's hungers can be aroused when they work intensively together in close quarters. In order to keep their own feelings in check and contain intense relationships at work, women sometimes desexualize themselves. They may take on the role of a daughter, sister, or mother figure, which is safer than being a three-dimensional woman. Other women create a "bubble," or shell, closing themselves off even from their own feelings, to stay safe.

So, largely as a product of our cultural history and norms, women and men may have mirror images of the same problem. Men more often have the problem of being uncontained. Their hungers, amplified in the workplace, get acted out. Until recently, that harmed women, and a man's soul and family, but it had few consequences to his position of authority at work, and may even have enhanced his reputation in some quarters.

In contrast, women are rarely rewarded for crossing that line. In response, many women have told us that they become overcontained. Because they expend a bit of energy all day long being mindful and wary, some women find it difficult to disengage from their professional role at the end of the day and let themselves relax into emotional and sexual intimacy.

We know we are treading on turf that, as men, is not our own. Moreover, this terrain is fraught with stereotypes. However, we mention the patterns as women have described them so that perhaps men and women can better understand aspects of our lives generally rendered undiscussable. To allow herself to be touched deeply, emotionally or sexually, a woman has to allow herself to trust. But it is challenging to open up your body and soul if you've just spent the whole day on guard. So, many women find it difficult to allow their human needs to be met, to be restored to themselves, even after they leave work and get home.

Many women, when they enter positions of authority and experience being the center of attention, have the same visceral response as many men. Being looked to in a special way, a woman's hunger for intimacy and sexual pleasure may increase. And just as people are attracted to men in power, people are attracted to women in power. Temptations abound. Some men, in the grip of their own desires, will sense her hungers and act seductively. But though she may find it arousing, the feelings are also a danger signal. Most women heed the warning. Some do not and, by crossing that threshold, damage themselves.

For example, remember our friend Paula in chapter 3, who did not survive her effort at reforming the state agency? The pressure and the position made her vulnerable to her desire for companionship. She took the job at a time in her life when she had significant unmet personal needs for affirmation and intimacy. Life at home was not easy: Her marriage seemed fragile and she felt stressed by the demands of raising two very young children. She also had nagging self-doubts about her professional life, wondering whether she had what it takes to handle a senior position of authority, where "the buck stops here."

She was not consciously aware of those needs. At least, she certainly was not aware of how those hungers would make her vulnerable. Inadvertently, by trying to meet her needs in inappropriate ways, by creating a too-personal relationship with a professional colleague, she colluded with her opponents, making herself a target for personal criticism. Once she became the issue, the conversation shifted to the nature of her appetites, and away from the important issues she wanted to address.

What Can You Do about It?

How do you learn to manage such visceral hungers? First, know yourself, tell yourself the truth about what you need, and then appropriately honor those human needs. Every human being needs power and control, affirmation and importance, intimacy and sexual pleasure. You cannot lead and stay alive by simply putting a silencer on yourself. Managing your hungers requires knowing your vulnerabilities and taking action to compensate for them. This begins with respecting your hungers. Here are two ideas that may be useful in regard to the need for sexual intimacy. We focus on this particular need because it's a very common, yet unspoken, area of vulnerability.

Transitional Rituals

Both women and men need transitional rituals to help peel away their professional roles so they can feel their own skins again. Otherwise, our well-protected professional selves can seep into our personal lives. It is too easy to keep the mask on, since it provides such a good defense against injury during the workday. Almost any simple act can serve to mark the transition between your public and private lives. To be restored to yourself, beyond any role, you might simply change clothes, take a shower, go to the gym, take a walk or run, meditate or pray, or drink a glass of wine. Any kind of activity, turned into a ritual and coupled with some mindful intent, can help you move from one state of mind and feeling to another. You will have to experiment and see what ritual will work for you.

Of course, some of us come to identify so completely with one particular role that it seems frightening or impossible to imagine stepping out of character. Indeed, in the digital age, the seductions of our self-importance grow more powerfully available, and we find ourselves plugged in nearly all of the time. "Surely someone must be looking for me now?" we tell ourselves.

Perhaps we need permission to stop working. How many mothers and fathers have trouble quieting themselves even after getting their children to sleep? Ironically, it takes discipline to unplug, slow down, and create moments of transition every day. It takes deliberate care to restore ourselves so that our need for intimacy can be known and fulfilled.

On the other side of these moments, however, you may find the raw experience of hunger in the form of loneliness and emptiness. So it may not be enough simply to create transition. You may then have to rekindle the capacity for intimacy and patterns of family and community that have been neglected. The transition is not useful if you have no place of intimacy to go to.

Rekindle the Sparks

All of us have the human need to be touched physically, as well as in our soul and heart. We are designed that way. In our tribe, Jews are supposed to make love on the Sabbath (with husband or wife), because the delights of love can provide the sensation of timeless heaven. The taste of divine eternity and union is meant not only for a man; according to Jewish law, a man must give full pleasure to a woman.

Sustained intimate relationships too often dry up. Yet it is especially important during periods of intensity in your professional life, when keeping your spirit alive is at risk, that you honor your hungers. And if they become unmanageable, get the assistance you need to pay proper respect to the intimate possibilities of life. Otherwise, as we've seen, the hunger spills over in destructive ways, or we abandon that aspect of our humanity altogether.

We live, perhaps for the first time in history, in an era when it is no longer taboo to get help in order to strip away the distrust, peel off our roles, and rekindle the sparks. There is little reason, in this day of every kind of therapy and workshop, to resign oneself to a dry relationship. We are even learning how to heal the wounds of pervasive abuse. As a society, we are just beginning to bring sexuality out of the shadows, and learn better and more honest ways to know these gifts. When we do, there will be less shame about seeking the kind of help many of us need in our private lives.

Of course, it takes courage to move past the embarrassment and cultural taboos that restrict us. We have deep loyalties to the people who both loved us in the best way they knew, yet taught us constricted ways of living. For example, in some cultures, women are taught that there is no joy in being touched. Sexual intimacy is just a service one has to perform for a man, and the future will be brighter because over time he will become less and less interested. We have heard many variations on this theme: "He hasn't come near me in four years; thank God I don't have to perform that service for him anymore!"

Yet any adaptive work, even at the individual level, requires investigating our loyalties, taking the best from the past, and discarding what's expendable. To give up the opportunity to experience the divine sparks in the vulnerability and joy of union seems a very high price to pay to maintain one's pride or loyal cultural assumptions. Restoring juice to a relationship seems the healthiest way to manage one's needs.

.   .   .

We are not designed to conduct the emotional currents produced by living in the midst of huge social networks. We were all designed to live in small bands under fairly stable conditions. It is entirely natural, therefore, to feel overwhelmed or hunkered down. Indeed, no matter how perfect your upbringing and the "software" your parents, culture, and community may have given you, you need ongoing practices to compensate for your vulnerabilities. You need anchors.

Anchor Yourself

To anchor ourselves in the turbulent seas of the various roles we take in life, professionally and personally, we have found it profoundly important to distinguish between the self, which we can anchor, and our roles, which we cannot. The roles we play in our organization, community, and private lives depend mainly on the expectations of people around us. The self relies on our capacity to witness and learn throughout our lives, to refine the core values that orient our decisions—whether or not they conform to expectations.

Many people experience a rude awakening when they leave high positions of authority. Former CEOs and politicians alike find that their phone calls to important and busy people do not get through as easily, their e-mails are not answered as quickly, their requests for favors and special treatment from "friends" no longer get quick results. Such is the harsh realization that the benefits they enjoyed in the past were at least as much a function of the role they played, the position they held, as they were a product of their character.

Distinguish Role from Self

It is easy to confuse your self with the roles you take on in your organization and community. The world colludes in the confusion by reinforcing your professional persona. Colleagues, subordinates, and bosses treat you as if the role you play is the essence of you, the real you.

In the 1980s, Alan Alda starred in the movie *The Seduction of Joe Tynan*. Alda plays a United States senator contemplating a run for president. The seduction takes two forms. In a traditional physical seduction story, costar Meryl Streep plays a liberal activist, and it isn't clear who seduces whom. But the title has another meaning as Alda gets increasingly caught up in his role as an effective, popular senator and presidential possibility. He begins to make speeches to his own kids, just like he does on the floor of the Senate, and treats his wife like a staff person who needs to toe the party line. He begins to think that he *is* the public and professional role that he plays. The movie ends before we know whether Alda wins the presidency, or whether his marriage survives his delusion. But the danger is clear: the all-too-common pitfall of losing yourself in your role.

Confusing role with self is a trap. Even though you may put all of yourself into your role—your passion, values, and artistry—the people in your setting will be reacting to you, not primarily as a person, but as the role you take in their lives. Even when their responses to you *seem* very personal, you need to read them primarily as reactions to how well you are meeting their expectations. In fact, it is vital to your own stability and peace of mind that you understand this, so that you can interpret and decipher people's criticism before internalizing it.

Thus, you have control over whether your self-worth is at stake. If you take what is said personally, your self-esteem becomes an issue. "You are a jerk" is not necessarily a personal attack, even though it is framed that way. It might mean that people don't like the way you are performing your role. Perhaps you have not been tactful enough in making your challenge. You may have raised the temperature too high or too quickly, or you may be raising an issue people would rather leave alone. In fact, they may be right to criticize your sensitivity or your pacing, and you may have a lot to learn to correct your style, but their critique is primarily about the issue, not about you.

In the guise of attacking you personally, people are trying to neutralize the threat they perceive in your point of view.

Indeed, say you put forth an idea and it is attacked. If you accept the notion that the purpose of your intervention is to stimulate the group's work, then the attack becomes a form of the work. It is an opportunity. The resistance you receive is not a criticism of you, or even necessarily a dismissal of your point of view. On the contrary, it suggests that your input was worth reacting to, that it provoked engagement with the issue.

Elizabeth Cady Stanton described how people responded in what became the first women's rights convention in the United States.[1] As Stanton tells the story, one summer afternoon in 1848, she told a group of friends about her encounters with the outrageous, entrenched positions of men, including teenaged boys, workmen, and policemen, when she organized and managed the refurbishment of a property in Seneca Falls, New York. The discussion made it obvious to at least some of those present that something had to be done to change how men and women thought about women. They decided not only to meet again the next week, but also to begin writing a declaration of women's rights.

After several meetings, they adopted a declaration of women's rights and resolutions demanding that American men change the laws to allow women to vote. Stanton described the resulting uproar throughout the country: "So pronounced was the popular voice against us, in the parlor, press, and pulpit, that most of the ladies who had attended the convention and signed the declaration, one by one, withdrew their names and influence and joined our persecutors. Our friends gave us the cold shoulder and felt themselves disgraced by the whole proceeding."[2]

The response, with its personal costs, was hard not to take personally. Stanton said at the time, "If I had had the slightest premonition of all that was to follow that convention, I fear I should not have had the courage to risk it, and I must confess that it was with fear and trembling that I consented to attend another, one month afterward, in Rochester."[3]

Anchoring yourself may enable you to sustain the furious opposition even of your own friends and former collaborators, who may remake your role overnight from a darling to an outcast. But if you can anchor yourself, you may find the stamina to remain responsive, focused, and persistent. Progress may take decades. The Seneca Falls convention in 1848 was the beginning of Stanton's work on women's suffrage. It took her thirty more years to tackle the constitutional flaws that underlay the problem in America. In 1878, Stanton drafted a federal suffrage amendment, introduced and rejected by every Congress for the next forty years. When in 1918 the House finally approved the essence of Stanton's draft for Senate approval of what would become the Nineteenth Amendment, Stanton had been dead for sixteen years.

Like Stanton, if you are to be authentic and effective, you must play your role in accordance with what you believe so that your passions infuse your work. You need to realize that you cannot have it both ways. If you are attacked, discredited, ostracized, or fired, you may feel that you have experienced a kind of assassination. But you cannot expect people to seriously consider your idea without accepting the possibility that they will challenge it. Accepting that process of engagement as the terrain of leadership liberates you personally. It enables you to make room for others to get just as involved in working on your idea as you are, without withdrawing or becoming entrenched in a personal defense.

Again, distinguishing yourself from your role is just as important with regard to praise as it is to criticism. When you begin to believe all the good things people are saying about you, you can lose yourself in your role, distorting your personal sense of identity and self-image. Also, people can gain control over you because of your desire to maintain their approval. Losing yourself in your role is a sign that you depend on the institution or community for meeting too many of your personal needs, which is dangerous, as we saw in chapter 8.

Do not underestimate the challenge of distinguishing role from self. When people attack you personally, the reflexive reaction is to take it personally. We all find it exceedingly difficult in the midst of a personal attack to get to the balcony, maintain an interpretive stance, and identify the way our messages generate distress in other people. As Stanton discovered, it is especially hard when your friends and the people whose support you seek are doing the attacking. But being criticized by people you care about is almost always a part of exercising leadership. When Bill Clinton successfully reached across party lines in 1993 to fashion with Newt Gingrich a crucial deficit-reduction bill that raised taxes and reduced government spending (contributing to a decade of prosperity), his wife Hillary was sharply critical of the president and his advisers. Front the president's point of view, that was her job.[4]

Indeed, leadership often means going beyond the boundaries of your constituency and creating common ground with other factions, divisions, and stakeholders. Adaptive work rarely falls in the lap of any one faction. Each has its work of adjustment to do. In crossing boundaries, you may appear a traitor to your own people, who expect you to champion their perspective, not turn around and challenge their view. Violating their expectations generates a sense of betrayal, perhaps expressions of outrage. However, little of this is personal, even when it's coming from your compatriots, friends, spouse, or partner.

When you take "personal" attacks personally, you unwittingly conspire in one of the common ways you can be taken out of action—you make yourself the issue. In an election campaign, a candidate's character and personal qualities are accepted as appropriate subjects of debate. But in most situations, even in politics, the attack is a defense against the perspectives you embody, which threaten other people's own positions and loyalties. As we've asked before, does anyone ever critique your personality or style when you hand out big checks or deliver good news? We don't think so. People attack your style when they don't like the message.

It's the easy way out to attack the person rather than the message itself. For example, some might accuse a courageous woman of being pushy if she seeks a change in the culture of the organization.

By making her style or character the issue, those who are threatened distract people in the organization from her message. Discrediting her reduces the credibility of her perspective.

Although Bill Clinton provided plenty of ammunition for his detractors, would people have attacked him so unceasingly had they liked everything about his points of view on the issues facing America? It is no accident that those attacking him on the character issue also disagreed with him on many of his policies, and moreover were furious with his appropriation of some of their positions as he moved to the political center. It is also not surprising that the people more forgiving of Clinton's character flaws agreed with key elements of his agenda. Feminists were almost unanimous in defending him in the impeachment process, rather than attacking him for his exploitation of women, because he had strongly supported their agenda.

Ironically, though the Clintons and their political consultants prided themselves on mounting a quick and effective defense, their attack-defense dynamics focusing on character served them poorly. Every time the attackers succeeded in generating a defensive response from the White House, they siphoned public attention from the issues. The more the Clintons acted defensively (by withholding documents, fashioning legal arguments, using legalistic language, or lying), the more they added momentum and intensity to the attack.[5] Reacting defensively to the literal substance of personal attacks colludes with the attackers by perpetuating the diversion. This work avoidance mechanism almost always succeeds simply because it's so natural to take a personal attack personally.

Of course, everyone could learn better styles of communicating a challenging message. Unfortunately, there is no way around the fact that it is just plain difficult to pass out bad news. It is easy, even enjoyable, for a doctor to say to a patient, "Here's your penicillin. You'll be cured." But what if the news is grave? "I don't think I can save you. I wish I could, but I don't think I can. Let me help you and your family grasp what you are about to face, so that you can make the appropriate adjustments in your lives." It is hard to imagine a message more painful to deliver or to receive than this. Nearly any teacher would prefer to give out A's than C's. Nearly any boss would prefer to hire than fire. But if the doctor, teacher, or boss gets deflected from the goal of helping people take in the message, and instead becomes the issue, the work won't get done and precious time will be lost.

Even physical assassination, the ultimate form of attack, is not personal. Though this is no comfort to the victim, it can help supporters and surviving family comprehend and survive the tragedy. Moreover, knowing that even physical attacks are not personal can bolster courage, helping the person exercising leadership to take needed risks. If you understand this, then, in your heart you may feel that even if you lose your life, the essence of your intent will continue to infuse meaning in the lives of others.

Clearly, for example, Martin Luther King, Jr., was killed for no other reason than to eliminate the role he played in the changing of America. Yigal Amir, the assassin of Yitzhak Rabin, claimed that his purpose was to silence Rabin, and killing him was the only way to do that. It was Rabin's message—his role—that was threatening, not Rabin himself.[6]

Failing to distinguish role from self can also lead you to neglect the proper levels of role-defense and role-protection. Rabin risked his life many times during his career as a soldier. By the time he became prime minister of Israel, he was well accustomed to physical peril. So when his secret service informed him of the increasing risks of assassination and advised him to use a bulletproof vest before leading a massive public rally, he refused. Having crossed that threshold of risk years back in the army, and perhaps with some lingering pride in his personal, physical courage, he made himself and his role more vulnerable than necessary. The irony is tragic.

Had Rabin distinguished role from self, he might have worn that vest, not in self-protection, but for role-protection—he might have recognized the increasing need to protect the crucial part he was playing in the Middle East peace process. Had he stepped back, moved to the balcony, and considered the stakes at risk, he surely would have agreed with his bodyguards. Instead, in the fleeting moment of decision, he calculated the risks according to his personal level of risk tolerance, rather than assessing the risk to his historic role in the future of Israel and the Middle East.[7]

Of course, a more common example of role-protection occurs when new parents find themselves becoming risk-averse because of the significance of their new roles. Fortunately, most people who seek to lead do not have to weigh the risks to their lives. The physical dangers do not loom so large as the everyday ways people push back personally when you introduce a controversial idea.

To draw people's attention back to the issues after you have been attacked or unduly flattered, you have to divert them from your personality, personal judgment, or style. The absolute best long-term defense against personal attack is to be perfect and make no mistakes in your personal life. But, of course, none of us is perfect. Our human hungers and failings are there always, causing us to lose our tempers in public, to hit the send button before thinking twice about the effects of an email, to lie reactively when we feel cornered, to make an off-handed remark that offends people we are trying to reach. We have been susceptible to these behaviors ourselves—everyone has. The key, however, is to respond to the attack in a way that places the focus back where it should be, on the message and the issues.

In their campaigns for president, the press accused both Gary Hart and Bill Clinton of philandering. They responded in very different ways. Hart counterattacked. He criticized the reporters who had shadowed him. He questioned *their* scruples. He got defensive. Bill Clinton took a very different road. He went on *60 Minutes* right after the Super Bowl, sat before the cameras holding hands with his wife and essentially admitted that he had strayed. Hart responded personally; Clinton, strategically, and more honestly.

No one watching Hart or Clinton knew for sure how many women either of them had romanced. What everyone could know and judge was how both men handled the situation. People made up their minds about these men not by poring through the accounts of their dalliances, but by observing the data at hand. That's what people see. *Your management of an attack, more than the substance of the accusation, determines your fate.* Even though the attacks were deeply personal, Clinton understood them to be political attacks on his credibility. He responded with a disarmingly honest, non-defensive defense to gain trust and put the issue away, and was then able to return the conversation to the policy issues in the campaign.

Remember our friend Kelly, who tried to stay out of the fray in order to secure her appointment to the Denver Civil Service Commission? She was criticized publicly and repeatedly during the process. But she realized that the criticism (and occasional praise) was not really about her, but about what she represented for different factions of the community. Had she taken the attacks to heart, she would have been inclined to react defensively, and would have placed herself in the midst of a crisis that was not hers. She might well have put her appointment in jeopardy.

There is also a long-term value to distinguishing role from self. Roles end. If you are too caught up in your role, if you come to believe that you and your role are identical, what will happen to you when your role ends? Will Jack Welch find the strands of himself after playing the part of "Jack Welch: CEO of General Electric"? After putting all of himself into that role for so many professional years, will he know where to look?[8]

While parenting is a part of one's personal life, it provides a powerful example of the need for the self/role distinction in all aspects of our lives. When Ron starting having children, Marty told him, "You know you will have succeeded as a parent when your child acts really badly toward you and you don't take it personally. And you won't figure it out until the second child."

Ron then proceeded to discover the truth of that prediction. At his worst as a father, he says, he took it personally when his children got angry and were disrespectful to him. First he yelled inside his own head, "Why don't you kids appreciate all I do for you, and all that you have?!" Before long that internal sob story leaked out. He started yelling out loud, shamefully losing his temper, and then, feeling guilty about having lost his temper, compounded it all by yelling at his kids further for making him lose his temper. "Why are you making me yell, don't you know how I hate losing my temper!" After a few minutes of this craziness, he withdrew defeated to his study where he licked his wounds. By the time he rejoined his family, he had lost sight of whatever may have precipitated the incident.

At his best, Ron stayed calm. Instead of taking his children's behavior personally, he remembered his job: He corrected their behavior by setting limits of some kind, and then he started listening to find out the problem. If he kept listening for a day or two, the story eventually came out: Inevitably, something upsetting had happened in a friendship, on the ball field, or in class. Having identified the issue, he could then help the child solve that problem, whatever it was. Rather than turn his attention inward to tend his wounds, he focused outward, where the problem was located.

It may be obvious from this example, but it's worth emphasizing that we are not talking about playing a role at a distance from yourself, or separating yourself from your role. We use the word distinguish because we want you to *differentiate* self from role, not distance or withhold yourself. Indeed, we hope you can find ways to put all of your heart and soul into many of the roles you take in relationship to the people and institutions in your lives. In other words, distinguishing between self and role does not mean you need to avoid *embodying* important issues, though there are dangers when you do so, as we've discussed earlier. There are some situations in which you have no choice. Whether you like it or not, you will embody issues in the eyes of other people, and sometimes they will attack you when they see you running with the ball down the field. If you choose to play, you will incur these dangers because it is the only way to move the issue forward.

This role/self distinction becomes extremely hard to practice when we get tackled in surprising ways that cut close to the bone.

At those times, we find it far more difficult to get to the balcony and see that the challenges we represent to others remain distinct from our own essential identity.

For example, when Geraldine Ferraro ran for vice president in 1984 and was attacked mercilessly regarding her husband's business dealings, she held a massive news conference. Some of you will remember. She told the reporters that she would stand up and answer every one of their questions, however long it took, to clear her name. And in fact, the news conference lasted hours.

Did it actually let her bring the attention back to the real issues? No. The media, on behalf of their readers and viewers, kept inventing newer variations of the attack even when she answered their questions, because her family finances were never the issue anyway. They were merely a distraction, and indulging the media and the public in this diversion with a marathon news conference was precisely the wrong move. The issues she *embodied* were real issues, and they were intensely provocative in America: What does it mean for a woman to be powerful and professional? What would it mean for a woman to be second in line to the most powerful position of authority in the world? What has the sexual revolution done to our families? These continue to be challenging questions in our society, as we've seen in public debates and elections through the present.

With disastrous results, the campaign managers in 1984 advised Ferraro to stay away from the issues she embodied. She was told to stick to international security, poverty, taxes, and the budget, but not to talk from a woman's perspective; moreover, she was advised to avoid issues of particular urgency to women, like equal opportunity. Ironically, by following this advice, expressing a generic perspective on the issues rather than one more authentically shaped by her own experience, she may have indirectly roused the media to search for something distracting in her personal life.

As the first female vice presidential candidate, she could not escape her role, even if she had wanted to, because in the eyes of the nation she inevitably embodied questions regarding women's ability and perspective. As a leader, she needed to play the role fully, which she finally allowed herself to do with great inspiration in the last four days of the campaign.

> We can win Olympic gold medals *and* we can coach our daughters' soccer teams. We can walk in space *and* help our children take their first steps. We can negotiate trade agreements *and* manage family budgets. . . . The choices are unlimited. We can be all these things. But we don't have to be any of them. . . . My candidacy is not just for me; it's for everyone. It's not just a symbol. It's a breakthrough. It's not just a statement. It's a bond between women all over America. My candidacy says America believes in equality. And the time for that equality is now.[9]

Joseph Lieberman, America's first Jewish vice presidential candidate learned from her. He played the role of religious Jew fully throughout the 2000 campaign. In nearly every speech and occasion, he spoke about the role of faith in America. Instead of begging the issue and avoiding the role the public ascribed to him, he spoke to the issue he embodied. Had he done otherwise, he would have made himself vulnerable to personal attack.

Remember, when you lead, people don't love you or hate you. Mostly they don't even know you. They love or hate the positions you represent. Indeed, we all know how quickly idealization turns into contempt when suddenly you disappoint someone. Surely, if Monica Lewinsky had met Bill Clinton in a supermarket behind a shopping cart, he would have been just another middle-aged guy getting burgers.

By knowing and valuing yourself, distinct from the roles you play, you gain the freedom to take risks within those roles. Your self-worth is not so tightly tied to the reactions of other people as they contend with your positions on issues. Moreover, you gain the freedom to take on a new role once the current one concludes or you hit a dead end.

No role is big enough to express all of who you are. Each role you take on—parent, spouse, child; professional, friend, and neighbor—

is a vehicle for expressing a different facet of yourself. Anchored in yourself, and recognizing and respecting your distinct roles, you are much less vulnerable to the pains of leadership.

Keep Confidants, and Don't Confuse Them with Allies

The lone warrior strategy of leadership may be heroic suicide. Perhaps no one can be sufficiently anchored from within themselves for very long without allies, whom we discussed in chapter 4, and confidants.

Allies are people who share many of your values, or at least your strategy, and operate across some organizational or factional boundary. Because they cross a boundary, they cannot always be loyal to you; they have other ties to honor. In fact, a key aspect of what makes allies extremely helpful is precisely that they do have other loyalties. That means they can help you understand competing stakes, conflicting views, and missing elements in your grasp of a situation. They can pull you by the collar to the balcony and say, "Pay attention to these other people over here. You're not learning anything from your enemies." Moreover, if persuasive, they can engage their people in the effort, strengthening your coalition.

Sometimes however, we make the mistake of treating an ally like a confidant. Confidants have few, if any, conflicting loyalties. They usually operate outside your organization's boundary, although occasionally someone very close in, whose interests are perfectly aligned with yours, can also play that role. You really need both allies and confidants.

Confidants can do something that allies can't do. They can provide you with a place where you can say everything that's in your heart, everything that's on your mind, without it being predigested or well packaged. The emotions and the words can come out topsy-turvy, without order. Then once the whole mess is on the table, you can begin to pull the pieces back in and separate what is worthwhile from what is simply ventilation.

Confidants can put you back together again at the end of the day when you feel like Humpty Dumpty, all broken to pieces. They can remind you why it's worth getting out there and taking risks in the first place.

When you ask them to listen, they are free to care about you more than they do about your issue. They either share your stakes completely or, better, they may not care about your issue at all, one way or the other.

Confidants must be people who will tell you what you do not want to hear and cannot hear from anyone else, people in whom you can confide without having your revelations spill back into the work arena. These are people you can call when a meeting has gone sour, who will listen as you recount what happened and tell you where you screwed up. You can reveal your emotions to them without worrying that it will affect your reputation or undermine your work. You do not have to manage information. You can speak spontaneously.

When you do adaptive work, you take a lot of heat and may endure a good measure of pain and frustration. The job of a confidant is to help you come through the process whole, and to tend to your wounds along the way. Moreover, when things are going well, you need someone who will tell you that you are too puffed up, and who will point out danger signals when you are too caught up in self-congratulation to notice them.

Almost every person we know with difficult experiences of leadership has relied on a confidant to help them get through. A governor who is making painful choices in bringing the state out of a perilous financial condition plays pool at night with an old friend who lives down the street. A businesswoman trying to change the values and culture of her company to meet new competition has long phone calls with her sister late in the evening. A bureaucrat trying to lead difficult change in his organization e-mails a new professional colleague thousands of miles away whom he just met at an intensive two-week seminar. A spouse, too, can be an excellent confidant, except of course when the issues are about the spousal relationship or family dynamics. Sometimes a confidant can be explicitly engaged. "I'm about to start a difficult process here at work. Do you mind if I call you from time to time and just pour my guts out so you can tell me what you hear?" Sometimes, of course, the dynamic is more spontaneous.

When you are discouraged and feeling low, think about an old friend, a roommate you have not seen in a decade or more, an employer or teacher who helped train you—someone who cares about *you* rather than any particular role you play. Give them a call. Ask them for time to hear you out. If they agree, then tell them the story, no holds barred, as well as how you feel so they can get a full picture of what is going on inside you as well as around you.

When you need someone to talk to in difficult times, it's tempting to try to turn a trusted ally into a confidant as well. Not a good idea.

Remember Sara, the newspaper designer we introduced in chapter 4? She understood that her staff, the designers she recruited to join the paper and carry out the work, consisted of allies—as committed to the issue as was she. Indeed, they were terrific advocates and effective troops, bringing good design to every aspect of the paper, creating relationships of their own, and winning friends among reporters and editors who were reluctantly being brought along into the visual era.

But this was difficult and lonely work for Sara. She was a long way from her old colleagues in the Midwest. She had no family. She really had no one outside the newspaper in whom to confide. So she began to take into her confidence her young recruits, telling them how frustrated she felt, how difficult she found it to deal with some of the senior management and recalcitrant editors and reporters. In particular, she complained about the old-timers running the presses, who didn't have the patience or the intelligence, she said, to cope with all the sophisticated changes she was introducing and her high standards of quality production.

Now, the pressmen walked on hallowed ground at this newspaper. Most of them came from lower-class backgrounds, fiercely proud of their heritage and their craft. Typically, they had been with the newspaper for years, through good times and bad. Many of them had relatives at the paper, sons or daughters who worked on the business side or even as reporters and editors. They were family.

In turning to her younger colleagues, Sara confused allies with confidants. Don, her deputy, was one of them. Don was talented, demanding, and high strung, and as committed as she was to the new visual emphasis of the paper. He was an effective ally, but this did not mean he was with her personally. On the contrary, Don found Sara abrasive and difficult to deal with, and thought her personality added to the already tricky problem of changing people's attitudes and habits.

He also wanted her job. He believed he could do much more, much faster, to advance the cause than Sara. Unfortunately, caught up in her need for a confidant, she ignored clues to his doubts and envy. In fact, Don took every opportunity to undermine her. When she would air her critical thoughts about colleagues, he would later repeat them, sometimes to the colleagues themselves. When she would trust him to provide a safe harbor where she could ventilate her feelings, he would tell others that she threw tantrums and describe her unbecoming behavior. Sometimes the stories got her into trouble, but only momentarily. The newspaper's editor mostly viewed them as unsubstantiated rumors and continued to stand by her.

Then Sara gave an interview to a design industry magazine. She was talking to her own community, and her guard was down. Ordinarily, pressmen would not read the magazine, so she didn't worry about everything she said the way she did in the newsroom. She made some very disparaging comments about the pressmen, ridiculing their intelligence and their competence. Don, a subscriber to the magazine, read the interview and saw the offensive remarks. He made several copies, highlighted the provocative quotes, and circulated them to senior management.

The editor was now faced with hard evidence, a smoking gun. Though Sara's change efforts at the paper had been quite successful, he could no longer defend her. Within weeks she was gone and Don was announced as her replacement.

Sara made a common mistake. When battling loneliness, insecurity, stress, or other pressures, the need to open up to someone can be almost overwhelming. In this frame of mind, it's very easy to mistake allies for confidants. Sara thought that because she and Don were together on the issue, he backed her personally as well. When you try to turn allies into confidants, you never know when circumstances may force them to choose between their commitment to their own priorities and people, and their commitment to you. Since their previous commitment to the issue came first, it's likely that their prior loyalty will prevail.

Why make them choose? With Don, it was easy. He didn't like Sara in the first place, and he thought their issue would be better and more quickly advanced if he were at the helm. She gave him ammunition, and it was only a matter of time before one of the bullets hit home. But if your ally is committed to you as well as to the issue, you put him in a terrible spot by asking him to be loyal to both. It is better, whenever possible, to keep the two separate.

Allies can be the closest of friends. They may confide in each other about many aspects of their lives. At work, however, they have overlapping, not identical, stakes and loyalties. To protect their relationship, it becomes crucial that they also respect the boundary that separates them, and honor each other's loyalties when those come into conflict. This is easier said than done in nearly every profession except legislative politics, where representatives are accustomed to stating up front how the pressures of their constituencies conflict. Tom Edwards and Bill Monahan, whom you met in chapter 4, were unusual in their ability to speak openly after dinner about their competing interests, and thereby protect the relationship. "I'm sorry, Tom, I can't back you on this one." Far more frequently, your ally, caught between two loyalties, won't know what to say. The likely consequence is the developing of distance between you.

In our experience, when you try to turn allies into confidants, you put them in a bind, place a valuable relationship at risk, and usually end up losing on both counts. They fail you as a confidant, and they begin to slip away even as reliable allies.

Seek Sanctuary

Like a loyal confidant, having a readily available sanctuary provides an indispensable physical anchor and source of sustenance. You would never attempt a difficult mountain journey without food or water, yet countless people go into the practice of leadership without reserving and conserving a place where they can gather and restore themselves.

A sanctuary is a place of reflection and renewal, where you can listen to yourself away from the dance floor and the blare of the music, where you can reaffirm your deeper sense of self and purpose. It's different from the balcony, where you go to get a wider perspective on the dynamics of your leadership efforts. Analyzing from the balcony can be hard work. In a sanctuary, you are out of that world entirely, in a place where you feel safe both physically and psychologically. The rules and stresses of everyday life are suspended temporarily. It is not a place to hide, but a haven where you can cool down, capture lessons from the painful moments, and put yourself back together.

Too often, under stress and pressed for time, our sources of sanctuary are the first places we give up. We consider them a luxury. Just when you need it most, you cut out going to the gym or taking your daily walk through the neighborhood, just to grab a few more minutes at the office. Clearly, it's when we are doing our most difficult work that we most need to maintain the structures in our lives that remind us of our essential and inviolable identity and keep us healthy.

We're not peddling a particular type of sanctuary. It could be a jogging path or a friend's kitchen table where you have tea. It could be a therapist's office, a 12-step group, or a room in your house where you sit and meditate. It could be a park or a chapel on the route between home and workplace. It doesn't matter what your sanctuary looks like or where it is. It doesn't even need to be a quiet place; your sanctuary might be as noisy as the pounding surf. What matters is that it fits you as a structure that promotes reflection, and that you protect it daily. Once a week is not enough.

At a particularly difficult time in Ron's life, when he struggled and felt pulled in too many directions both professionally and personally, he started picking up his children at school every day. He resigned from several committees, cut back on travel obligations, and cleared his afternoons. His kids usually got out at 3:30 P.M. They were then in first and second grade, and he found picking them up to be a challenging experience.

In fact, when three o'clock came around he had to pry himself out of his office—there were "important" calls left unmade, wonderful projects to do, money left on the table. (He usually could be seen racing out the door at 3:10 P.M.)

He would drive like a madman, and by the time he arrived at the school, he usually had to wait behind a long line of cars. With cell phone in one hand and dictating machine in the other, he would frantically try to make the most of every moment. "What am I doing here? I've got so many important things to do!" he would moan to himself. Finally, after inching his way to the front of the line, he would see their little round faces. He would ask them to get in one at a time, but did they listen? Throwing in their backpacks, always helter-skelter, they would crawl over each other to get to their usual seats. And then out would come the stories, stories Ron never used to hear at dinnertime, because apparently they only told them once, to whoever was there first. (Later he learned that if he stayed quiet at bedtime, they would do a second telling.)

Quite quickly, Ron would be transformed. He left behind the frenzied professional and recovered himself in being a father. After only three or four minutes the stories, the laughter, and even the kids' problems would work their curative magic. He felt anchored in a different world.

. . .

Everyone seeking to exercise leadership needs sanctuaries. We all need anchors to keep us from being swept away by the distractions, the flood of information, the tensions and temptations. As you provide leadership to people, you should expect to encounter emotions you cannot handle unless you have a time and place to sort them out.

Human beings were not designed to deal with the nonstop modern world, so we must compensate. Getting anchors and keeping them is, at root, a matter of self-love, discipline, and purpose. It is a serious recognition that we need to care for ourselves in order to do justice to our values and aspirations. Without antidotes to the modern world, we lose perspective, jeopardize the issues that matter, and risk our future. We forget what's on the line.

10

What's on the Line?

We have focused in this book on practical advice that addresses the question, How can you lead and stay alive? And we have offered a variety of answers, none of them easy. Some solutions stem from your ability to analyze a situation and understand the issues, stakes, and pace of change appropriate for the people around you. Some answers lie in creating strategic holding environments for conflicts. Others emerge from your tactical ability to respond quickly to changing situations, work avoidance patterns, and deviations from the plan. And some answers can be found in the strength of your personal life, your relationships, and in your practices of renewal.

But we have not yet explored the root question: Why lead? If exercising leadership is this difficult, why bother? Why put yourself on the line? Why keep pressing forward when the resistance feels unbearable? Where can you find the drive to keep going, like Lois in that circle of chairs, when nobody shows up at the meetings you call?

Neither of us is a theologian. Marty comes out of politics and the press, and Ron's background is in medicine and music. But we believe, plain and simple, that the only way you can answer these questions is by discovering what gives meaning in your life.

For most of us, surviving is not enough. If survival were the point, in the end we would surely fail: We don't live forever. However, accepting that obvious fact is never easy. It may seem ironic that in a book whose theme has been staying alive, we would promote the idea of accepting death. But the freedom to take risks and make meaningful progress comes in part from the realization that death is inevitable. Even the word "lead" has an Indo-European root that means "to go forth, die."[1] As our Northern Irish colleague, Hugh O'Doherty, reminds us, "In the end they are gonna get you." Nothing is forever; the point is to make life meaningful while you can.

Think once again about the passengers on United Airlines Flight 93, whose plane crashed into that Pennsylvania field on September 11, 2001. Unlike the passengers on the planes that flew into the World Trade Center, those on Flight 93 knew they were going to die. Facing certain death, they gave profound and heroic meaning to their lives by diverting the hijackers' plan and thus saving an untold number of people on the ground.

Fortunately, there are endless sources of meaning and significance that do not occur in the context of death: the amazement of the biologist who uncovers mysteries in the study of DNA synthesis; the joy of a pianist in playing a Bach suite; the satisfaction of a business owner who creates jobs and prosperity for the men and women of a community; the profound quiet of a sleeping child's breathing.

Some sources of meaning are rare; much depends on the talent, opportunities, and experiences that come our way. There is, however, at least one source available to each of us, at all times, in all circumstances. People find meaning by connecting with others in a way that makes life better.

Having listened to people facing the end of their days, we have never heard them say, "I wish I had spent more time at the office." Instead, they talk in countless variations about the other joys of life: family, friendships, the many ways in which their lives touched people, and how their work meant something to others. When people hold fast to life, they want more time to experience those connections.

The utter simplicity of such meaning reveals itself in the cauldron of the battlefield. What makes a soldier willing to risk death? Not obedience to authority, although that counts for something. Not high ideals, although they matter, too. Not even their own survival, although that is obviously important as well. Soldiers crawl forth from the trenches into battle because they care about their buddies in the platoon. If they don't go, they will put their pals in jeopardy. Loyalty and feeling for their fellows impel them forward.[2]

In the words of Phil Jackson, "The most effective way to forge a winning team is to call on the players' need to connect with something larger than themselves." For Maggie Brooke, it was saving her Native American community by helping her friends and neighbors give up alcohol. For Yitzhak Rabin, it was mobilizing the Israeli community to adjust to the reality that they could not have both all the land of their biblical roots and the peaceful existence they so deeply desired. For John Patrick and David Grossman at IBM, it was helping a once-great company—a community in which they worked and for which they cared deeply—adapt to a changing world so that it might thrive anew.

In each of these cases, and in every case of leadership we recite in this book, leadership was driven by the desire of one person to contribute to the people with whom he or she lived and worked.

So the answer to the question "Why lead?" is both simple and profound. The sources of meaning most essential in the human experience draw from our yearning to connect with other people. The exercise of leadership can give life meaning beyond the usual day-to-day stakes—approval of friends and peers, material gain, or the immediate gratification of success—because, as a practical art, leadership allows us to connect with others in a significant way. The elemental word we use for that kind of connection is love.

To some, talking about love in this context may seem soft and unprofessional, but it seems undeniable that love lies at the core of what makes life worth living. Love gives meaning to what you do, whether in a corporation, a community, a classroom, or a family. We take risks for good reason: We hope to make a difference in people's lives. Leadership enables and challenges us to love well.

Love

Human beings have always created communities, beginning with the extended families that formed the basic social unit of human existence for more than a million years. Recently (ten thousand years ago), with the invention of agriculture, people began to give up the nomadic way of life. Humans began to stay in one place, store wealth, form large organizations, and create settlements and societies. The enduring basis for all civilization, however, lies in the formation of attachments to one another, and these loyalties are based upon the ability to love, care, or take interest in other people. The capacity for family attachment serves as the foundation for social living. And the building block for family attachment is the mammalian capacity to nurture and defend offspring.

The challenge presented by the increasing complexity of civilization during the last ten thousand years has been the extension of our sphere of loyalties beyond the family, beyond the town, beyond the tribe. Indeed, as the world enters the third millennium, humanity is exploring and experiencing the risks and opportunities in the globalization of human societies. The European Union, for example, is a bold experiment in creating an architecture within which the diversity of nations can thrive. Can people sustain loyalties so diffuse as these, across so many boundaries of culture, ethnicity, faith, language, and historical conflict? The scourge of terrorism that struck the United States in September 2001 is one of many horrible testaments to the difficulty of this challenge.

In this sense, the human enterprise is an experiment in love and community. As we learn to tolerate and then enjoy so much diversity, we strive to create communities in which more and more of our members can thrive together. When a CEO delights in corporate success, enabling the creation of new jobs, new wealth, or new sources of efficiency or pleasure, in some essential way the sense of meaningfulness comes from having made a difference in the lives of other people: customers, employees, and shareholders. Making such a difference, at its root, taps into the gratifications of love.

At Medtronic, the highly successful company that makes cardiac pacemakers, defibrillators, and other medical devices, shareholder value grew from 1985 to 2001 at a compound rate of 37 percent per year. The CEO, Bill George, known in the press for boldly declaring at the annual shareholders meeting, "Shareholders come third," puts it this way: "Medtronic is not in the business of maximizing shareholder value. We *are* in the business of maximizing value to the patients we serve. Shareholder value comes from giving superior service to customers because you have impassioned employees serving them." As he tells it, "The Medtronic mission— restoring people to full life—transcends the everyday struggles, the battles for market share, the vicissitudes of the stock market, the regular changes in the executive ranks. Its light beams on the company's 25,000 employees like the North Star, providing a constant reference point against which each of us can calibrate our internal compass."[3]

The compass heading that orients people most directly, even when you get blown off course, is loving and being loved. That's the mammalian experience, the mother's attachment to her nursing child, from which human beings have developed a generalizable capacity for love at ever-greater distances from home. The contribution of your work may seem less direct than that of the Medtronic folks, who literally keep hearts ticking, but you need only scratch the surface of your imagination to see that your successes put you back in touch with the pride of your parents, teachers, family, or friends. Success serves as a proxy for their love. In other words, an important part, perhaps the very heart, of feeling successful comes from reexperiencing the bonds of those you love.

If the acts of leadership, available to all of us, are such a potent source of meaning, then it is worth considering again the words with which we began this book. Every day, opportunities for leadership present themselves to us. Why do we refuse most of them?

We have devoted most of this book to exploring the dangers of leadership that make us hold back, as well as ways to diminish these obstacles and lessen the perils. In our work with thousands of men and women over more than thirty years, two final reasons for hesitation appear again and again.

- People get stuck in the myth of measurement.

- People forget that the form of the contribution does not matter.

The Myth of Measurement

For some people, stepping out on the line is worth the risk only if success can be seen, touched, felt, and, most of all, counted. But trying to take satisfaction in life from the numbers you ring up is ultimately no more successful than making survival your goal.

Meaning cannot be measured. Yet we live immersed in a world of measurement so pervasive that even many of our religious institutions measure success, significantly, by market share. Who's winning in the missionary competition? Catholics, mainline Protestants, Mormons, Evangelicals, Muslims, Buddhists, Hindus? How many Jews have left the fold?

We even witness religious organizations distorting their mission to mean "reaching more people," as if souls were a measurable commodity. Indeed, the mission of bringing the applications of spirit, which is by nature beyond measure, to our daily efforts to live good and honorable lives seems estranged in the competition that measurement fosters. All too often, "mission" is something we do to outsiders, not something that drives the work inside the community itself. We seem to forget at times that "If you save one life, you save the world."[4]

Of course, measurement is a profoundly useful device, but it cannot tell us what makes life worth living. The challenge is to use measurement every day, knowing all the while that we cannot measure that which is of essential value. In medicine, for instance, we often have to engage in triage because we don't have the resources or the time to treat everyone needing help: We select those with the best chance of benefiting from whatever help we can give. And sadly, those with the worst odds get the least help. But one cannot imagine practicing medicine without the tools of measurement to assess blood pressure, heart rate, blood chemistries, and so forth. We save lives with these tools. In business and public policy, we continuously measure the value of our products and respond accordingly to increase value. In our household budgets, we allocate money to those activities that we value most. Yet, however useful these tools are, they mislead us when we apply them indiscriminately by habit.

Do many believe that when it is their turn to pass on, the Angels of Judgment will ask them, "Why did you teach 5 children to read, and not 16? Why did you create 803 jobs, and not 23,421? Why did you save 433 lives, and not 718?" Historians estimate that Herbert Hoover saved more than 100,000 lives by organizing emergency relief during World War I. Should this matter less in light of his failure to restore the economy as president of the United States after the stock market crash of 1929 and during the Great Depression that followed? We have learned greatly from his presidential mistakes, but can anyone assess or diminish the value of his life efforts?

Before graduating from Columbia University, Ron went to speak with one of the great twentieth-century philosophers of science, Professor Ernst Nagel. Ron asked, "What questions do you ask?" Elderly in his years and gentle in his demeanor, Nagel replied, "I have been asking, 'What can be measured?'" Implying, of course, that not everything can be. Ron got excited: "Oh, as with Shakespeare when Juliet declares to Romeo, '. . . the more I give to thee, The more I have. . . .'"[5]

We have rarely met a human being who, after years of professional life, has not bought into the myth of measurement and been debilitated by it. After all, there is powerful pressure in our culture to measure the fruits of our labors, and we feel enormous pride as we take on "greater" responsibility and gain "greater" authority, wealth, and prestige. And well we should, to a degree. But using measurement as a device is not the same as believing that measurement captures the essential value of anything. You cannot measure the good that you do.

Perhaps no activity in the United States teaches more children about the arts of measurement than baseball. Indeed, every part of the game is measured, and every player is a walking set of "stats." Kids throughout this country memorize and traffic in these numbers.

By statistical accounting, Hank Greenberg was one of the greatest baseball players of his day, and fans throughout the 1930s and 1940s kept a running tab on his stats. Between 1937 and 1947, excluding the war years (Greenberg was one of the first major league players to enlist), he hit more home runs than anyone else in baseball. His career batting average, RBI totals, and home runs made him a shoo-in for the Hall of Fame. He is still among the all-time leaders in several hitting categories, including his tie for first with an average of .925 runs batted in per game. Elected into the Hall of Fame in 1956, he received 85 percent of the votes. In a sport where measurement is an obsession, Greenberg's numbers were outstanding, among the best of his era, or any era for that matter. Yet one of his major accomplishments, one of his great contributions to the game, was totally immeasurable.

Greenberg had played his entire career with the Detroit Tigers. After the war though he had clearly lost a step or two, he was still hitting well, having led the league in both home runs and RBIs. The Tigers had finished in a respectable second place. But after the 1946 season, in part based on a misunderstanding between Greenberg and Tigers' owner Walter Briggs, the Tigers shockingly and unceremoniously placed him on waivers, giving up their rights to keep him. None of the American League team owners claimed him, obviously suggesting that Briggs had gotten an agreement from them in advance. The National League Pittsburgh Pirates picked up his contract. For one of the greats of the game, what could possibly be the meaning in such a degrading end to a career? He went from a contending team to one at the bottom of the standings; from the American League to the National League; from Detroit, where he had spent his whole career, to Pittsburgh, where he knew no one. Who would want to finish out an outstanding career so displaced?

But the year was 1947, the year that Jackie Robinson broke the color line by signing with the Brooklyn Dodgers and becoming the first black person to play major league baseball. All around the league, fans and opposing players treated Robinson to vicious abuse. Greenberg, a Jew, had been subjected to considerable heckling in his own career, but having become through his persistence and success a revered figure in the game, he was now playing out his days with his new team and making the very best of it. While he knew it was tougher on Robinson than it had been on him, he had been subjected to mean-spirited racial abuse, and so he identified with Robinson. "I know how he feels," Greenberg said early in the season.[6]

Robinson and the Dodgers came to Pittsburgh to play the Pirates for the first time in mid-May. From the start, Jackie Robinson was razzed and insulted, not only by the fans, but also by some of Greenberg's teammates on the Pirates.

Here's the way Greenberg recalled the atmosphere that day: "Jackie came into Pittsburgh on a Friday afternoon, and the place was jammed. We were in last place and the Dodgers were in first. Our Southern ballplayers, a bunch of bench jockeys, kept yelling at Jackie, 'Hey, coal mine, hey coal mine, hey you black coal mine, we're going to get you. You ain't gonna play no baseball . . . you dumb black son of a bitch.'"

Early in the game, Robinson reached first base. He took a lead off the base, and then had to charge back when the pitcher tried to keep him close to prevent a steal. Robinson slid hard into the first baseman, Greenberg, demonstrating the kind of aggressive play that was to make him a superstar and member of the Hall of Fame.

The crowd quieted. Ordinarily, a player in Greenberg's position might say something aggressive in return, even cast a menacing glance. At the least, he would step back, leaving the player on the ground to get up and brush himself off. In response to Robinson's aggressive playing that year, many players in Pittsburgh and elsewhere would have become angry, taunting and swearing at Robinson as he got himself up.

But Greenberg did none of that. In a simple gesture, he leaned over, gave Robinson a hand, and helped him up. Everyone in the stands and on both benches could not help but notice.

The next time Robinson got to first base, he and Greenberg chatted, Greenberg asking him whether he had been hurt on the earlier play, telling him not to pay attention to the razzing and inviting him out to dinner that evening.

After the game, Robinson described Greenberg as a hero: "Class tells. It sticks out all over. . . ."

Greenberg's gesture meant not only a great deal to Robinson personally, but also helped put the Pirates and fans on notice that Robinson was here to stay. If he was OK with Greenberg, then he must be OK.

There is no way to quantify the value of Greenberg's gesture. A career's worth of home runs and RBIs gave him the credibility to make a difference to Robinson, baseball, and American society. The fans and his teammates took notice because the great "Hankus Pankus," as he was nicknamed, stood up for justice. But it may also be that his actions during his final year, playing for a losing team, gave new context and meaning for the years that went before, meaning that could never be captured by statistics that merely measured all the home runs and RBIs of a career.

Measurement is an extraordinarily useful tool. We don't mean to diminish its utility. Three quarters of the courses at the school where we teach are based on measurement: cost-benefit analysis, economic analysis, policy analysis, financial analysis. The same is true in medical schools and business schools. But measurement is simply one artifice among many that cannot capture the essence of what makes our lives and organizations worthwhile.

If you buy into the myth of measurement, what happens to you after being in a job for twenty or thirty years? After becoming a big and important person with a big and important role, what happens when you lose that role? You are likely to think the next job, the next form of your work, has to be just as "big and important." Otherwise, it isn't worth doing; otherwise, you cannot find yourself. Having bought into the myth of measurement, you cannot define new modes of loving and care, giving and mattering, unless they can be measured in the same terms as your previous work. We all know people who shriveled up inside after retiring or leaving a career because they could not find the big next thing to do.

Fortunately, some people escape this trap.

Ron's father, Milton, was considered one of the ten living masters of his craft—neurosurgery. He designed surgical instruments used by brain surgeons around the world. Directly and indirectly, he saved thousands of lives.

When Milton retired, he returned to one of the activities that he loved in his youth—stargazing. But finding the range of books on stargazing unsatisfying, he decided to write a book of his own.[7] Written with children in mind, Milton dedicated the book to his seven grandchildren, which of course included Ron's two kids, David and Anni.

On Halloween night, soon after the book's publication, Ron's parents were visiting. The children went out trick-or-treating with an old family friend, Rick Stemple, a music teacher who used to room in their house during his student years. At the end of a lively evening, as Rick was about to leave, Ron decided to give him a copy of his father's new book as a gift. As the family all crowded around, Rick thumbed through the book and then turned to Milton and asked him for a pen. Milton smiled, thinking about what he would write as he autographed the book for Rick.

Rick took the pen, but he did not hand the book to Milton. Instead, he got down on one knee, opened the book to the dedication page where the names of the grandchildren were listed, and asked David and Anni to sign the book.

Ron looked over and saw tears come to his father's eyes as he watched his young grandchildren sign their names, in their one-inch-high script, on the dedication page. After forty years of clinical medicine, with all of the lives he had saved, nothing for Milton could compare to the meaning of that moment.

The Form Doesn't Matter

Just as measurement will distract you from truer appreciations of life, the form of your contribution is far less important than the content. In Shakespeare's last great tragedy, *King Lear*, Lear himself is caught up in the role and forms of the royal court, so much so that he rejects Cordelia, the sincere daughter, finding her expressions of love too simple and sparse. Misled by pandering and pretensions of love, he bestows his kingdom upon his other two daughters. When Lear finally comes to his senses, he asks, "Where have I been? Where am I?" But by then it is too late: He loses both the kingdom and Cordelia.[8]

How are we to keep from making Lear's mistake, only to discover too late the difference between form and substance?

Early in his career, Ron worked at the Life Extension Institute, a health care facility in New York City that provides physical examinations for top business executives. He talked at length with many corporate presidents and vice presidents who looked back as they approached their late fifties at having devoted themselves to "winning in the marketplace." They had often succeeded remarkably, yet many were having difficulty making sense of their lives in light of what they had given up. They felt troubled, and some had begun to wonder if it were possible to create for their businesses a greater sense of mission. Some of these top managers described, with insight, the risk of questioning corporate purposes. They had seen predecessors and colleagues who, upon expressing the desire to bend the organization to larger social purposes or even create customer value, were "bumped upstairs" to the board—put out to pasture where they could be "visionaries on their own time." In the meanwhile, the company would recruit or promote the next hard-charging star in his or her forties with a single-minded focus on the bottom line. Often the cycle continued, from generation to generation.

These people felt "cheated." They had kept their eyes on the prize all right, and had reached the goal, only to find it wanting. The accomplishments for which they had sacrificed seemed empty. They were living with the discomfort of the growing gap between the goals that had been driving them and the aspirations that would make their lives worthwhile. They began to distinguish between form and substance, and many were now looking for the latter.

More recently we have come to know young high-tech billionaires who are asking themselves the same question but far earlier in their lives. What for? These folks are lucky, not just because they've made their money early on, but because they've discovered the essential questions early on.

When young people begin thinking about professional life, the world seems full of options. They believe that the newspaper ads will yield dozens of interesting and meaningful jobs. As they get older, chance, seemingly random events, friends and family, an inspiring teacher, an immediate job opening—all determine much of what people choose to do. And before long, they often become wedded to that choice and married to a professional role.

Typically, that choice works well for a while, maybe even a long while. Then, sometimes, a crisis hits. You might feel like you've been knocked off your horse. Perhaps you have reached the end of the line in a successful career, or you're a doctor and the structure and values of the health care environment have changed around you. Maybe your company has been taken over by a huge conglomerate and you are pushed aside. Perhaps you're actually fired from your job, or you're secure but something is gnawing away at you inside, suggesting that this is just not right for you, or enough for you, even though it has put food on the family table for twenty years. Or you've stayed at home to raise the kids, and now your nest is empty. Perhaps you lose reelection, or your boss does, and you are out of a job.

People experience disorientation at those times because they've mistaken form for essence. They've come to believe that the form of the work is what makes it important. They have identified themselves as their roles: I am the mayor, I'm a stay-at-home mom, I am a business executive. They confuse the form of their participation in life with the essence of its meaning and purpose.

If the essential ingredient of meaning in life is the experience of connection and contribution, then part of the magic of life in our organizations and communities lies in the human capacity to generate many forms for its expression. Meaning derives from finding ways, rather than any one particular way, to love, to contribute to the worldly enterprise, to enhance the quality of life for people around you.

In his best-selling memoir, *Tuesdays with Morrie*, author Mitch Albom recounts his visits with his mentor, Morris Schwartz, during Schwartz's last year of life. At one point Schwartz asks, rhetorically, "You know what gives you satisfaction?" "What?" responds Albom. "Offering others what you have to give."

"You sound like a Boy Scout," Albom observes, and that starts Morrie off again.

"I don't mean money, Mitch. I mean your time. Your concern. Your storytelling. It's not so hard. . . . This is how you start to get respect, by offering something that you have. There are plenty of places to do this. You don't have to have a big talent."[9]

Whatever vehicle you use is less consequential than realizing the continual possibilities for service that will surround you, right up until the end of your time. Morrie Schwartz continued to contribute even as his life ebbed away, teaching Albom how to die at the same time he was teaching him how to live.

Fundamentally, the form doesn't matter. Any form of service to others is an expression, essentially, of love. And because the opportunities for service are always present, there are few, if any, reasons that anyone should lack for rich and deep experiences of meaning in life. The most common failing, perhaps, is Lear's failing: We get caught up in the form, and lose sight of what's essential and true.

When Jimmy Carter left the White House a defeated and depressed man, his renewal took forms of service that no one would have imagined for a former president of the United States. He began in a tangible, straightforward way: building houses for poor people with the organization Habitat for Humanity. He then began to build upon his Camp David success, in which he had negotiated the Egyptian-Israeli peace agreement in 1978, by exploring ways to help communities and societies resolve their conflicts. Those efforts broadened to a variety of initiatives to serve emerging democracies. Now, many years after leaving the White House, Carter has made an undeniable contribution to people. To try to compare it to his record in the White House would be to miss the point completely. Deeply rooted in a personal philosophy of loving service, his capacity to create new forms of meaning is an inspiration for anyone in the midst of change.

Few roles are more mesmerizing than occupying the White House. But even less glamorous forms can be just as seductive. When people came to see Marty in the Massachusetts governor's office to explore opportunities for work in state government, they often had great difficulty imagining a way to contribute professionally other than through the form to which they were accustomed. They could see themselves heading a state agency, but they could not imagine themselves volunteering in a state hospital. Finding meaningful work became easily confused with all of the accoutrements of the job—access to the governor, title, salary, status, or size of the office.

Of course, these aspects of any job matter, not only because they are fun, but also for the leverage they may give in mobilizing action. But frequently, it's not the instrumental import of these forms and trimmings that matters to people as much as the symbolic import. The forms become a misleading proxy for the value and essence of what we do. As a consequence, not only do people lose sight of the essential opportunity, but they also allow their experience of self-worth and meaning to get tied to the wrapping, rather than the gift.

When Jerry Rice temporarily retired from the National Football League as one of the greatest wide receivers ever to play the game, he started a foundation for kids. To raise money, he gathered a group of his buddies from the NFL and formed a basketball team that played exhibition games around the country. Ron watched one of these games while on vacation with his family, marveling at the fun these men were having playing fairly good basketball against a state all-star team, lighting up the eyes of countless kids, and raising money. Jerry looked tired, to be sure—they had played three games in three cities in two days, and he clearly missed the thrill he had known as a pro player since he soon returned to the NFL. But he also looked pretty proud of the transition he had made and the meaning he was producing, in contrast to so many of his athletic colleagues who appear thoroughly lost for decades after leaving the limelight.

Having purpose differs from having any particular purpose. You get meaning in life from the purposes that you join. But after working in a particular discipline, industry, or job for twenty or thirty or forty years, you begin to be wedded to that specific purpose, that particular form.

When you lose that purpose, that specific form, you think you have no meaningful options. We know a seventy-seven-year-old man, Bennie, who can retire with full salary and medical benefits. He's been in the same job for forty years. He no longer has the strength to do the tasks that go with the job. He refuses to quit, he says, because he does not know what he will do with his days.

Bennie fears retirement because he can't redefine the purposes in his life. Minus the form, he thinks he will lose his source of meaning. But what Bennie really has lost is something that he probably once had as a child: a sense of purpose. Children have generative power. They create meaning as they busily connect with whatever is happening. But grown-ups often forget that ability. They tend to lose that playful, adventuresome, creative generativity by which they can ask themselves: What's worth doing today?

The vehicles we find for meaning obviously take some tangible form, and certainly that form matters in significant ways. Some jobs suit your interests, personality, skills, and temperament; others do not. The point here is not to diminish the importance of finding forms and taking roles that personally gratify you, but simply to rekindle that youthful capacity to imagine a host of possibilities. Then, when you are forced to compromise, or when you suffer a deep setback, you can recover your natural ability to generate new forms of meaningful expression.

.   .   .

Exercising leadership is a way of giving meaning to your life by contributing to the lives of others. At its best, leadership is a labor of love. Opportunities for these labors cross your path every day, though we appreciate through the scar tissue of our own experiences that seizing these opportunities takes heart.

11

Sacred Heart

Exercising leadership is an expression of your aliveness. But your life juice—your creativity and daring, your curiosity and eagerness to question, your compassion and love for people—can seep away daily as you get beat up, put down, or silenced.

In our work with men and women all over the world, in all walks of life, we have seen good people take on a cloak of self-protection to insulate themselves from the dangers of stepping out. Self-protection makes sense; the dangers are real.

But when you cover yourself up, you risk losing something as well. In the struggle to save yourself, you can give up too many of those qualities that are the essence of being alive, like innocence, curiosity, and compassion. To avoid getting hurt too badly, it is easy to turn innocence into cynicism, curiosity into arrogance, and compassion into callousness. We've been there. Maybe you have as well.

No one looks in a mirror and sees a cynical, arrogant, and callous self-image. We dress up these defenses, give them principled and virtuous names. Cynicism is called realism, arrogance masquerades as authoritative knowledge, and callousness becomes the thick skin of wisdom and experience. The following table summarizes the common tendencies that take over when people lose heart.

Losing Heart

Quality of Heart		Becomes		Dressed Up As
Innocence	→	Cynicism	→	Realism
Curiosity	→	Arrogance	→	Authoritative knowledge
Compassion	→	Callousness	→	The thick skin of experience

Cloaking cynicism, arrogance, and callousness in more accept-able language does not hide the consequences of adopting them in the first place. Cynicism, arrogance, and callousness may be the saf-est ways to live, but they also suffocate the very aliveness we strive to protect.

Indeed, realism must capture both the ugly *and* the amazing in our lives, unvarnished. To interrogate reality unflinchingly takes courage. The cynical brand of realism, which assumes the worst will happen, is a way of protecting yourself by lowering your aspi-rations so that you will never be disappointed. It's like an insur-ance policy. If things go well, boy, that's terrific. But if you never expect anything to work out, you're never surprised, and, more to the point, you never have to experience betrayal.

Furthermore, authoritative knowledge depends upon curios-ity to teach you when and where to take corrective action. Main-taining doubt when the people around you yearn for certainty can strain you to the limits of your integrity. But how can you possibly learn if you do not retain a healthy measure of curiosity? And how can you continue to be authoritative unless you continue to learn?

As for the thick skin of wisdom and experience, it is natural to develop some protective cover as you grow in your role and bear the vicissitudes of life. Otherwise the slings and arrows might be intolerable. But it is too easy to buy in to the common myth that you cannot survive a demanding professional role without a tough exterior, as if you have to check your compassion at the office door. Calloused fingertips lose their sensitivity. Your listening becomes less and less acute, until you fail to hear the real messages from people around you, and cannot identify the songs beneath their words. You listen to them only strategically, as resources or obstacles in the pursuit of your objectives. In the effort to protect yourself, you risk numbing yourself to the world in which you are embedded.

Moreover, the deepest wisdom and the most profound expressions of your experience are rooted in compassion. How can you possibly guide and challenge people without the capacity to put yourself in their shoes and imagine what they are going through? How otherwise can you identify the sources of meaning that can sustain them through the losses of change?

The hard truth is that it is not possible to experience the rewards and joy of leadership without experiencing the pain as well. The painful part of that reality is what holds so many people back. As we have described, the dangers of leadership will come from many people and places, and take many forms, not only from known adversaries, but also from the betrayal of close associates and the ambivalence of trusted authorities.

Cynicism, arrogance, and callousness can come in very handy. It may often seem as though, without their protection, there is nothing between you and the experience itself. They get you through the day. In reality, however, they undermine your capacity for exercising leadership tomorrow. Perhaps even more critically, they disable an acute experience of living.

A Reflection on Sacred Heart

The most difficult work of leadership involves learning to experience distress without numbing yourself. The virtue of a sacred heart lies in the courage to maintain your innocence and wonder, your doubt and curiosity, and your compassion and love even through moments of despair. Leading with an open heart means you could be at your lowest point, abandoned by your people and entirely powerless, yet remain receptive to the full range of human emotions without going numb, striking back, or engaging in some other defense. In one moment you may experience a loss of all faith, but in the next, compassion and forgiveness. You may even experience such swings in the same moment and hold those inconsistent feelings in tension with one another. A sacred heart allows you to feel, hear, and diagnose, even in the midst of your daily work, so that you can accurately gauge different situations and respond appropriately. Otherwise, you simply cannot accurately assess the impact of the losses you are asking people to sustain, or comprehend the reasons behind their anger. Without keeping your heart open, it becomes difficult, perhaps impossible, to fashion the right response and to succeed or come out whole.

Several years ago, Ron was invited to give a talk on leadership in Oxford, England, on a weekend that coincided with the Jewish New Year, Rosh Hashanah. The morning after the talk, he embarked on a short trip through the English countryside en route to London, where he expected to attend synagogue services. Early on he came upon a very charming village called Castle Combe, where the original movie version of *Dr. Doolittle* was filmed. A beautiful old manor, hundreds of years old, arose at the edge of the town, with expansive lawns and clusters of old trees. The manor now operated as an inn, so Ron decided to stay there for the night. It was the afternoon before Rosh Hashanah, and as the evening approached, he wondered how he would celebrate the holy day so far from any Jewish community.

Just before sundown, which marked the start of the New Year, he discovered a lovely old Anglican church at the edge of the manor. More than 600 years old, the small, well-built stone building seemed to have no more than twenty rows of pews. He wandered in and sat down in front, a Jew in an Anglican church, facing Jesus on the cross. Only weeks before, Ron had attended a Jewish workshop on deep ecumenism given by Reb Zalman Schachter-Shalomi. (Reb is an endearing form of the word *rabbi,* which means teacher.) In the workshop, Reb Zalman explained sacred heart as the essence, or heart, of God's promise, not to keep you out of the fire and the water, but to be with you in the fire and the water.[1]

Ron looked up at the image of a man being tortured for his beliefs—a frightening sight perhaps for anyone who has not been acclimatized to it, but more so for a Jew, conscious of a history of persecution. After decades of feeling a smoldering outrage with the violent abuses of Christianity, Ron found sitting in that church a challenging leap across a deep divide. As he reflected on his complex feelings, he began to wonder what this holiday might have been like for Jesus in his lifetime. He thought a bit wistfully, "Reb Jesus, you were one of our great teachers. We are the only Jews close by, and nobody else is here to celebrate with us. Why not keep each other company on the New Year?"

Ron looked at Jesus and meditated. "Reb Jesus, will you tell me your experience? What was it like for you on the cross? This is Rosh Hashanah, when we contemplate Abraham's willingness to sacrifice his son, Isaac. Can you give me a message?" After sitting for a while, Ron got very excited. He went outside into the clear late afternoon day and sat beneath an enormous old pine tree.

As he thought about his experience in the church, he lay down, stretched out his arms wide, and just stayed there for a long time looking up into the branches of the tree. How did he feel? Vulnerable.

And then Ron thought, "That's the message. That's what sacred heart is all about—the courage to feel everything, everything, the capacity to hold it all without letting go of your work. To cry out like King David in the wilderness, just when you desperately want to believe that you're doing the right thing, that your sacrifice means something, 'My God, my God, why have you forsaken me?' But in nearly the same instant, to feel compassion, 'Forgive them, Father, for they know not what they do.' Jesus's heart stayed open. He held it all."

A sacred heart means you may feel tortured and betrayed, powerless and hopeless, and yet stay open. It's the capacity to encompass the entire range of your human experience without hardening

230 * Leadership on the Line

or closing yourself. It means that even in the midst of disappointment and defeat, you remain connected to people and to the sources of your most profound purposes.

Our underlying assumption in this book is that you can lead and stay alive. Leadership should not mean that you must sacrifice yourself in order to do good in the world. But you will encounter dangers and difficulties, as you may have experienced already, where you are likely to *feel* as if you are being sacrificed. Can you imagine the sense of abandonment that Maggie Brooke's Lois must have felt week after week as she faced a circle of empty chairs, surrounded by a community struggling with alcoholism? Or the anguish of Jamil Mahuad, working tirelessly to serve his country, only to end up being forced by a military escort to abandon his office? Or the pain of Yitzhak Rabin, as he lay dying from an assassin's bullet?

A sacred heart is an antidote to one of the most common and destructive "solutions" to the challenges of modern life: numbing oneself. Leading with an open heart helps you stay alive in your soul. It enables you to feel faithful to whatever is true, including doubt, without fleeing, acting out, or reaching for a quick fix. Moreover, the power of a sacred heart helps you to mobilize others to do the same—to face challenges that demand courage, and to endure the pains of change without deceiving themselves or running away.

Innocence, Curiosity, and Compassion: Virtues of an Open Heart

You choose to exercise leadership with passion because a set of issues moves you, issues that perhaps have influenced you for a long time. These issues might have roots that were planted before you were born, in your family or in your culture; they may reflect questions that live within you and for which you've decided to devote a piece of your life, perhaps even the totality of your lifetime. Keeping a sacred heart is about protecting innocence, curiosity, and compassion as you pursue what is meaningful to you.

Innocence

The word *innocent* comes from a Latin root that means, "not to injure and harm," as in "not guilty." We are not using that legal definition. Rather, we use the term in the sense of childlike innocence, naiveté—the capacity to entertain silly ideas, think unusual and perhaps ingenious thoughts, be playful in your life and work, even to be strange to your organization or community.

Adaptive challenges disturb the norms of a culture and therefore require some abnormality. It does not mean that all norms change, but some norms must. For change to take place, some idea has to be imported from a different environment, or exploited internally from a deviant voice from within that environment.[2] That deviant voice may have it wrong 80 percent of the time, but that means the other 20 percent of the time, the strange, naive, but ingenious idea might be just what is needed.

When you lead people, you often begin with a desire to contribute to an organization or community, to help people resolve important issues, to improve the quality of their lives. Your heart is not entirely innocent, but you begin with hope and concern for people. Along the way, however, it becomes difficult to sustain those feelings when many people reject your aspirations as too unrealistic, challenging, or disruptive. Results arrive slowly. You become hardened to the discouraging reality. Your heart closes up.

As an organ, a healthy heart opens and closes every second. So how do we keep the spirit in our hearts opening, and not just closing, while in the midst of such difficult work? How do we maintain the innocence along with a realistic appreciation for the dangers involved in exercising leadership? How can you celebrate your desire to love and care effectively, even as you recognize the tough realities you face, which may hurt you?

Maintaining your innocence does not mean taking unnecessary grief. As one former student of ours expresses it, "For twenty-five years, every time I have to terminate somebody's employment, whether for economic or performance reasons, it is enormously painful to me, and I suffer for it. I don't think it is supposed to get easier every time, but I also don't think I have to be stupid and not fire someone who is hurting the organization. So it doesn't mean that I don't act. But perhaps I don't have enough calluses. How do I prevent this pain from becoming destructive, yet still stay smart about it? In a sense, every time I fire someone, I lose a little bit of innocence; I have to have mechanisms within myself and colleagues around me to rebuild that innocence or reconnect with it."

We all reach our limits. At times, Jesus may have been overwhelmed, too. He got tired. He retreated. He tried occasionally to set limits on the people he chose to heal. In response to reaching your own limits you have a choice. You could say respectfully to yourself, "You know, I can't take anymore of this today. I can't witness any more today. Time to turn on an old movie, look back at some family pictures, take time off, and reacquaint myself with the sweetness of life, because that sweetness exists all the time, too." You can allow your heart to close by developing a thick callus or becoming cynical about people, but you don't have to.

Curiosity

Nearly all of the rewards of professional life go to the people who know, rather than the people who do not. Every day, even in a great university dedicated to learning, we see many colleagues more eager to show what they know than reveal what they do not. In business, assuredness goes a long way. People overstate their confidence in their products routinely. In politics, candidates express certainties far beyond their predictive powers. In the short run, your people may trust you less when you share your doubts, as they worry about your competence; but in the long run, they may trust you more for telling the truth.

The dynamic starts early. By the time children reach adolescence, they already form deep attachments to having it "right." They begin to lose that wonderful curiosity that comes from knowing what they do not know, when they assume that people with a different point of view are there to learn from, not just argue with. But the sense of mystery and wonder so precious in the early years fades fast as the routine debates develop the characteristic structure:

"I'm right,"

"No! I'm right!"

"No! I'm right!"

The unlucky ones keep winning and become the "best and the brightest." They are unlucky because the awakenings, like King Lear's, often come late, after the mistakes and the waste. Then, the deflating of a grandiose self-assurance becomes particularly painful and laced with regret. A few, like Robert McNamara, who played a key role in the Vietnam War, demonstrate the extraordinary heart to revisit their mistakes and reclaim their doubts. The fact that McNamara would write deeply thoughtful memoirs analyzing his errors of judgment should stand as an inspiration for anyone taking on the risks of leadership.[3] How many prominent people can say the same about their own memoir? Instead, layers of self-justification reinforce one another to protect some misguided notions of pride. Lessons for posterity are lost.

If Jesus, at the end of his ministry, could question God, then surely we can question ourselves.

Is it possible to retain that childhood virtue, curiosity, even as we hone our capacity to reality-test assumptions? Are there ways to maintain a sense of the mystery of it all?

To succeed in leading adaptive change, you will need to nurture the capacity to listen with open ears, and to embrace new and disturbing ideas. This will be hard because, the pressures on you will be to know the answers. And in your "inspired moments," you will persuade yourself that, indeed, you do! And then you may say about your detractors, "How can they possibly doubt the value of what I am offering? Of this new technology? Of this new program?" When Bill George became the CEO of Medtronic in 1989, the company had a tradition of dividing the physicians into two categories: "our customers" and "competitive docs," those with loyalties to competitor companies and their products. He found that many of the engineers did not like dealing with the "competitive docs" because they were too critical and challenging. "Of course," reflects George, "they were precisely the doctors from whom we could learn the most." Against resistance, George quickly moved to ban the term "competitive docs" and to bring them and their ideas into the company.

Most of the time, if you are honest with yourself, you know that your vision of the future is just your best estimate at the moment. As we've said, plans are no more than today's best guess. If you lack the heart to engage with "competitor" ideas, how can your organization possibly do the adaptive work needed to thrive in that competitive environment?

The practice of leadership requires the capacity to keep asking basic questions of yourself and of the people in your organization and community. Our colleague Robert Kegan teaches the difference between assumptions that you hold and assumptions that hold you. The assumptions that hold you constrain you from seeing any other point of view. But we have a special and righteous name for them: We call them truths. Truths are assumptions for which doubt is an unwelcome intruder. And truths are held in place by a lack of heart to refashion loyalties within key relationships.

Compassion

Aristotle described God as the unmoved mover. In contrast, the twentieth-century philosopher, Abraham Joshua Heschel, described God as "the most moved mover."[4] If God is moved, shouldn't we allow ourselves to be moved, too, by the triumphs, the failings, and the struggle?

At root, compassion means, *to be together with someone's pain.* The prefix *com-* means "together with," and the word *passion* has the same root as the word *pain,* as in the phrase "the passion of Jesus." We have described throughout this book both practical and transcendent reasons to maintain a reverence for the pains of change. The advice to "keep your opposition close" rests on many strong strategic and tactical arguments, for example, but it also draws upon the insight that the people who fight the hardest also have the most to lose; and therefore, they deserve the most time, attention, care, and skill.

When you lead, you cannot help but carry the aspirations and longings of other people. Obviously, if your heart is closed, you cannot fathom those stakes, or the losses people will have to sustain as they conserve what's most precious and learn through innovation how to thrive in the new environment.

Like innocence and doubt, compassion is necessary for success and survival, but also for leading a whole life. Compassion enables you to pay attention to other people's pain and loss even when it seems that you have no resources left.

As he lay in his hospital bed during what he and everyone else knew was his last week of life, Marty's father made extraordinary use of the time he had left to attend to the impact of his death on his family. He arranged a private conversation with each of his four grandchildren, probing them about their values and delivering the benefits of his nearly eighty years of experience. He gave his grand-daughter a rousing pep talk before she retook her driving test. (She passed.) He met alone with his former daughter-in-law, who had always felt distanced from him after she and his son were divorced. He told her that he loved her, and that he thought she had been a great mom. Finally, an hour before he breathed his last, he asked Marty to get him a beer.

"What kind?" Marty asked.

"Bud."

"Light or regular?"

"Light's fine."

Tears streaming down his face, Marty ran down the hospital stairs and across the street to the liquor store. He bought a six-pack and returned to the hospital room so his father could deliver a last gift. The son poured a beer for each of them. Father and son clinked glasses one more time to celebrate his life and his love.

In the formal language of this book we might say Marty's father led his family, and perhaps himself too, through the adaptive challenge of his death. Probably a better way to say it is that Marty's father, in spite of his own pain and loss, taught everyone he touched that week something about how to live, how to die, about how to take advantage of any opportunity to love and make a difference to people.

·   ·   ·

Opportunities for leadership are available to you, and to us, every day. We believe the work has nobility and the benefits, for you and for those around you, are beyond measure. But putting yourself on the line is difficult work, for the dangers are real. We have written this book out of admiration and respect for you and your passion. We hope that the words on these pages have provided both practical advice and inspiration; and that you have better means now to lead, protect yourself, and keep your spirit alive. May you enjoy with a full heart the fruits of your labor. The world needs you.

Notes

Preface

1. Deborah L. Ancona, Thomas W. Malone, Wanda J. Orlikowski, and Peter M. Senge, "In Praise of the Incomplete Leader," *Harvard Business Review*, February 2007, 92–100.

Chapter 1

1. This story is adapted from Sousan Abadian, "From Wasteland to Homeland: Trauma and the Renewal of Indigenous Communities in North America" (Ph.D. dissertation, Harvard University, 1999). The names have been changed and the story altered to maintain confidentiality.

2. This case is based on Ronald Heifetz's observations and interviews with key parties during this period in Quito, including numerous conversations with President Jamil Mahuad.

3. Gary Hamel, "Waking Up IBM: How a Gang of Unlikely Rebels Transformed Big Blue," *Harvard Business Review* 78, no. 4 (July–August 2000): 138. For the full story on which this is based, see Gary Hamel, *Leading the Revolution* (Boston: Harvard Business School Press, 2000), 154–166.

4. Hamel, *Leading the Revolution,* 155.

5. Hamel, "Waking Up IBM," 138.

6. Ira Sager, "Inside IBM: Internet Business Machines," *Business Week,* 13 December 1999. P. EB38.

7. Ira Sager, "Gerstner on IBM and the Internet" (interview with IBM Chairman Louis V. Gerstner, Jr.), *Business Week,* 13 December 1999. EB40.

8. Hamel, "Waking Up IBM," 143.

9. Mark Moore, personal communication with author, 16 October 2000.

Chapter 2

1. A more comprehensive version of this story can be found in "Diversity Programs at the New England Aquarium," Case C116-96-1340.0 (Cambridge, MA: Kennedy School of Government Case Program, Harvard University, 1996).

2. See Ronald A. Heifetz, *Leadership Without Easy Answers* (Cambridge, MA: The Belknap Press of Harvard University Press, 1994), chapter 7.

3. Warren Bennis, *The Unconscious Conspiracy* (San Francisco: Jossey-Bass Publishers, 1989).

4. Lani Guinier, "The Triumph of Tokenism: The Voting Rights Act and the Theory of Black Electoral Success," *Michigan Law Review* 89, no. 5 (March 1991): 1077–1154.

Chapter 3

1. On the skill of reflection in action, see Donald A. Schön, *The Reflective Practitioner: How Professionals Think in Action* (New York: Basic Books, 1983); and M. Weber, *Politics as a Vocation,* H. H. Gerth and C. Wright Mills, trans. (Philadelphia: Fortress Press, 1965).

2. Lee Kuan Yew, *From Third World to First: The Singapore Story 1965–2000* (New York: HarperCollins Publishers, 2000).

3. Metaphor courtesy of Jack Bridenstein, U.S. naval officer, personal communication with author, 11 August 1982.

4. Lee Kuan Yew, personal communication with author, 17 October 2000.

Chapter 4

1. John Greenwald, "Springing a Leak," *Time,* 20 December 1999, 80. For additional accounts of Ivester's tenure and demise from which much of this material was gleaned, see also: Betsy McKay, Nikhil Deogun, and Joanne Lublin, "Tone Deaf: Ivester Had All Skills of a CEO but One: Ear for Political Nuance," *Wall Street Journal,* 17 December 1999, A1; and Matt Murray, "Deputy Dilemma: Investors Like Backup, but Does Every CEO Really Need a Sidekick?" *Wall Street Journal,* 24 February 2000, A1.

2. This case is based upon a lecture by Leslie Wexner at the John F. Kennedy School of Government, Harvard University, Cambridge, Massachusetts, 13 September 2000.

3. For a full account of Nelson Poynter and his stewardship of the *St. Petersburg Times,* see Robert N. Pierce, *A Sacred Trust: Nelson Poynter and the St. Petersburg Times* (Gainesville, FL: University Press of Florida, 1993).

4. Robert Haiman, telephone interview by author, 24 April 2001.

Chapter 5

1. See Donald Winnicott, *The Maturational Process* (New York: International Universities Press, 1965); Arnold H. Modell, "The 'Holding Environment' and the Therapeutic Action of Psychoanalysis," *Journal of the American Psychological Association* 24 (1976): 285–307; Edward R. Shapiro, "The Holding Environment and Family Therapy with Acting Out Adolescents," *International Journal of Psychoanalytic Psychotherapy* 9 (1982): 209–226; Robert Kegan, *The Evolving Self* (Cambridge, MA: Harvard University Press, 1982); and Edward R. Shapiro and A. Wesley Carr, *Lost in Familiar Places* (New Haven: Yale University Press, 1991).

2. See Ronald A. Heifetz and Donald L. Laurie, "The Work of Leadership," *Harvard Business Review* 75, no. 1 (January–February 1997): 124–134.

3. Arthur Schlesinger, Jr., *The Coming of the New Deal* (Boston: Houghton Mifflin, 1958), 538.

4. Delivered on the steps of the Lincoln Memorial on August 28, 1963.

5. For a more comprehensive treatment of this story, see "Ricardo de la Morena and the Macael Marble Industry (A)," Case 16-90-971.0 (Cambridge, MA: Kennedy School of Government Case Program, Harvard University, 1990).

Chapter 6

1. There are many versions of this story. We have relied on two of them: one found in the David Shields's profile of Phil Jackson, "The Good Father," *New York Times Magazine,* 23 April 2000, 60; and Phil Jackson and Hugh Delehanty, *Sacred Hoops: Spiritual Lessons of a Hardwood Warrior* (New York: Hyperion, 1995), 189–193. The core facts are in accord.

2. According to a *New York Times*/CBS News poll, Carter's approval rating went up from 26 percent to 37 percent the day after the speech; see "Speech Lifts Carter Rating to 37%; Public Agrees on Confidence Crisis," *New York Times,* July 18, 1979, p. A1, and Howell Raines, "Citizens Ask if Carter Is Part of the 'Crisis'," *New York Times,* August 3, 1979.

Chapter 7

1. For a more comprehensive version of Selecky's story see "Principle and Politics: Washington State Health Secretary Mary Selecky and HIV Surveillance," Case 1556 (Cambridge, MA: Kennedy School of Government Case Program, Harvard University, 2000).

2. Heifetz, *Leadership Without Easy Answers,* chapters 6 and 9.

3. The full story of the U.S. Post Office reorganization can be found in "Selling the Reorganization of the Post Office," Case C14-84-610 (Cambridge, MA: Kennedy School of Government Case Program, Harvard University, 1984).

4. This account of the relationship between Lehman and General Dynamics is primarily drawn from "John Lehman and the Press," Case C16-89-917.0 (Cambridge, MA: Kennedy School of Government Case Program, Harvard University, 1989). More comprehensive accounts can be found in Jacob Goodwin, *Brotherhood of Arms* (New York: Times Books, 1985); and Patrick Tyler, *Running Critical* (New York: Harper & Row, 1986).

Chapter 8

1. David Gergen, *Eyewitness to Power: The Essence of Leadership, Nixon to Clinton* (New York: Simon & Schuster, 2000), 261.

2. "The Real Story of Flight 93: Special Report: 'Let's Roll,'" *The Observer*, 2 December 2001, 15.

3. See David Gergen's account of Hillary Clinton and her impact on Bill Clinton's strategy toward health care reform in *Eyewitness to Power*, 296–309.

4. William Shakespeare, *Julius Caesar,* Act I, Scene 2.

5. "Workshop on Leadership, Religion, and Community," Plymouth Congregational Church, Seattle, WA, 4 March 2000.

Chapter 9

1. Elizabeth Cady Stanton, *Eighty Years and More* (New York: Source Book Press, 1970), 148.

2. Ibid., 149.

3. Ibid., 149.

4. Gergen, *Eyewitness to Power*, 298–299.

5. Ibid.

6. Nurit Elstein Mor, Head of Department of Labor Disputes, State Attorney's Office, Israel, personal communication with author, September 2000.

7. Of course, no one can know what was in the mind and heart of Rabin during those moments of decision. Our interpretations are based on personal communication with people in his political circle, but they remain interpretations, meant mainly to illustrate the role/self distinction rather than write biographically about Rabin.

8. See Jack Welch, *Straight from the Gut* (New York: Warner Books, 2001).

9. Speech at Valley College, Van Nuys, California, November 1984, in Geraldine Ferraro, *Ferraro: My Story* (New York: Bantam, 1985), 292 (italics in the original).

Chapter 10

1. *American Heritage Dictionary,* fourth edition (New York: Houghton Mifflin Company, 2000).

2. S. L. A. Marshall, *Men against Fire: The Problem of Battle Command in Future War* (New York: William Morrow, 1947), chapters 9 and 10; and Edmund Shils and Morris Janowitz, "Cohesion and Disintegration in the Wehrmacht in World War II," *Public Opinion Quarterly* 12, no. 2 (Summer 1948): 280–315.

3. William W. George, "A Mission for Life," unpublished manuscript, 2001; and personal communication with the author, November 2001.

4. The Talmud, Koran, and other sacred teachings. *Mishnah, Tractate Sanhedrin,* chapter 4, *Mishnah 5*; and *Surat al-Ma'idah* (translation: *The Table Spread*) (Sura 5), verse number 32 in the *Qur'an.*

5. William Shakespeare, *Romeo and Juliet,* Act II, Scene 2.

6. Hank Greenberg with Ira Berkow, *Hank Greenberg, The Story of My Life* (Chicago: Triumph Books, 2001), 181. The relationship between Greenberg and Robinson is described on pages 181–183 and also noted in "The Life and Times of Hank Greenberg," an award-winning documentary written, produced, and directed by Aviva Kempner, 1998.

7. Milton D. Heifetz and Will Tirion, *A Walk through the Heavens: A Guide to Stars and Constellations and Their Legends* (New York: Cambridge University Press, 1998).

8. William Shakespeare, *King Lear,* act IV, scene 7.

9. Mitch Albom, *Tuesdays with Morrie* (New York: Doubleday, 1997).

Chapter 11

1. "Deep Ecumenism," a workshop at Elat Chayyim, Concord, NY, in July 1998 with Rabbi Zalman Schachter-Shalomi.

2. See Richard Pascale, Jerry Sternin, and Monique Sternin, *The Power of Positive Deviance: How Unlikely Innovators Solve the World's Toughest Problems* (Boston: Harvard Business Press, 2010).

3. Robert S. McNamara with Brian VanDeMark, *In Retrospect: The Tragedy and Lessons of Vietnam* (New York: Vintage Books, 1996); and Robert S. McNamara and James G. Blight, *Wilson's Ghost: Reducing the Risk of Conflict, Killing, and Catastrophe in the 21st Century* (Public Affairs, LLC, June 2001).

4. Abraham Joshua Heschel, *God in Search of Man: A Philosophy of Judaism* (Northvale, NJ: Jason Aronson, Inc., 1987), xxxiii.

Index

accepting casualties, 98–100

access, 75

actions
  as interventions, 137–139
  moral justification for, 114
  and taking the heat, 142–145

adaptation to change, 119

adaptive work, 13–20, 30, 33. *See also* technical work
  accepting casualties during, 98–100
  acknowledging loss as part of, 92–95
  on an individual level, 185–186
  distinguishing from technical, 55–62
  problems of, 200
  providing context for, 104
  versus technical, 108

affirmation, 169–176

Albom, Mitch, 220

alienation of constituents, 78

allies/alliances, 152. *See also* partners/ partnerships
  confusing confidants with, 199–204
  creating, 81, 82

knowing others', 84

versus lone warrior strategy, 199

relationships with, 89–90

risks of losing, 83–84

Amir, Yigal, 193

anchors, 179, 190, 205

anger, 141–146

apologizing, 77

Aristotle, 234

arrogance, 225–227

assassinations, 11, 42, 193

assumptions, challenging, 114

attacks. *See also* terrorism
  personal, 40–45, 188–189, 191–192
  physical, 41–42, 193

attention, 148, 154–159. *See also* focus

authority
  compared to leadership, 25
  during crises, 169–170
  gaining, 123
  going beyond your, 20–26, 153
  lack of, 34–35, 152, 157–158
  loss of benefits of, 187
  marginalization of, 35–36

authority (*continued*)
  restoring order using, 113
  risks of losing, 181–182
authority figures, 67–74

balcony metaphor, 53, 65–67, 135, 165
behavior, 95–98, 107, 108–109
Bennis, Warren, 40
betrayal, 31
blaming others, 90–92
Bork, Robert, 43
Both, Hennie, 105–107
boundaries, 182, 191
Bratton, William, 24
Briggs, Walter, 214
Bush, George H. W., 61–62
Bush, George W., 42, 113, 169

callousness, 225–227
capacity for reflection, 51
Carter, Jimmy, 135, 220–221
casualties, accepting, 98–100
challenges
  adaptive, 13–20
  identifying adaptive, 105–106
  of leadership, 102
Chandler, Otis, 134
change
  adaptation to, 119
  adaptive, 13–20
  generating significant, 96–98
  mobilizing, 13
  to norms, 231
  respecting pain of, 146
  sweeping, 117
  willingness for, 92
character attacks, 43
Cheney, Dick, 42

civil rights movement, 26, 28, 38, 93,
  147–148. *See also* King, Martin
  Luther, Jr.
Clinton, Bill
  character of, 42–44, 192
  credibility of, 152–153
  going beyond boundaries by, 191
  health care and, 148
  health care reforms by, 117
  hungers of, 177–180
  philandering by, 194–195
  physical condition of, 164
  reelection of, 119
Clinton, Hillary, 43
clues, reading authority figures
  for, 67–74
Clymer, Adam, 42
collusion
  with attackers, 45
  with constituency, 88–89
  with marginalizers, 35
  unconscious, 172
commitment, signaling, 98–100
compassion, 227, 234–236
composure, keeping your, 44
compromising, 46–47
confidants versus allies, 199–204
confidence, loss of, 95–96
conflicts
  controlling the temperature of,
    107–116
  creating a holding environment for,
    102–107
  pacing the work of, 116–120
  persistence of, 61
  personality, 124
  placing at right location, 128–129
  showing the future for, 120–122
  types of, 101
"constituency problem," 47

"Contract with America," 118–119
control, hunger for, 166–169
controlling the temperature, 107–116
controversial issues, 142–145
corporate culture
    changing, 106–107
    diversity as mission of, 32–35
    IBM's changes to, 22–23
    making changes to, 79–81
    recognition of change by, 151–152
    study of, 103–104
Coughlin, Father, 111
creating a holding environment,
    102–107
credibility, 20, 146
    gaining, 123
    loss of, 153
crises
    authority during, 169–170
    as indicator of adaptive issues, 61
    leadership during, 15–17
    shifting attention during, 148–149
    urgency generated by, 151
curiosity, 107, 232–234
cynicism, 225–227

Daley, Richard, 138
defeat, reasons for, 163–164
defending against attacks, 192
defense mechanisms, 45
demagogues, collusion with the
    grandiosity of, 172
denial, 154
dependency, fostering, 174
devaluation by "invisibility," 52
Diallo, Amadou, 25
Digital Equipment Corporation
    (DEC), 174
disappointing your supporters, 46

disloyalty, 27, 29, 89
disorientation, 219–220
distress, experiencing, 227–228
diverting attention, 38–40, 44
doctors as leaders, 12
dysfunction, 14, 105–106

Ecuador crisis, 15–18, 63
effectiveness, loss of, 48
Eisenhower, Dwight D., 73, 118
embodying the issue, 37, 196, 197
emotional realities, 111–112,
    116–117, 166. See also hungers
employees, showing the future to,
    121–122
equilibrium, attempts to restore,
    153–154
ethical issues, of pacing work, 119
exhaustion, 164
expectations, 20, 46, 127
externalizing issues, 127

Ferraro, Geraldine, 197–198
finding partners, 75–84
Flight 93 heroism, 168. See also
    September 11, 2001, attacks
focus. See also attention
    on authority figures, 68
    derailing your, 45
    on issues, 154–159
    loss of, 38
form, unimportance of, 218–223

Gates, Bill, 174
gender issues, 32–33
George, Bill, 211, 234
Gergen, David, 164

Gerstner, Lou, 23
Gingrich, Newt, 117–119, 178
Giuliani, Rudolph, 24, 94–95
Good Friday peace agreement, 46
Gore, Al, 113
grandiosity, 171, 172, 173
Greenberg, Hank, 214–216
Grossman, David, 21–23, 157, 209
Guinier, Lani, 43–44

habits, abandoning, 27–28
Haiman, Bob, 97
Hart, Gary, 194–195
Health, Education, and Welfare (HEW),
    U.S. Department of, 32–37
heat. *See* taking the heat
Heifetz, Milton, 217–218
heroism, 168, 208
Heschel, Abraham Joshua, 234
hierarchical structures, 3
holding environments, creating,
    102–107
honesty with yourself, 234
Hoover, Herbert, 213
hostility, 88
hubris, 171
human enterprise, 210–211
hungers
  for affirmation and importance,
      169–176
  for intimacy and sexual pleasure,
      176–183
  managing, 184–186
  for power and control, 166–169
Hussein, Saddam, 61

Iacocca, Lee, 98
IBM, 21–23

"I Have a Dream" speech, 121, 159.
    See also civil rights movement;
    King, Martin Luther, Jr.
illusions, sustaining, 169
impeding progress, 54–55
importance, need for a sense of,
    169–176
information, withholding, 119
initiative, 24, 152
innocence, 230–231
insatiability, 176
inspiration versus fear, 118–119
insubordination, 125–127
internal disagreements, 39–40
interpretations, 57, 66, 136–137
interventions, 134–139, 158–159
intimacy, 176–183, 185
invulnerability, 87
Iran-Contra affair, 25
issues
  avoidance/denial of, 154
  controversial, 142–145
  crises as indicator of adaptive, 61
  cultural, 60
  embodying, 37, 196, 197
  ethical, 119
  externalizing/internalizing, 127
  focusing on, 154–159
  gender, 32–33
  missing core, 63–64
  nonroutine, 156–157
  physical stress, 164
  political, 168
  ripening of, 146–154
Ivester, M. Douglas, 76–78

Jackson, Phil, 125–128, 209
Johnson, Lyndon, 37, 138,
    148, 153

Jordan, Michael, 125–127
Julius Caesar (Shakespeare), 171

Kegan, Robert, 234
Kerasiotes, James, 167–168
King, Martin Luther, Jr. *See also* civil
    rights movement
  agenda of, 38
  assassination of, 193
  "I Have a Dream" speech, 121
  message sent by, 138
  risk taking by, 151, 152, 159
  seizing of the moment by, 149
King Lear (Shakespeare), 218
Kissinger, Henry, 181
Koedijk, Ruud, 103–107
Kohnstamm, Abby, 23

Landrey, Wilbur, 97
Laurie, Donald, 103
leadership
  compared to authority, 25
  dangers of, 11–13, 26–30, 227
  exercising without authority, 153
  myth of measurement and,
    212–218
  opportunities for, 236
  reasons for, 208–212
Leadership Without Easy Answers
    (Heifetz), 5
learning, continuing, 225–226
Lehman, John, 155–156
Lewinsky, Monica, 179–180
Lewis, David, 155–156
Lieberman, Joseph, 198
limits of relationships, 103
line of fire, 132–134. *See also* taking
    the heat

listening, 64–67
lone warrior strategy, 199
losing heart, 226
loss
  acknowledging, 92–95
  of authority, 187
  of confidence, 95–96
  as heart of danger, 26–30
Louima, Abner, 24
love, 210–212
loyalty, 27–28, 84, 199

Mahoney, Miles, 66–67
Mahuad, Jamil, 15–18, 63, 230
maintaining innocence, 231–232
Marcos, Ferdinand, 173
marginalization, 32–37, 52
McNamara, Robert, 37
meaning, 208–209, 212–218
measurement, myth of, 212–218
meetings, style of, 106
messages, failing to hear, 66–67
metaphor
  balcony, 53, 65–67, 135, 165
  football, 90–92
  musical, 165
military, control in, 168
minimizing opposition, 142
misrepresentations, 44, 45
missing the real concerns, 63–64
mistakes
  letting your guard down, 202–203
  reversing, 174
  taking responsibility for, 90–92
modeling behavior, 95–98, 108–109
momentum, sustaining, 119
moral authority, 146
moral justification for actions, 114
Moses, Robert, 81–83

Muskie, Edmund, attacks on wife of, 45
myth of measurement, 212–218

Nagel, Ernst, 213
needs, 172, 177. *See also* hungers
Nehru, Jawaharlal, 54–55
Netanyahu, Benyamin, 11
neutralization, 57–58, 65
neutralizing your message, 40–41
New England Aquarium, 32–35
Nixon, Richard, 43, 138, 149–150
nonroutine issues, 156–157
North, Oliver, 25

observations, 52, 72–73, 135–136
observing from the balcony, 53–55,
     64–67, 135, 165
O'Doherty, Hugh, 208
Odysseus, 179
Olsen, Ken, 174
O'Neill, Tip, 45
opportunities for leadership, 1–2
opposition, 81, 85–90, 142

pacing work, 116–120
parental roles, 195–196, 236
Parks, Rosa, 26
partners/partnerships, 75–84. *See also*
     allies/alliances
patience, 146–154
Patrick, John, 22, 23, 157, 209
Patterson, Gene, 96–98
Pentagon attack. *See* September 11,
     2001, attacks
perseverance, 20
persistence of conflict, 61
personal attacks, 40–45, 188–189,
     191–192

personality conflicts, 124
personalization, 37, 130
personal life, 185–186
Pertchuk, Michael, 87–88
physical attacks, 41–42, 193
physical stress issues, 164
Pinochet, Augusto, 112–113
Pippen, Scottie, 125–128
political thinking, 75–100
     accepting casualties and, 98–100
     accepting responsibility and,
          90–92
     acknowledging losses of others
          and, 92–95
     finding partners and, 75–84
     keeping the opposition close and,
          85–90
     modeling behavior and, 95–98
Powell, Pete, 173
power, 166–169, 181
Poynter, Nelson, 96–98
prejudice, 56–57
presidential election of 2000, U.S., 113
pressure, 58–59, 145
pride, 171, 214
problems
     accepting responsibility for,
          90–92
     of adaptive work, 200
     "constituency problem," 47
     of cooperation, 34
     technical solutions for adaptive,
          131
progress, impeding, 54–55
promotions, as diversions, 39
psychological needs. *See* hungers
psychological readiness, 146
purpose, having, 222

questions, 136, 158–159

Rabin, Yitzhak, 11, 42, 193–194, 209
realism, 225–227
reflection, capacity for, 51
rekindling sparks, 185–186
relationships. *See also* partners/
     partnerships
   with allies and opponents, 89–90
   limits of, 103
   personal, 75
   protecting, 203
   sharing within, 84
renewal, 220–221
repression, 113
reputation, 56, 77
resistance, 30, 69
   to adaptive work, 31
   to change, 35–36
   to learning, 175–176
respect for pain of change, 146
responsibility
   accepting, 90–92
   for mistakes, 97
   taking the heat, 141–146
retirement, 222
Rice, Jerry, 221–222
Richardson, Elliot, 131
ripeness, 56, 146–154
risks
   of drawing attention, 157
   of leadership, 3
   to life, 194
   of losing authority, 181–182
Robinson, Jackie, 214–216
Robinson, Tony, 173
roles
   becoming wedded to, 219
   defense/protection of, 193–194
   ending of, 195
   parental, 195–196
   playing your, 190
   "special person," 36

role-self distinction, 187–199,
     219–220. *See also* anchors
Roosevelt, Franklin D., 110–112, 135

sacred heart, 227–230
sacrifices, 93–94, 98
Sadat, Anwar, 42
safeguarding leadership, 64–65
Sanchez, Ricardo, 121–122, 128–129
sanctuary, seeking, 204–206
Schachter-Shalomi, Zalman, 228–229
Schlesinger, Arthur, 112
Schlesinger, Len, 91, 92
scruples, 194–195
seduction, 45–48
Seduction of Joe Tynan, The (film), 188
seeking sanctuary, 204–206
Selecky, Mary, 142–145
self-care, 184–185
self-definitions, 27, 129–130, 180
self-knowledge, 164
self-protection, 222
self-reflection, 51, 204
September 11, 2001, attacks, 19–20,
     94–95, 151, 168. *See also*
     terrorism
sexual dynamics, 181
sexual needs, 176–183
sexual pleasure, 176–183
shared dilemmas, 46–47
shouldering the work, 124–127
showing the future, 120–122
solutions, 207
   destructive, 230
   internalizing issues, 127
   technical, for adaptive problems, 131
sources of meaning, 208–209
"special person" role, 36
Stanton, Elizabeth Cady, 189, 190, 191
Stemple, Rick, 217–218

stress
  controlling the temperature and, 107–116
  physical, 164
style, personal, 55–56
subordinate, seeing oneself as, 28
success, as downfall, 174
Sun Microsystems, 21–23
sustaining leadership, 73–74

taking the heat, 141–146. *See also* line of fire
technical work
  versus adaptive, 14, 60, 108
  challenges of, 33
  distinguishing from adaptive, 55–62
temperature, controlling the, 107–116
temptations, managing, 180–181
tension, controlling, 109
terrorism, 151, 208. *See also* assassinations
  September 11, 2001, attacks, 19–20, 94–95, 151, 168
thinking politically, 75
Thomas, Clarence, 43
Three Mile Island, 150–151
tokenism, 32–37
tolerance, 57, 108–109, 113
transitional rituals, 184–185
transitions of authority, 35–36
trust, gaining, 90–100
Tuesdays with Morrie (Albom), 220
Twelve Angry Men (film), 114–116, 142

unconscious collusion, 172
Unconscious Conspiracy, 40
undermining of authority, 35–36
understanding people, 62–64

unmanaged hunger, 179–180
U.S. Post Office strike, 149–150
U.S. presidential elections, 113

values
  choosing, 30
  sources of our, 29
  transcendent, 109
verbal attacks, 42
Vietnam War, 37, 38, 138, 233
vulnerabilities. *See also* hungers
  to attacks, 42–43, 79
  experiencing, 229–230
  personal, 119

Welch, Jack, 83, 195
Weld, William, 47, 124
Wexner, Leslie, 83, 91–92, 98
Willes, Mark, 132–134
Williams, Glenn, 34–35
women
  and boundaries, 182–183
  marginalization of, 32–33
  rights of, 189–190
  sexual dynamics and, 180–181
work
  pacing the, 116–120
  placing where it belongs, 127–134
  shouldering the, 124–127
World Trade Center attacks. *See* September 11, 2001, attacks; terrorism

Yew, Lee Kuan, 54–55, 64

zealots, 170
Zone of Insatiability, 176

About the Authors

RONALD HEIFETZ cofounded the Center for Public Leadership at Harvard University's John F. Kennedy School of Government, where he pioneered leadership theory and education beginning in 1983. He advises heads of government, businesses, and nonprofit organizations around the world. President Juan Manuel Santos of Colombia commented on Heifetz's advice in his 2016 Nobel Peace Prize Lecture. Heifetz's first book, *Leadership Without Easy Answers* (1994), is a classic in the field and one of the ten most assigned course books at Harvard and Duke Universities. His research aims to provide a conceptual foundation for the study and practice of leadership and strategies to develop the adaptive capacity of organizations and societies. Heifetz is well known for developing transformative methods of leadership education and development. His courses at the Kennedy School have consistently been voted the "most influential" by the School's alumni. His teaching methods are the subject of the book, *Leadership Can Be Taught* (2005), by Sharon Daloz Parks. Heifetz and Linsky coauthored with Alexander Grashow *The Practice of Adaptive Leadership* (2009).

A graduate of Columbia University, Harvard Medical School, and the Kennedy School, Heifetz is both a physician and a cellist. He trained initially in surgery before deciding to devote himself to the study of leadership in public affairs. Heifetz completed his medical training in psychiatry. As a cellist, he was privileged to study with the great Russian virtuoso, Gregor Piatigorsky. He lives in Cambridge with his wife, Kathryn. Family, music, nature, and taking college classes anchor him.

MARTY LINSKY has been on the faculty at the Harvard Kennedy School since 1982. In 2002 he and Ron Heifetz cofounded Cambridge Leadership Associates, a leadership consulting practice that was sold to the staff in 2013. A graduate of Williams College and Harvard Law School, Linsky has been Assistant Minority Leader of the Massachusetts House, a writer for the *Boston Globe*, editor of the *Real Paper*, and Chief Secretary to Massachusetts Governor Bill Weld. He has authored or coauthored over a dozen books and chapters. His most recent publication is "Adaptive Design," published in the *Stanford Social Innovation Review*. For much too long, he has been working on a new book, tentatively titled "The Politics of Everyday Life: Relentless Optimism and Brutal Realism." Linsky has three married children and two grandsons. His wife, Lynn Staley, was *Newsweek's* design director and is a successful painter in her "retirement." Linsky has run nine marathons (never again!), exercises daily (to avoid a back operation), roots for his beloved Red Sox, enjoys good drink and vegetarian food (rewards for exercising), spends as much time as possible at his family's house in Italy, is into serious decluttering, and still collects baseball cards (25,000+).